PELICAN BOOKS

THE PELICAN HISTORY OF THE CHURCH
Volume Two

During the Middle Ages 'church' and 'state' did not exist. In the West they merged in the religious and political community known as Christendom. The Papacy spoke with an authority only challenged by the Emperor: even lay thoughts and activities were draped in clerical garb. Yet because the Church was so intimately involved with the world, it responded to intellectual and social pressures with a sensitivity far beyond that of the sectarian churches after the Reformation. Any history of the Church in the Middle Ages, therefore, must discuss the development of medieval society. This new book by the President of St John's College at Oxford is a profound study of the social mechanisms of religious change.

Professor Southern's general work, *The Making of the Middle Ages*, has already become a classic. Now he covers a wider period, from the eighth century to the sixteenth. After sketching the main features of each medieval age, he deals in greater detail with the Papacy, the relations between Rome and her rival at Constantinople, the bishops and archbishops, and the various religious orders. This is the story of the birth and decay of a great western ideal – an ordered human society, both religious and secular, as an integral part of a divinely ordained universe.

Richard William Southern, F.B.A., was born in Newcastle upon Tyne in 1912. He was educated at the Royal Grammar School there, and at Balliol College, Oxford. With the exception of five years' war service he has worked and taught in Oxford since 1932 as a Research Fellow of Exeter College (1933–7), a Tutorial Fellow at Balliol (1937–61) and Chichele Professor at All Souls (1961–9). In 1968 he was a visiting professor at Berkeley, University of California, and he has lectured widely in Britain, America and Australia. He is now Professor of St John's College, Oxford. He is also President of the Royal Historical Society, and an Hon.D.Litt. of Glasgow and Durham Universities. His publications include *The Making of the Middle Ages* (1953) – this has been translated into many foreign languages; *Western Views of Islam in the Middle Ages* (1962); *Eadmer's Vita Anselmi* (1963); *St Anselm and His Biographer* (1963); *Memorials of St Anselm* (with Dom F. S. Schmitt, O.S.B.) (1969) and *Medieval Humanism and Other Studies* (1970). He was knighted in 1975.

The cover shows marginal roundels from a French Book of Hours of c. 1470, showing (front) Franciscan and (back) Carmelite friars, in the Bibliothèque Nationale, Paris

R. W. SOUTHERN

Western Society and the Church in the Middle Ages

PENGUIN BOOKS

Penguin Books Ltd, Harmondsworth, Middlesex, England
Penguin Books, 625 Madison Avenue, New York, New York 10022, U.S.A.
Penguin Books Australia Ltd, Ringwood, Victoria, Australia
Penguin Books Canada Ltd, 2801 John Street, Markham, Ontario, Canada L3R 1B4
Penguin Books (N.Z.) Ltd, 182–190 Wairau Road, Auckland 10, New Zealand

—

First published 1970
Reprinted 1972, 1973, 1975, 1976, 1977, 1978

—

—

Made and printed in Great Britain by
Hazell Watson & Viney Ltd,
Aylesbury, Bucks
Set in Monotype Baskerville

The Pelican History of the Church

GENERAL EDITOR: OWEN CHADWICK

Contents

Contents

Charts and Maps

Preface

THIS book has required much more time and work than I expected when it was first undertaken. It has also become a different kind of book. The difficulty of treating so large a subject in a single volume was always apparent, but at first it seemed that the difficulty might be overcome by describing the life of the church at selected moments through the centuries in a series of essays. In the course of time, however, the relations between ecclesiastical development and social change took so strong a hold on the work that the plan had to be altered. The present volume is the result, and I am grateful to the General Editor and the publishers for their readiness to accept a volume which fits somewhat awkwardly into their general plan.

A bald statement of the problems discussed in this task might seem to threaten the reader with a formal or doctrinaire treatise. I hope that any alarm on this score will prove unfounded. There can be no doctrines in these matters, only perceptions; and I have tried to receive these only at first hand.

I greatly regret some of the omissions that the plan of the work has made necessary, and if circumstances are favourable I hope to write a second volume to fill some of the gaps. Meanwhile I have put together elsewhere some essays on subjects that are only lightly touched on here. Most of them were written while this work was in progress as excursions from the main work and as indications of some of the ways along which it might progress in future.[1]

The debts incurred in writing any book are so numerous that it is difficult to remember them all when the moment for parting with it comes. My first debt is to All Souls College where most of the work was done in surroundings that must make any work seem inadequate to the opportunities. My second is to Mrs Jayakar and Miss Julia Hunt

1. *Medieval Humanism and other Studies.*

who have typed the work in its various stages; and to those
friends who have helped me, especially in reading proofs and
saving me from errors – Professor Owen Chadwick, Dr
R. W. Hunt, Mrs. P. E. Letts, and my wife above all. The
last and greatest debt is to all those who have given me the
stimulus of discussion in lectures and classes over many
years, to the members of Oxford University in the first
place, to those at York University who took part in the
discussions on the Heslington Lectures in 1968 and to the
members of the Southeastern Institute of Medieval and
Renaissance Studies at Duke University in 1966. I would
dedicate this book to them if I thought it could in any way
express the extent of the debt that I owe them.

List of Abbreviations

1

Church and Society

I

THE history of the Western church in the Middle Ages is the history of the most elaborate and thoroughly integrated system of religious thought and practice the world has ever known. It is also the history of European society during eight hundred years of sometimes rapid change, when the outlines of our institutions and habits of thought were drawn. To attempt to write this history in a single volume is to attempt the impossible, and some limits must be set to bring the task within manageable proportions. The chief aim of this book is to understand the connexion between the religious organizations and the social environment of the medieval church. In order to keep within these limits it has been necessary to exclude a great part of that spiritual and intellectual activity which must form the best memorial of the medieval church and its chief claim to our regard. This is a great deprivation. We have here a grimmer, more earthy church than that of scholastic theology or monastic contemplation. Although the portrait that emerges has many features that hint at the existence of spiritual and intellectual energy, this energy is not our main subject. The study of the individuals who most fully display this energy must be left for a later volume.

Yet, limited though the objective must be, it is important to appreciate the forces which confined and directed the development of the church, for ecclesiastical history is often written as if these forces did not exist, or existed only to be overcome. The truth is that they could not be overcome because they were invisible to contemporaries. The historian can recognize them in retrospect only because he can observe their influence over a wide field of human behaviour. When historians write of the church as if it could be separated from secular history, they are simply repeating the mistake made by medieval ecclesiastical reformers, who were never more clearly the captives of their environment than when they spoke of their freedom from it. The only freedom they could conceive was itself a confinement within a contemporary system, and the words in which they dissociated themselves from the world are a striking testimony to the narrow bounds of human freedom and to the enduring limitations of the church as an organized institution.

The medieval centuries have a special importance in any inquiry into the ways in which religious ideals, and the organizations designed to protect and perpetuate these ideals, are influenced by their social environment. In the first place, these centuries were very prolific in the creation of religious organizations, and these creations have shown an astonishing power of survival. The medieval social environment still haunts the modern world in institutions which were formed by its pressures. One reason for their survival is the success with which they were built into and conformed to the pattern of the society that produced them. Church and society were one, and neither could be changed without the other undergoing a similar transformation. This is the clue to a large part of European history whether secular or ecclesiastical.

II

The identification of the church with the whole of organized society is the fundamental feature which distinguishes the Middle Ages from earlier and later periods of history. At its widest limits it is a feature of European history from the fourth to the eighteenth century – from Constantine to Voltaire. In theory, during the whole of this period only orthodox and obedient believers could enjoy the full rights of citizenship. But in western Europe it was not until the seventh century that this doctrine became a practical reality; and by the seventeenth the system was becoming riddled with so many exceptions and contradictions that it was ceasing to be plausible even as an ideal. In the intervening centuries, however, the exceptions were rare and it was reasonable to suppose that they would get rarer, and might even in time disappear.

There were always indeed some outsiders, even within the geographical area of western Christendom, but at best they were people with very limited rights, and at worst they had no right even to live. At best they were Jews. The lives and basic possessions of the Jews were protected by ecclesiastical law and the self-interest of princes; they could not be killed just because they were Jews; they could not be forcibly converted; their children could not be taken from them to be brought up as Christians; they could practise their religion, so long as they did not attempt to spread it. But rulers owed them no more than a bare permission to survive if they could: 'Because of their sins' (of unbelief) – wrote Thomas Aquinas –

they are subject to perpetual servitude, and their goods are at the disposition of the ruler; only he must not take from them so much that they are deprived of the means of life.[1]

If this was the case with the most privileged class of outsiders, the licensed enemies of God, not even the right to live could be allowed to those who fell away from the orthodox Christian faith and became outsiders by their own free choice. They were harried out of existence by popular zeal, by ecclesiastical censure, and above all by remorseless logic:

Heresy [again the words are those of Thomas Aquinas] is a sin which merits not only excommunication but also death, for it is worse to corrupt the Faith which is the life of the soul than to issue counterfeit coins which minister to the secular life. Since counterfeiters are justly killed by princes as enemies to the common good, so heretics also deserve the same punishment.[2]

In a word, the church was a compulsory society in precisely the same way as the modern state is a compulsory society.

1. *De Regimine Judaeorum ad Ducissam Brabantiae* (*Aquinas: Selected Political Writings*, ed. A. P. d'Entrèves, 1948, p. 84).
2. *Summa Theologiae*, 2, 2, qu. xi, art. 3.

Just as the modern state requires those who are its members
by the accident of birth to keep its laws, to contribute to
its defence and public services, to subordinate private
interests to the common good, so the medieval church
required those who had become its members by the accident
(as one may almost call it) of baptism to do all these things
and many others.

The problem of determining how someone becomes a
committed member of a political community was one
which gave much trouble to the theorists of the early
modern state. But it was the easiest of all problems for the
theorists of the medieval church-state, for the answer lay
ready to hand in baptism. In baptism the godparents made
certain promises on behalf of the child which bound him
legally for life. From a social point of view a contractual
relationship was established between the infant and the
church from which there was no receding. For the vast
majority of members of the church baptism was as involuntary as birth, and it carried with it obligations as binding
and permanent as birth into a modern state, with the
further provision that the obligations attached to baptism
could in no circumstances be renounced.

Baptism was not the only involuntary tie which bound a
medieval man: secular serfdom, if he was so unfortunate as
to be born into this condition, was another. Serfdom, however, could be revoked by purchase, or flight, or free gift;
and the higher forms of secular obligation were all in some
degree voluntary – a man could take them up and, in
certain conditions, renounce them. But the obligations
assumed in baptism were there for ever, and they brought
secular obligations and penalties in their train no less than
spiritual ones.

In this extensive sense the medieval church was a state.
It had all the apparatus of the state: laws and law courts,
taxes and tax-collectors, a great administrative machine,
power of life and death over the citizens of Christendom and
their enemies within and without. It was the state at its
highest power, such as even Hegel among modern prophets
of the state scarcely contemplated. This sounds very un-

attractive. But we must remember two points. In the first place, those who bore authority in the church were agents with very limited powers of initiative. They were not free agents. Doubtless they were responsible for some terrible acts of violence and cruelty, among which the Albigensian Crusade holds a position of peculiar horror. But on the whole the holders of ecclesiastical authority were less prone to violence, even against unbelievers, than the people whom they ruled. Every day they were reminded that the misuse of their authority on earth would be rewarded by an eternity of punishment hereafter. And, in so far as they were not restrained by this consideration, they were restrained by practical impotence.

To rule men at a distance requires an army of willing and disciplined collaborators, capable of being reached by a word of command, of moving when commanded, and of coercion when necessary. Very great efforts were made, especially by successive popes, to give western Christendom an effective centralized government sufficient for directing the main areas of human life. Popes dreamed of a militia of St Peter, of secular rulers obedient to command, of knights sworn to faithful service, of mercenaries paid to act as agents of the church. Popes claimed the sole right of initiating and directing wars against the unbelievers. They raised armies, conducted campaigns, and made treaties of peace in defence of their territorial interests. They put the whole weight of their spiritual and temporal authority behind these efforts. But they failed to gain the acquiescence which must be the basis of any state. No sufficient body of powerful men was ever persuaded that they had a Christian duty to support the popes in these tasks.

There was a further ultimate impotence that prevented the medieval church-state from becoming a police-state. It had no police. It had no dependable army. Even the Inquisition, the most efficient instrument of coercion in the hands of the church, was swallowed up in a mêlée of local interests. Over most of Europe the worst terrors ordinary people had to face were archdeacons and rural deans. They were seldom men of liberal outlook, but they wanted a quiet life and kept most of their thunder for village lechers, drunkards, and adulterers.

When we speak of a church-state therefore we say too much, for the church was weak in the means of coercion. In the end, the decisive factor in the exercise of coercion was the consent and cooperation of independent secular rulers, who were mainly concerned to safeguard their own inherited interests. If the secular ruler refused, there was nothing to be done except resort to excommunication. This was the great weakness of the medieval church as a state. It had only one sanction: outlawry by means of excommunication, and even this was only effective if the secular ruler lent it his support. The full consequences of this division of sovereignty (as it would be called in a later age) could not at once be recognized. There were many forces which combined to persuade secular rulers to harry and burn excommunicates, and to submit in the end if they themselves incurred excommunication. Apart from their own faith and the faith of their magnates, the force of public opinion and the widespread dislocation of life which followed excommunication all inspired obedience. So long as these forces of persuasion were fully operative the system worked, but in the long run it was bound to break up.

All systems of government depend ultimately on consent, and the medieval church came in the end to depend on the consent of a few secular rulers, who possessed increasingly effective alternative machines of government. Moreover long familiarity taught them to look with equanimity on the terrors of excommunication. In the early thirteenth century King John lived for nearly four years as an excommunicate. During the whole of this time and for eighteen months previously, his kingdom was under an interdict and all the ordinary services of the church – marriages, masses, Christian burials, everything except baptism and the last rites – were suspended. The situation was accepted with astonishing calm. Not a mouse squeaked. If the king had not had political enemies and military failures, it might have lasted much longer. A contemporary chronicler says that the king thought of becoming a

Moslem, and he gives a detailed account of the steps he took in this direction.[3] This is probably only one of those wild outbursts which are familiar in any highly integrated system. But there was one thing the king never thought of doing, and that was to cast off the authority of Rome, to keep the churches open on his own authority, and to accept papal excommunication as a permanent condition. This was wholly out of the question in the thirteenth century: three hundred years later it was not. When this happened, the medieval system – in Catholic countries no less than Protestant – was finished.

The medieval church was therefore less than a state because the forces of coercion were ultimately not within its control. But in another sense it was much more than a state. In the first place it was not, and could never be simply, *a* state among many: it had to be *the* state or none at all. As soon as there were other states similarly equipped to rule, the church was on its way to becoming a voluntary association for religious purposes.

Until this happened, there were several ways in which the unique statelike character of the church could be conceived. It could be envisaged as a universal society directed by a Christian emperor, or by the pope, or by the two of them together, or by the Christian community as a whole. All these are medieval ideas, but undoubtedly the idea that came nearest to practical success, and the one that everyone thinks of in connexion with the Middle Ages, is the theory of papal monarchy. We shall have later to examine the practical meaning of papal monarchy in the Middle Ages; for the moment it is enough to remark that, though men differed about the instruments to be employed, they all agreed that a universal coercive power resided in the church. Whether in the hands of pope, emperor, king, or community, the purpose of human government was to direct men into a single Christian path. There was no liberalism in the Middle Ages. Only a few scoffers thought that there might be many paths, all equally good as far as

3. Matthew Paris, *Chronica Majora*, ed. H. R. Luard, *R.S.*, 1874, ii, 559–64.

men could see. There were many sensible people who saw that excessive coercion might defeat its own ends; but everyone thought that coercion should be used as long as it was likely to succeed, and that it should be used to promote the doctrine and discipline of orthodox Christianity. In directing men along this road the church was the sole legitimate source of coercive power.

But of course the church was much more than the source of coercive power. It was not just a government, however grandiose its operations. It was the whole of human society subject to the will of God. It was the ark of salvation in a sea of destruction. How far there could be any rational social order outside the ark of the church was a disputed question, but at the best it could only be very limited. It was membership of the church that gave men a thoroughly intelligible purpose and place in God's universe. So the church was not only *a* state, it was *the* state; it was not only *a* society, it was *the* society – the human *societas perfecta*. Not only all political activity, but all learning and thought were functions of the church. Besides taking over the political order of the Roman Empire, the church appropriated the science of Greece and the literature of Rome, and it turned them into instruments of human well-being in this world. To all this it added the gift of salvation – the final and exclusive possession of its members. And so in all its fullness it was the society of rational and redeemed mankind.

One of the greatest achievements of the Middle Ages was the detailed development of this idea of a universal human society as an integral part of a divinely ordered universe in time and in eternity, in nature and supernature, in practical politics and in the world of spiritual essences. Nearly everything of importance that was written in the Middle Ages, until the system began to break up in the fourteenth century, was written with some consciousness of this cosmic background. Naturally, both the cosmic background and the practical details were subject to many changes in the course of seven or eight centuries. The very largeness of the attempt to describe the whole cosmos and men's place in it, and to regulate the details of human life in the light of this description, made the medieval church (all unknown to contemporaries) deeply sensitive to intellectual and social change – much more sensitive than the post-Reformation churches with their more limited aims and powers. It is therefore to the main outline of this changing environment that we must now turn.

2

The Divisions of Time

THE Middle Ages may be defined as the period in western European history when the church could reasonably claim to be the one true state, and when men (however much they might differ about the nature of ecclesiastical and secular power) acted on the assumption that the church had an overriding political authority. This is of course not the way in which those who first invented the term 'Middle Ages' would have defined the period. For them it meant the age of barbarism, superstition, and ignorance, lying between the two ages of civilization, ancient and modern. Almost no one now thinks that this is at all a fruitful way of looking on the period from the collapse of the Roman Empire to the collapse of the western church-state. But great historical generalizations, even when exploded, have some elements of truth which cannot be ignored. The fall of the Roman Empire left a mental and spiritual as well as a political ruin which it took centuries to repair. The collapse was a long and complicated business, but in the West it was complete by the end of the seventh century. It was then that the work of rebuilding began. The dominating ideal in the rebuilding was that the unitary authority of the Empire should be replaced by the unitary authority of the papacy. Hobbes's gibe about the papacy being the ghost of the Roman Empire sitting crowned upon the grave thereof has a greater truth than he realized. An imperial papacy was the main articulate principle behind the medieval reconstruction of society. Hence the importance of the secular and religious movements of the sixteenth century which destroyed for ever the possibility of recreating the Roman Empire on a religious basis.

It was this attempt at imperial reconstruction under papal auspices that gives a measure of unity to the Middle

Ages – not as the coiners of the phrase imagined, by abandoning the ideals of the ancient world, but by attempting
to give them new life. If for Roman law we read canon
law, if we replace the frontier legions of Rome by Crusaders,
if we look on medieval kings as tributary dynasties under
the general supervision of the Roman pope, and if we
think of Dante as the Virgil of the new Rome, we shall
begin to see that the attempt to keep the Roman Empire
alive was not entirely chimerical. Looked on in this
perspective it is not absurd to say that the Roman Empire
achieved its fullest development in the thirteenth century
with Innocent IV playing Caesar to Frederick II's Pompey.

The unity of the period from the seventh to the sixteenth
century comes from the more or less effective preservation
of a unity that draws its strength from the ancient world.
The modern world begins when that strength, despite all
the talk of humanists about the rediscovery of classical
literature and culture, ebbed away. Of course the Roman
unity which was shattered in the sixteenth century had
long been very shaky. Intellectually the break-up had been
conceivable for two centuries before it happened; but when
it came it released many long-repressed impulses, and the
initial cracks were progressively widened in ways that no
one could have anticipated. The ultimate destruction of the
whole medieval social, political, and intellectual framework
was foreshadowed in the religious cleavages of the Reformation.

During the whole medieval period there was in Rome a
single spiritual and temporal authority exercising powers
which in the end exceeded those that had ever lain within
the grasp of a Roman Emperor. Of course the papacy
changed greatly in the course of these centuries. Its pretensions were never the same as its practice, and even its
strongest advocates differed about the legitimate limits of
the papal primacy. Nor did it lack open enemies. The
Greek church in its slow decline, the majority of secular
rulers at one time or another, and a wide variety of anti-
hierarchical critics throughout the Middle Ages opposed a
steady resistance to the most cherished claims of the papacy.

It is an illusion to think of the Middle Ages as a time of unanimity. The nature of the papal monarchy and the medieval objections to it will need careful consideration. But it would be foolish to make too many qualifications at the outset. For the whole of this period – from the age of Bede to that of Luther, from the effective replacement of imperial by papal authority in the West in the eighth century to the fragmentation of that authority in the sixteenth, from the cutting of the political ties between eastern and western Europe to Europe's breaking out into the wider western world beyond the seas – the papacy is the dominant institution in western Europe.

The commanding position of the papacy gives the Middle Ages its unity. Consequently there is a tendency to think of the shape of medieval history in terms of the rise and decline of the papal monarchy. In this scheme of things the twelfth and thirteenth centuries, when this monarchy was theoretically and practically at its most effective, mark the climax; what goes before is a period of preparation, and what comes after is decline. In a sense there is nothing very wrong in this. Nearly everything that is essential to the understanding of the medieval church reached its fullest development, its most satisfactory exposition, and its most successful practical application in this short central period of the Middle Ages. But on a closer inspection, there is a serious distortion in viewing the Middle Ages as a time of the rise, maturity, and decline of a single idea. Firstly, this point of view conceals the extent to which independent and contradictory ideals helped to determine the course of events. And secondly, it ignores the individual character of various periods of the Middle Ages, which are in fact as distinct from each other as the pre-industrial age in British history is from the post-industrial age. The political background, the social formation, the intellectual outlook of the early, middle, and late Middle Ages are very different. So are their religious ideals and institutions. Within the general unity of medieval Europe it is necessary to make some initial distinctions if we are to understand the nature of the medieval church.

All divisions of time are arbitrary, but as a preliminary to further discussion it will be useful to attempt a characterization of three main periods.

I. THE PRIMITIVE AGE,
c.700–c.1050

The first thing that stands out in this period is the inferiority of western Europe to its Greek and Moslem neighbours. The Greek political and religious system was the direct descendant of the Christian Roman Empire and therefore the rival of the Latin West on its own ground; Islam, on the other hand, offered itself as an alternative to the whole Christian and Roman tradition, and was therefore the enemy of Greeks and Latins alike. Both the Greek and Islamic systems were immensely richer, more powerful, and intellectually more sophisticated than that of western Europe. The West was the poor relation of Byzantium, making, after the manner of poor relations, strident claims to a superiority which were derisory by any objective test. Similarly with Islam. Moslem invaders during this period occupied most of Spain and nearly all the islands of the western Mediterranean, including Sicily. Western Christendom was a beleaguered citadel which only survived because its greatest enemy, Islam, had reached the end of its lines of communication, and its lesser enemies (the Slavs, the Hungarians, and the Vikings) were organized only for raids and for plunder.

This situation permitted survival, and even brought about the independence of the West, but it made life very constricted. The main reason for constriction was poverty. As a result of plague, famine, destruction, and commercial atrophy, the whole of the West was thinly populated, with no towns of more than a few thousand inhabitants, with no important industries, with a rural population practising a primitive agriculture in adverse circumstances. There are indeed signs that whenever peaceful conditions prevailed the level of population at once rose. A powerful

aristocracy, which needed manpower and desired luxuries
only obtainable by foreign trade, provided a basis and incentive for expansion. In judging the latent energies of this
population it is a significant fact that in this period of
deepest economic depression water mills, which had been
known but not widely exploited in the Roman Empire,
spread everywhere in north-western Europe. In England
alone the imperfect statistics of Domesday Book record the
existence of some six thousand mills in 1086.[1] Clearly it
would be wrong to characterize as stagnant a society which
(in contrast to the society of the ancient world) took readily
to the exploitation of mechanical power; but its powers of
organization and expansion were limited, and men were
more conscious of their powerlessness than of their modest
and unnoticed expansive energies.

Cardinal Newman long ago designated the period of the
Middle Ages before the twelfth century as the Benedictine
Age, and from a religious point of view no better name for
it can be found. As a religious ideal the Benedictine Rule
had a monopoly in western Europe throughout this
period. Already by the early eighth century it was driving
all rivals from the field, and by the middle of the eleventh
its hold on the minds and affections of the whole population seemed to be complete. All the greatest figures of the
intervening centuries were Benedictine monks or founders
and patrons of Benedictine monasteries. It was universally
agreed that man's best chance of eternal salvation lay in
the strict observance of the Rule or (as second best) in
contributing to its maintenance and extension. Everyone
concurred in admiring the solemn ritual and elaborately
organized life of the great monasteries. The Benedictine
monasteries were the symbol of stability and immutability
in a world of flux; they were the gate to heaven; they were
replicas of heaven on earth. They were institutions designed
to stem the tide of change. The idea of a changeless society

1. M. T. Hodgen, 'Domesday Water Mills', *Antiquity*, xiii, 1939,
pp. 261–79; see also R. Lennard, *Rural England 1086–1135*, 1959, p. 278,
where Miss Hodgen's total is described as 'almost certainly too low'.

forever enshrined within the fleeting shadows of the world
was written into their title-deeds and discipline:

Amid this fleeting and transitory world, all visible things hasten
to their end more quickly than the wind, but the things which are
not seen remain fixed and immutable forever. Seeking therefore
to use our transitory and temporal riches to procure eternal
rewards and lasting joys . . . I give to the bishop and monastery of
Worcester this piece of land to remain free from all human service
till the end of time.[2]

This document expressed the spirit of the founders and
benefactors of monasteries in this period: they were snatch-
ing a small portion from the world of meaningless change
to make it a replica of eternity. Outside there was visible
aimless flux; within, the image of invisible immutability.

This great divide ran through the whole of life. The
monasteries were living symbols of immutability in the
midst of flux, and there were many other such symbols.
The majority of people must mainly have been aware of
the Christian religion as an intrusion of the supernatural
into their lives in the form of miracles and ritual ceremonies.
The practical meaning of religion was imprinted on man's
mind in the awe-inspiring ceremonies of judicial ordeals,
by which a divine judgement was sought in the common
affairs of life. We have many accounts of the ceremonies on
these occasions. In one account for example we see suspected
criminals fasting with a priest for three days, and then receiving the holy Sacrament while the priest says 'The Body
and Blood of our Lord Jesus Christ be for you a means of
proof this day.' After this the priest prepared the water for
the ordeal saying these words:

I adjure you [the water] by the holy name of the Trinity, by
whom the water was divided for the Israelites to pass through with
dry feet, that you reject these men if they are guilty.[3]

2. *Hemingi Cartularium Ecclesiae Wigornensis*, ed. T. Hearne, 1723, ii, 345.
There are many similar formulas in this splendid collection of ancient
documents.
3. The full form of ordeal is printed in F. Liebermann, *Die Gesetze der
Angelsachsen*, 1903, i, 401; there are parallel rites from the Continent in
K. Zeumer, *Formulae Merov. et Karol. Aevi, M.G.H. Leges*, v, 601–722.

The accused then kissed the Gospels and the Cross; he was sprinkled with holy water and lowered into the bath. He whom the pure element of water, thus prepared, rejected was guilty. It were well for a man to sink and hope to be pulled out in time.

In these ceremonies and in all similar tests and trials whereby the transitory things of the world were brought before an eternal tribunal, we see the same spirit as that which moved the monastic founders. They sought stability and safety through some physical association with eternity.

Most of all, they sought this association through their contact with the relics of saints. Throughout these centuries relics were the most important feature in the religious landscape. In them the power of the unseen world was more accessible than anywhere else. Every church, every altar, every nobleman, every king, every monastery, had relics, sometimes in great quantity. They were brought out to authenticate the work of justice; they were carried out with the armies; they were borne in procession to encourage the drooping crops; they were instruments of state, of law and order, of personal well-being. From the eighth century, when the incessant demand for relics caused the bodies of the early saints and martyrs to be broken up, they were the object of a huge commerce. If we were able to draw up statistics of imports into England in the tenth century, relics would certainly come high on the list. They were necessary for every important undertaking. Even the pope, whatever theoretical claims were made for him, in practice owed most of his authority to the fact that he was the guardian of the body of St Peter. This brought men to Rome and made them listen to the voice of St Peter mediated through his representative on earth.

Secular rulers buttressed their feeble resources with the power of the saints. Charlemagne's throne in Aachen, built to the measurements of Solomon's throne, was constructed with cavities which were filled with relics. The Holy Lance, which had pierced the side of the Saviour, was the most important political possession of the tenth-century emperors. The fact, or fiction, that it had belonged to Constantine, the first Christian emperor, added a further dimension to its rich store of power and meaning. The great victories of the Ottonian emperors over the heathen were gained under its protection. But this was only the greatest relic of state. All kings had relics in their crowns and round their necks. In the relic collections of the king lay the safety of the kingdom. They compensated for his powerlessness before man and nature.[4]

This was the importance of relics, and of the rituals and symbols with which they were entwined, in the lives of all men. As human beings men were powerless. They could only survive through their dependence on the supernatural, and they sought to clothe themselves in the power of the unseen world. Relics were the main channel through which supernatural power was available for the needs of ordinary life. Ordinary men could see and handle them, yet they belonged not to this transitory world but to eternity. On the Last Day they would be claimed by the saints and become an integral part of the kingdom of Heaven. Among all the objects of the visible, malign, unintelligible world, relics alone were both visible and full of beneficent intelligence. For the rest, the visible world was either meaningless or filled with evil.

Human government was especially subject to the curse of meaningless flux. It combined two of the chief features of the transitoriness of worldly things: violence and impotence. It was therefore especially necessary that the ruler should seek a supernatural sanction to mark him off from other men and give him a divine right to rule as the Vicar of Christ. Men had no confidence in mere policy or in the human machinery of government; and rightly so, for policy was nearly always frustrated and the contrivances of government were seldom effective. Whatever sprang from

4. Some of the most important reliquaries of the western Emperors are illustrated in H. Fillitz, *Die Insignien u. Kleinodien des heiligen Römischen Reiches*, 1954. For Charlemagne's throne in Aachen and its importance in the religious and political framework of empire, see *Karl der Grosse, Lebenswerk und Nachleben*, ed. W. Braunfels, 5 vols., 1965–8, esp. iii, 306–7, 452, 464–79, 501–5.

unsanctified human policy belonged to the kingdom of sin and death. It was not enough that kings should carry relics on their expeditions; they needed some sanctification at the heart of their office. And this they found. At their anointing and on ceremonial occasions they wore vestments essentially ecclesiastical; they were anointed with holy oil used in the consecration of bishops; the sword, sceptre, ring, and crown they received were blessed in formulas appropriate to ecclesiastical ordination. For three centuries, from about 750 to 1050, the kings who emerged from these ceremonies exercised an authority which (they were encouraged to think) gave them a sacred character and set them above bishops and priests in the government of the Christian community. In 775, one of Charlemagne's advisers wrote to him:

Always remember, my king, that you are the deputy of God, your King. You are set to guard and rule all His members, and you must render an account for them on the Day of Judgement. The bishop is on a secondary plane.[5]

And a few years later Alcuin pressed home the same point in writing to the king, his patron:

Our Lord Jesus Christ has set you up as the ruler of the Christian people, in power more excellent than the pope or the emperor of Constantinople, in wisdom more distinguished, in the dignity of your rule more sublime. On you alone depends the whole safety of the churches of Christ.[6]

Similar thoughts were still a commonplace of political thought in the early eleventh century:

Our kings and emperors, vicars of the Supreme Ruler in this our pilgrimage, are alone responsible for the appointment of bishops; and this is right, for it would be incongruous if the pastors, who rule in the likeness of Christ, were set under the authority of any except those who are set above other men by the glory of benediction and coronation.[7]

5. *M.G.H. Epistolae Karolini Aevi*, ii, 503.
6. Ep. 174 (*M.G.H. Epistolae Karolini Aevi*, ii, 288).
7. Thietmar of Merseburg, *Chronicon*, i, 26 (ed. R. Holtzmann, *M.G.H. Scriptores in Usum Scholarum*, pp. 34–5).

In the three centuries which I have called the first period of the Middle Ages there were no thoughts more venerable than these. They had their practical expression in gorgeous ceremonies which conferred a mysterious power on the anointed ruler, and if they could not make government effective they at least associated it with the dignity and stability of the supernatural world.

One result of this massive dependence on the supernatural was that the individual was of little account. The individual was swallowed up in his community or (if he were a great man) in his office. And both community and office drew their strength from the supernatural. The rules of life for monks and laymen alike emphasized the littleness of man, the impersonal majesty of the spiritual world, the dignity of an order which was only attainable in this life in symbolic ritual, and the peace of spirit which could be found only in a rigid discipline. Thus in a paradoxical way it came about that the feebleness of man, his insecurity, his weak grasp of the laws of nature, and his ineffectiveness in government, all combined to impose an extraordinary appearance of strength and stability on the products of this first period of the Middle Ages. In all that men did, whether in secular ceremonial or liturgy or building, they aimed at producing an image of an eternal world within a world of change. These creations were made to last for ever, and many of them survived the disappearance of the social and intellectual system which had brought them into being. Buildings, indeed, were easily pulled down when architectural tastes changed; but the elaborate liturgical routine of the Benedictine monasteries, the institution of the payment of tithes based on the legislation of the Old Testament, the organization of dioceses and parishes, the loyalty to Rome which developed in these centuries in the West, proved almost indestructible. These were the lasting contributions of this primitive age to the future. The sacred ruler however, who seemed to contemporaries the strongest of all the products of the age, turned out to be of all things the most fragile.

II. THE AGE OF GROWTH,
c. 1050–c. 1300

The social and religious order which has just been sketched showed little sign of breaking up in the year 1050. Whether we look at western Europe's general economic condition, its religious ideals, its forms of government, or its ritual processes, there is little to suggest that a great change was at hand. And yet within the next sixty or seventy years the outlook had changed in almost every respect. The secular ruler had been demoted from his position of quasi-sacerdotal splendour, the pope had assumed a new power of intervention and direction in both spiritual and secular affairs, the Benedictine Rule had lost its monopoly in the religious life, an entirely new impulse had been given to law and theology, and several important steps had been taken towards understanding and even controlling the physical world. The expansion of Europe had begun in earnest. That all this should have happened in so short a time is the most remarkable fact in medieval history.

The main development

At present we understand very little of the causes of rapid change on this scale, but it is possible that the most important factor was a great acceleration in economic development in the late eleventh and early twelfth centuries. Intermittent growth had probably been going on for several centuries, but by the end of the eleventh century this growth had changed its character. From being uncertain and easily reversible it became rapid, ubiquitous, and for a time apparently limitless. That moment of self-generating expansion, for which economists now look so anxiously in under-developed countries, came to western Europe in the late eleventh century. There was no single outstanding technical innovation behind this expansive movement, but a combination of many circumstances: growing accumulation of capital, rising population, the return of the Mediterranean to western control, the political decline of the Greek and Moslem empires, all helped to open up ever-enlarging prospects to the West.

When it had once started, the expansion became irresistible. Increasing rewards encouraged the settlement of waste lands, the improvement of rivers, roads, and canals, the introduction of new methods of farming, the organization of markets and credit. All over northern Europe we find new villages where previously there had been only waste-land. The contraction of urban population, which had marked the end of the Roman Empire and remained a feature of the first period of medieval history, was now decisively reversed. Colonization began on all the frontiers of western Europe, and with colonization there began the familiar process of military aggression. For the first time in its history western Europe became an area of surplus population and surplus productivity, and it developed all the assertive and aggressive tendencies of a rapidly developing and self-confident community. An active and bloodthirsty sense of superiority took the place of the fear and resentment towards the outside world which had characterized the earlier period. The old romantic view of the Middle Ages with its head in the clouds and one foot in the grave is, for this period of the Middle Ages at least, as wrong as an idea can well be. For two centuries after 1100 the West was in the grip of an urge for power and mastery to which there appeared no obvious limit.

It was this new drive that did more than anything else to break down the old social and religious harmonies of the primitive age. Increasingly complex problems demanded more refined solutions than the old rituals could provide. As population grew, the problems of rights and obligations became more numerous and difficult; the methods of war, trade, and finance all became more refined, and the scope of these activities became greater. In every sphere of life the demand for expert knowledge became more urgent. Administration and specialization took the place of ritual as the chief instrument of government.

All this took time, but the beginnings are clearly apparent

by the first quarter of the twelfth century, and it is against this background that the religious changes of the period must be seen. Indeed it is misleading to speak of 'background' in this connexion: religious and economic changes are part of the same movement, both stimulating and being stimulated by the wider movement of expansion. The effect of this movement on the papacy, the clergy, the monasteries, on law and government, will have to be discussed later in some detail. For the present it is sufficient to point out the main effects of these changes.

In the first place, the area of life directly controlled by an appeal to supernatural power was slowly and inexorably reduced. As a corollary of this, new methods and new efforts to enlarge the area of intelligibility in the world are the most prominent features of the new age. These two complementary movements have many aspects. The secular ruler lost his supernatural attributes. The clerical hierarchy asserted its claim to be the sole channel of supernatural authority. Both secular and spiritual hierarchies, becoming more clearly distinct in their offices, developed new techniques of government and a new range of expertise. Relics retained their importance in the personal life, but lost their central importance in government and judicial processes.

It might seem at first sight that this movement, which in a very broad sense can be called 'scientific' in that it enlarged the scope of human reason and contrivance, would have increased the importance of the laity at the expense of the clergy. But the main effect was exactly the opposite.

The rise and limits of clerical supremacy

The movement which stripped the lay ruler of his supernatural pretensions had a complicated origin. On the one hand, it was part of a determined effort to claim for the ecclesiastical hierarchy the main role in directing human society to its goal of peace and salvation. But it was also an inevitable result of the growing complexity of society which called for organized government rather than ritual for the

solution of its problems. It often happens at critical moments
in history that ideas which have long held the field almost
unchallenged are suddenly discovered, not to be wrong, but
to be useless; then almost everyone can see they are absurd.
So it was around the year 1100. Even men with very little
ability suddenly knew that the religious pretensions of
kings had no foundation. They could see through them
without difficulty:

> Perhaps there are babblers who with windy eloquence contend
> that the king is not to be numbered with the laity since he is
> anointed with priestly oil. But there is a plain reason which mocks
> this folly: the king is either a layman or a clerk. Is he a clerk?
> Then he must be a doorkeeper, lector, exorcist, acolyte, sub-
> deacon, deacon, or priest. But he is none of these. Therefore he is
> not a clerk. So he is a layman pure and simple, unless perhaps
> you think he is a monk. But if he is a monk, how can he have a
> wife and bear a sword? No. He is neither monk nor clerk; just
> a layman; nothing more.[8]

It is amazingly simple to knock over cherished theories
when they no longer satisfy the needs of the time. The
thoughts on which royal government had acted for several
centuries were blown away like airy nonsense. Almost no
one bothered to defend them. The old sacred kingship
had no place in the new world of business.

In the long run this discovery helped to enlarge the area
of secular action and pointed forward to a purely secular
state. But immediately its chief result was to emphasize the
superiority of the sacerdotal element in society which could
not be cut down to human proportions. The spiritual
nakedness of the lay ruler only disclosed more fully the
indefeasible claims of the spiritual hierarchy. Moreover,
with the secularization of the lay ruler, that whole broad
stratum of society which he particularly represented – the
laity – suffered a corresponding demotion. Henceforth it
became increasingly natural to speak of the ecclesiastical
hierarchy as 'the church'. Of course everyone knew that

8. Honorius Augustodunensis, *Summa Gloria de Apostolico et Augusto, P.L.*
172, 1261–2.

there was another, more ancient, sense of the word which
embraced the whole body of the faithful, but even when the
word 'ecclesia' was used in this wide sense the rôle of the
laity began to be seen as a very humble one. The ideal
church of the twelfth and thirteenth centuries was a society
of disciplined and organized clergy directing the thoughts
and activities of an obedient and receptive laity – kings,
magnates, and peasants alike.

In theory, therefore, the whole body of the laity suffered
a severe setback as a result of the transformations that took
place in society in the late eleventh and early twelfth
centuries. Nor was this demotion of the laity simply a
theoretical one. The new techniques of government depended increasingly on expert knowledge, and this enhanced
the practical importance of those who were equipped by
intellectual training to provide this commodity. As it
happened, the long process whereby the laity had relin-
quished all claim to participate in scholastic training above
an elementary level was virtually complete by the end of
the eleventh century – the very moment when the practical
importance of advanced scholastic training first became
apparent in medieval Europe. This gave the clergy a
monopoly of all those disciplines which not only determined
the theoretical structure of society but provided the instruments of government.

We must not suppose that the laity felt injured by this
inferiority. Some of them gloried in it. They felt that they
employed the clergy to perform tedious and unpopular
tasks. But the inferiority remained all the same, and at a
time when most secular rulers were strictly illiterate (i.e.
unable to read Latin, which was the vehicle of government
as well as learning) a clerical wit invented a phrase which
was certainly not respectful to the majority of rulers: *rex
illiteratus est asinus coronatus* – 'an illiterate king is a crowned
ass'.[9]

One reason why the laity did not feel themselves injured

9. For the origin of this phrase, see V. H. Galbraith, 'The Literacy of
the Medieval English Kings', *Proceedings of the British Academy*, 1935, xxi,
212–13.

by the intellectual superiority of the clergy was that there was no such thing as a lay *esprit de corps*. Sentiments of unity, and organizations for the protection of common interests, existed among barons, peasants, craftsmen, and knights, but not among the laity as such. There was no general lay interest that called for protection. But there was very conspicuously a general clerical interest. Clergy of every degree and kind had an interest in protecting clerical 'liberties' as they were called – that is to say the exemption of clerks from the rough justice of secular courts, the protection of clerical goods from secular taxation, the exclusion of secular interference in ecclesiastical appointments, and so on. All this had the effect of giving the whole clerical order from top to bottom a sense of cohesion and common interest. This unity was by no means complete, but in the expansive period of the Middle Ages, it was the most effective single force in western society.

Gilds, formed to preserve interests threatened by the violence or intrusion of outsiders, were one of the characteristic features of the age, and the ecclesiastical hierarchy was by far the greatest gild or trade union of them all. It made rules for its own members wherever they might be. It created a massive system of courts and penalties to enforce these rules and to lay down the conditions on which its members would serve the community. Since these services were essential to the community, one may say that the medieval ecclesiastical hierarchy was a trade unionist's paradise.

In saying this, however, we express one important truth and ignore another. Like all trade unionists the ecclesiastical hierarchy formed part of the society in which it was placed. However much a clerk might be bound to the other members of the clerical order by common training, common ideals, and common interests, on most matters he thought like other men of his own social class. He therefore tended to acquiesce in those things which his social equals found tolerable, and he kept his severest censures for those things which they were prepared to think intolerable. Thus ecclesiastical rules and theories kept pace with the changes in secular society and offered very little hindrance to its continuing development.

The underlying identity of outlook between clergy and laity, however greatly separated they might be in their legal pretensions and intellectual equipment, can be seen very clearly in the development of those parts of ecclesiastical law which dealt with secular life. In the matter of trade, for instance, canon law in the early twelfth century still spoke of it as an occupation scarcely compatible with Christianity. But as the growing needs of society produced more elaborate forms of commercial organization, the ecclesiastical lawyers began to have other thoughts. They modified some principles and interpreted others until a large field was cleared for commercial enterprise, and the restrictions that remained were largely ignored or circumvented.

Similarly with war. It was still a grave sin in the eleventh century to kill a man in a battle waged for secular ends. Even the victors of the Battle of Hastings, a battle blessed with papal approval and fought against a perjurer on holy relics, were subject to severe penances for the deaths they had inflicted in battle. But by the middle of the thirteenth century a theory of the 'just' war had been evolved which gave the wars of almost all responsible secular rulers the benefit of the doubt, unless they were against the interests of the papacy or those to whom the pope had extended his protection. Apart from these limitations it became very difficult to say that any properly authorized war was unjust. The complacency of the ecclesiastical hierarchy towards secular society in the twelfth and thirteenth centuries has here had results that have long outlasted the medieval divisions of society.[10]

Similarly with taxation. Ecclesiastical law insisted that secular rulers should not tax ecclesiastical revenues without clerical consent separately and specifically obtained. It was sometimes not easy to get this consent, but the consent of the clergy was certainly not more difficult to obtain than that of the laity. This easy acquiescence became so conspicuous

10. For the rights of secular rulers in waging war in the mid-thirteenth century, see Thomas Aquinas, *Summa Theologiae*, 2, 2, qu. xl, art. 1.

that in 1296 Pope Boniface VIII tried to stiffen clerical resistance by insisting on the necessity for papal authorization for all clerical taxation by secular rulers. The pope's action represented the last stand of the papacy for the effective control of western society. It was a total failure. Within a few months, the pope was forced to explain away the terms of his decree, and soon everything went on as before.[11] It was not possible for the pope or anyone else to move far away from the consensus of lay opinion.

The ecclesiastical organization elaborated between 1050 and 1300 was the most splendid system, both theoretically and practically, that the church has ever known. It was provided with the most formidable array of teeth to be used against offenders, but they could seldom be used effectively against the current of any widespread secular interest. This was the inescapable dilemma. The rules of law could be immensely elaborated, and within the limits imposed by human craft and frailty they could be made effective within the clerical body. But outside this body they were only effective when they coincided with the general run of secular interests.

The attempt to impose a general clerical control on the spiritual and secular affairs of western Europe had indeed some remarkable successes. The theory of clerical superiority and the mechanism for enforcing it were developed to a formidable state of perfection. But the theories and mechanisms of secular society also developed. The world did not stand still while the clerical ideal was realized, and gradually it became clear to almost everyone that the ideal was losing the race against the facts.

The positive achievement

The moment of this realization can be dated to the early years of the fourteenth century. But before turning to con-

---

11. See T. S. R. Boase, *Boniface VIII, 1294–1303*, 1933, pp. 138–53, for the stages by which Boniface receded from his initial intransigence to a recognition that the king was the judge in deciding whether or not a tax should be levied without consulting the Holy See.

sider these disruptive forces, we cannot leave the central
period of the Middle Ages without a brief sketch of its
achievements. It was above all an age of rational and
coherent advance. In every sphere of life and thought, an
amazing variety of complicated detail was fitted into a
general system that was at once firm, authoritative, and
grounded in rational inquiry and widespread consent. We
can observe this in law, natural science, and in the practical
art of government no less than in theology and philosophy;
and the great artistic achievements of the age are a reflection of the same confident spirit.

The lines of development are firm and clear from 1050 to
1300; before this they are faint and uncertain; afterwards
they are often lost in a sea of conflicting tendencies. From
the beginning to the end of this relatively short period, we
progress step by step towards systematic completeness. The
papacy moves from the first aggressive statements of papal
supremacy by Cardinal Humbert and Gregory VII,
through the lawyer-popes Alexander III, Innocent III,
Innocent IV, Boniface VIII, to the final elaboration of the
papal system of government. All these popes added something distinctive to the same general plan; and their successors were left with the task of trying to keep the system
in repair.

The development of canon law took a similar course.
As a science it had scarcely begun in 1050; by 1300, the
system was complete and closed. So also in theology. The
first attempts at succinct systematic statement belong to
the late eleventh or early twelfth century: by the time of the
death of St Thomas Aquinas in 1274 the great days of the
system-makers were over. It is the same with the religious
orders. In 1050 the Benedictine monopoly was unchallenged; by 1300, almost every possible variety of religious
organization had been established: the Carthusians and
numerous Orders of hermits; the Templars and a similar
profusion of military Orders; the various branches of
Canons Regular; the Cistercians; the four great Orders of
friars; hospitals of many different kinds; organizations for
the relief of prisoners. All these Orders and organizations

had their own constitutions, widely different in type and aim but all elaborated under papal protection and direction.

There have been periods in European history in which more rapid progress has been made in some directions, and in which there has been a greater variety of individual genius, but there has never been a period which has displayed so great a variety of achievement in the service of a single aim.

The social situation necessary for these achievements can in its essentials be described in a few words. Obviously western Europe throughout this period was an expanding society – internally expanding in organization and population; externally expanding in territorial aggression and commercial enterprise. These conditions enlarged the horizons and the ambitions of a previously constricted society. Nevertheless, despite the growth of towns and trade, western Europe as a whole was still predominantly agrarian. Agriculture was still the main source of wealth and political power. The greatest and most successful rulers retained the outlook of country gentlemen. They treated their magnates as friends, their clergy as intellectual superiors, and their own wealth as a fund to be used for lavish display and good works. They thought of participation in a Crusade as their final goal, often indeed postponed but never relegated to a never-never land. Every man had his station in society, and few men were allowed to sink very much lower or to rise very much higher than the station into which they had been born. Despite all its violence and the rapidity of its changing face it was reasonable to think of society as stable, for the growth of wealth on the whole increased the well-being of the traditional rulers of society. The intellectual predominance of the clergy and the success of their scholastic procedure in solving practical and theoretical problems gave unity to the creations of the age. The rapid diversification and development of every form of activity ensured fecundity of invention. The growth of the papal monarchy, the proliferation of the religious Orders, the systematic expansion of the range of intellect, all bore the imprint of a society which was expanding without yet being torn by great social upheavals.

We must now consider what happened when the balance of society became seriously disturbed.

III. THE AGE OF UNREST,
c. 1300–c. 1550

There are many indications in the early fourteenth century of some far-reaching changes in the structure of society and in the theoretical system which interpreted and helped to develop this structure. Things happened and were said which are scarcely conceivable in the previous two hundred years. The violent attack on Boniface VIII by French troops who invaded the papal palace at Anagni in 1303 was a staggering reversal of the collaboration between the popes and the kings of France which had been a steady force in European politics for nearly two centuries. The settlement of the pope at Avignon in 1309 might have been looked on as just another exile similar to many others in the past, if it had not lasted for nearly seventy years. The destruction of the Order of Templars in 1312–14 removed one of the main expressions of militant Christianity so warmly welcomed by St Bernard two centuries earlier. The condemnations of the Spiritual Franciscans and other popular urban religious movements associated with them in 1317–18 reflected both the growing strength of ideas that had been stirring convulsively for a century or more and the growing hostility which they aroused. Finally a succession of papal condemnations in the 1320s showed that the papacy stood in a new relationship to the intellectual and spiritual currents of the age. For two centuries the papacy had on the whole encouraged new ideas and new organizations. Innovators had instinctively sought papal protection and approval. Now the balance suddenly changed. The condemnation of the Franciscan doctrine of poverty in 1323 was an important turning point. It signalized the growing papal fear of extremism, and it led by devious routes to the further condemnation of William of Ockham, Marsilius of Padua, and Eckhart. These condemnations may all have been amply justified, but they opened up a new vista of a Europe that was no longer under papal control, of new movements of thought that could no longer be guided but only opposed. They helped to establish a pattern of opposition, which soon led to new extremism and new opposition. The able and clear-sighted Pope John XXII, who started this round of condemnations, found himself in his turn subjected to more virulent criticism than any pope since Gregory VII and suffered the unprecedented indignity of having his own cherished doctrine of the Beatific Vision condemned by his successor.

This condemnation of a publicly defended papal doctrine was a remarkable sign of a new instability in the papal office, though the doctrine itself was a personal idiosyncrasy of no lasting importance. The other condemnations, however, were in varying degrees related to two major changes in the structure of European society – the growing confidence and assertiveness of secular rulers and their advocates; and the growing menace to established institutions of great urban populations and the movements which they inspired. Neither of these factors was new in the early fourteenth century. Towns and secular governments had been growing in size and scope for two hundred years, but it was in the early fourteenth century that they first found their voice: Marsilius of Padua was the first impressive spokesman for secular rulers – for the flamboyant rhetoric of Frederick II's pamphleteers was only a sham – and Eckhart was the first impressive spokesman for the religion of articulate townspeople.

The changing environment

This moment when new voices were heard cannot be very strictly related to a new phase in the development of either town life or secular government. The subtle changes in balance which lead men to have different expectations about the future from their predecessors largely elude our observation. But there are a few points which stand out sufficiently clearly to be observed.

In the first place there seems to have been a distinct change in the rate of growth of population as between urban centres and rural areas in the early fourteenth century. There was a check in the steady growth of rural population at the moment when some towns experienced an unprecedented expansion. In Florence, for instance, it has been estimated that the population grew from about 10,000 to 30,000 in the century before 1300, and from 30,000 to about 120,000 between 1300 and 1345. No doubt this was quite exceptional, but towns seem in general to have maintained their momentum of growth while the growth of the rural population became uncertain. Towns with a population of 50,000 or more were to be found in many places in Europe in the early fourteenth century, especially in Flanders, the Rhineland, and northern Italy. Economically and politically the urban communities of western Europe were more important than they had been since the fourth century.

This had important consequences for the history of the church. There is something about urban life which provokes dissent. The comparative stability and isolation of rural life does not encourage the expression of unauthorized opinions. One man who does not think as his neighbours had better keep quiet. But when rebels and eccentrics come together in twenties and thirties instead of twos and threes, they find safety in numbers, they encourage each other to speak, and even men of quiet disposition begin to say what they think and to think strange thoughts. Moreover the discontents of town life are more acute than those of the countryside: the proximity of abject poverty and blatant wealth, the capriciousness of unemployment, the sense of exclusion, all add anguish to the common sufferings of life. There is plenty of evidence that all this was present in towns in the twelfth and thirteenth centuries. Articulate lay opinion about religion, often crude and generally subversive, began in the towns. This in its turn stimulated preachers and organizers to give form and coherence to

these opinions, and sometimes to oppose and denounce
them. By the fourteenth century these movements were too
strong to be repressed. They were the great new feature in
the religion of the later Middle Ages.

This new feature may be seen from two points of view.
On the one hand it was a threat to that hierarchical stability
which had been the dominant aim of the last two centuries.
Many observers had seen the threat growing. At first they
had seen it mainly as a threat to individual salvation: trade
encouraged usury; it promoted hypocrisy; it turned men
from productive labour; it caused avarice to flourish and
raised up men who profited from the misfortunes of their
neighbours; and so on. Then, as the threat developed, it
was seen as a threat not simply to the individual soul but
to the stability and good order of society. *Communia est
tumor plebis, timor regni, tepor sacerdotii* – 'the municipal
commune is a tumult of the people, a terror to the kingdom,
and a cause of clerical slackness' – so wrote an English
observer of the late twelfth century.[12] Aristotle, who taught
men to think about social problems, encouraged this line of
thought, and it was taken up by St Thomas Aquinas with
characteristic thoroughness. His argument is succinct and
uncompromising: the more self-sufficient a community is,
the more perfect it is; since commerce makes a community
less self-sufficient, it makes it less perfect; moreover it makes
a community less fit for war, for merchants grow soft; and
paradoxically it makes the community less peaceful, for
it brings many people together in a confined space; besides
(as Aristotle pointed out) trade encourages too much
talk and lays a community open to the contagion of bad
morals and false opinions.[13] But despite these doubts and
criticisms, trade and towns continued to grow, and in the
course of the thirteenth century they began to produce new
types of religious organization and a new intensity of personal religion. Both these movements represented a move

12. Richard of Devizes, *De Rebus Gestis Ricardi Primi*, p. 416 (*Chronicles
of the reigns of Stephen, Henry II and Richard I, R.S.*, 1886, iii).
  13. *De Regno*, ii, c. 3 (*S. Thomae Aquinatis Opuscula Omnia*, ed. P.
Mandonnet, 1927, i, pp. 350–51).

away from the clerical and hierarchical ideals of the age,
and to this extent they justified the critics of town life.

Emotion is the leading characteristic of urban religion.
It takes men out of the pressures of business, out of the
perplexities of prices, wages, and interest rates, out of the
miseries of intermittent over-employment and unemployment, out of the conflicts of classes and gilds, and it trans-
ports them into a world of the spirit where (as Eckhart
taught them) 'God begets his Son in the soul' and 'in this
way, as some of the authorities say, the soul is made equal
to God'.[14]

These themes in one way or another spread throughout
the towns of northern Europe. They were not necessarily
heretical. They were sometimes compatible with a strict
regard for ecclesiastical discipline and respect for the
spiritual hierarchy. But they were a threat to stability
because they made the institutions of religion seem less
important, and, if not wrong, perhaps irrelevant.

Political change and reaction

This tendency to view established institutions as irrelevant
was all the more dangerous because it coincided with a
changing attitude to politics. Here too the hierarchical
structure which had been raised up with so much painful
effort began to seem impracticable and probably wrong.
Everyone could see that secular governments with no
theoretical pretensions were growing in strength and
independence, and this cast doubt on the relevance, and
then on the validity, of elaborate theories of papal over-
lordship, universal rule, and sacerdotal supremacy. At the
same time everyone could see a wide gap between papal
actions and papal pretensions. In itself, this was only to be
expected. But there began to be a widespread suspicion
that the gap was growing, and that it was growing because
the theory behind the pretensions was unsound. This
appeared to different people in different ways. Dante was

14. I have examined Eckhart's contribution to urban religion more
fully in *Medieval Humanism and Other Studies*, 1970, pp. 19–26.

especially outraged by the way in which papal secular pretensions became in practice a vehicle for the family ambition of the ruling pope, ruinous alike to the spiritual government of the church and the well-being of Italy. But even secular rulers with none of Dante's insight could see that in most matters the pope was simply one of themselves, moved by similar motives, confined by the same practical limitations, and open to the same arguments of profit and loss.

In these circumstances there was a new urgency in the questions whether a universal lordship was theoretically necessary; whether, if necessary, it rightly belonged to the pope; whether, if it belonged to the pope, it embraced secular as well as spiritual affairs. It is often thought that theories were evolved in the Middle Ages without too much regard for facts. But this is a mistake. Theory and practice had the same relationship in the Middle Ages as at any other time. That is to say, when theories had practical success, they developed rapidly and in time outran the limits of immediate practicability. When this point was reached, the sense of failure quickly communicated itself to the universities, and new views then developed that helped to shape events in a new pattern.

This interaction of practice and theory produced a new emphasis on individual experience, on the values of secular life, on the role of the community as the source of political and spiritual authority. These ideas, formulated in quite new ways in the early fourteenth century, were immeasurably important for the future, but immediately they were much less successful than the clerical and hierarchical ideas of the eleventh century in bringing about a re-orientation of European society. There were many reasons for this. In the first place Europe was no longer the primitive society it had been in the eleventh century. The earlier revolution had found almost no rival organization to sweep away. Europe had needed new forms of government, and whoever first provided them was placed in a position of great strength. But by the early fourteenth century there was an elaborate system of ecclesiastical government penetrating to every parish in Europe, controlling much of the wealth, and closely integrated with the organs of secular rule. Whatever doubts there might be about the theoretical validity of the system, any possible cure seemed worse than the disease. The weight of established institutions was overwhelming: it could not be shifted without a vast upheaval; and this was a prospect which every ruler in the fourteenth century came to dread.

There was another reason for the lack of practical success of revolutionary thinkers like Marsilius, Ockham, and Wycliffe. Although intellectually they were no less powerful than the prophets of hierarchical government in the eleventh century, they spoke for no widespread body of powerful opinion. The critics of the old order of society in the eleventh century had represented a combination of interests, mainly clerical but partly also lay, that was irresistible. But in the fourteenth century the critics of the ecclesiastical hierarchy appealed to lay rulers who were neither sufficiently united, nor sufficiently powerful, nor sufficiently interested to follow their advice. The most powerful critics, Marsilius and Ockham, committed their fortunes to the German king, Louis of Bavaria, who turned out to be a negligible factor in European politics. The most effective anti-clerical force in Europe was the king of England, but he had very limited objectives – a little more taxation of the clergy, a little less papal interference with ecclesiastical appointments, a little more jurisdiction for the royal courts. As for the rulers of Italian cities and states, they looked on the pope as a potential ally or enemy, to be dealt with in political not ideological terms. Secular rulers everywhere found that they could live quite comfortably with the ecclesiastical machine. Most of them had no love for it, but they could more surely improve their position by threats and compromises than by a full-scale conflict. The greatest strength of papal government in the fourteenth century was that it had lost most of its teeth. It threatened no one. On the other hand, the ecclesiastical hierarchy could not be seriously attacked without a threat to the whole social order. Looking back over the thirteenth century,

Boniface VIII might declare that long experience had shown that every layman was an enemy to the clergy. What the fourteenth century showed was that they were enemies who could not live without making room for each other at the top.

This can be very clearly illustrated from events in England. England was the home of the most radical political, social, and religious movements in Europe – yet it was also one of the most conservative parts of the western church. The combination is not difficult to understand. The secular hierarchy of king and magnates, despite a fairly constant hostility to clerical interests, had more in common with the ecclesiastical hierarchy than with that dangerous and amorphous body 'the people'. It was all very well in 1327, on the occasion of Edward II's deposition, for the archbishop of Canterbury to preach on the theme 'The voice of the people is the voice of God.'[15] By the 'people' he meant the magnates. He would scarcely have preached on this theme when Wat Tyler brought his men to London in 1381. The real 'people' had then arrived, and they had in fact signalized their arrival by murdering the archbishop. This was the second English prelate to be murdered by the people in the fourteenth century, and it is significant that – unlike Thomas Becket two centuries earlier – they were both murdered, not as clergy, but as agents of royal government.

The solidarity between the secular and ecclesiastical hierarchies, which became closer as the threats from below became more perilous, is the most important factor in the exterior history of the medieval church during its last two centuries. Most secular rulers made some gains at the expense of the clergy – at the expense, that is to say, of what in the two previous centuries would have been called 'the liberty of the church' – but they recognized that they could not go too far without undermining their own position. This explains why the English government, for example, encouraged anti-papal legislation in detail, but drew back from a more general attack and especially from anything

15. See the account of this sermon in *Lanercost Chronicle*, ed. J. Stevenson, 1839, pp. 257–8.

with a subversive tendency. King and aristocracy became
the chief supporters of conservatism in the church. While the
old identity of interest between pope and clergy became
weakened, a new identity of interest between all supporters
of the hierarchical principle, whether secular or spiritual,
took over the task of safeguarding the achievements of
the eleventh-century reformers. The ecclesiastical system,
established as a result of the efforts of these reformers,
survived the last two centuries of the Middle Ages as an
indispensable instrument of secular government and social
order. So long as this alliance of secular and ecclesiastical
hierarchies lasted, the system survived; when it collapsed,
a new crisis was at hand.

To talk in these terms is to speak of medieval Europe in
a modern way. If we were to attempt to speak in a way that
might have been intelligible to contemporary observers,
we should have to use quite different categories. We might
for instance describe the three ages of the Middle Ages in
the terms used by the visionary writer Joachim of Fiore
in the late twelfth century. He made a bold division of
history into three ages of the Father, Son, and Holy
Spirit. Those who took him seriously found themselves
involved in many disappointing experiences. But if we take
his divisions as an allegory, they have a curious relevance
to medieval history. The first age down to the eleventh
century is the stern age of creation and survival, when the
basic institutions of Europe emerged. The second age is the
age of reason and intelligible system. In the third age, there
is less emphasis on system and more on intuition, less on
reason and more on will, love, and a freely moving spirit –
and like Joachim's third age of the Spirit it was also the
prelude to catastrophe.

3

The Divisions of Christendom

I. THE SEEDS OF DISUNITY

THE Middle Ages began with a united church and ended with a congeries of churches in a state of mutual schism and recrimination. That at least is the western view. But taking a larger view, the Middle Ages began with division. About the year 700 Christendom was in process of losing to Islam a large part of the lands that had been Christian for hundreds of years. North Africa, Syria, Palestine, and Spain had been, or were being, engulfed in the tide of Islamic expansion. In this process three of the five ancient patriarchal churches disappeared as forces in Christendom and lost touch with the rest of the church: henceforth Alexandria, Antioch, and Jerusalem counted for nothing in the counsels of the church. From this date the West knew little or nothing about the state of Christians in the earliest bishoprics of the ancient world, and a similar ignorance prevailed on their side. A Christian of Antioch in the eleventh century has left the revealing remark that no certain succession of the patriarchs of Rome was known in Antioch after the time of Pope Agatho who died in 681.[1] After this date the church at Antioch lost contact with the outside world. It had just enough strength to survive – no more.

This destruction of the churches left Constantinople and Rome to share between them what was left of the Christian world. In 700 they did not yet think of each other as enemies. In the seventh century the unity of these great patriarchal churches, on which the future of a united Christendom depended, had been natural and unquestioned.

[1]. *Histoire de Yaha-ibn-Said*, ed. A. Vasiliev (*Patrologia Orientalis*, 1924, xviii).

They were parts of a single political unity, sorely battered and shrinking, but still intact – the Christian Empire. The emperor at Constantinople was still the more or less effective ruler of large parts of Italy including Rome itself. The bishop of Rome was his secular deputy in the Roman duchy, and Byzantine officials were a common sight in the streets of Rome. The main route from Rome led to Ravenna, the capital of Byzantine government, and thence to Constantinople. The Mediterranean as far west as Marseilles was still a Byzantine highway. In a sense the unity of this whole area had become closer, and the links between Rome and Constantinople were stronger as a result of the disasters that had befallen the patriarchates of Alexandria, Antioch, and Jerusalem. Palestine, Syria, and Egypt had after all never been part of the Roman world in the same way as Rome and Constantinople. They had been centres of alien and disturbing influences. Now that they had gone the old Rome and the new Rome might be expected to draw together to protect their common civilization and religion in the face of a common enemy.

To some extent this did in fact happen. In the century between about 650 when the Islamic threat began and 750 when it had almost reached its limit in the West, Rome was more ecumenical than it had ever been. It was full of Greek and Syrian monks, refugees from the Islamic flood, who helped to keep Greek speech and customs alive in the Roman church. The nationality of the popes reflected this state of affairs. From 654 to 752 only five out of seventeen popes were of Roman origin; five were Syrian, three were Greek, three came from the strongly Greek island of Sicily, and one from some unknown part of Italy. In other words, eleven out of seventeen popes during this century had a mainly Greek, and only six a mainly Latin, background. This was in marked contrast to the century before 654 when thirteen out of fifteen popes had been Roman or Italian. From the point of view of Christian unity the growth of the Greek element in the Roman church was a hopeful sign: it meant that the two halves of the Christian world could still hold familiar discourse together.

This familiarity was more than a fact of language and culture: it was a fact of political life, and it had every appearance of permanence. In 663 the Greek emperor visited Rome and he was received as its lawful ruler. In 710 the pope visited Constantinople, and he was received with every mark of reverence by the emperor in a ceremonial scene identical with that used for his predecessor in 536. More important still, in 680 the pope sent legates to a council at Constantinople and they joined in condemning as heretical the teaching of four patriarchs of Constantinople and one pope.[2] This was (or might have been) highly significant, for it foreshadowed the possibility of compromise in a long controversy about the primacy of Rome among the patriarchal churches. If the pope could err like any other patriarch, even in the proportion of one to four, there was some chance that the two churches might agree that the Roman primacy, whatever else it might imply, did not present a contrast between absolute infallibility at Rome and recurrent error at Constantinople. If agreement could have been reached on this point, the two churches might yet have worked together. Unlike Jerusalem and Antioch, Constantinople had no serious claims to primacy among the Christian churches. The emperor recognized this when he prostrated himself before the pope and gave him honours in his own capital which he denied to the patriarch of Constantinople. The only important question at issue was the nature of the Roman primacy, and the most important aspect of this question was papal fallibility. The judgement of the Council of 680 might have been a milestone on the road to agreement on this point. But events decided otherwise.

Behind the hopeful façade of unity there were forces working for its destruction. At first these can be seen only in isolated and apparently trivial episodes, but they announced a transformation in the whole European scene. For example, no one at the time would have thought that 668 was a specially fatal year, but looking back it displays

2. On this Council and its decrees see E. Caspar, *Geschichte des Papsttums*, 1933, ii, 620.

some very sinister features. The Emperor Constans II was murdered in this year in Sicily by some members of his entourage, and this was bad; but it was much worse – though no one could have known – that he died making the last serious attempt to hold together North Africa, Italy, and the eastern Mediterranean under Byzantine rule. The political unity of the eastern Mediterranean which goes back fitfully to the fourth century B.C. came to an end in this obscure act of violence.

Divergent habits

The prospect in 668 was not all black. In this same year in Rome, the pope made a most beneficent and hopeful appointment: he appointed Theodore, a Greek-speaking monk from Tarsus, as archbishop of Canterbury. No one could better have exemplified the unity of the Greco-Roman world. Born in a Byzantine city, educated at Athens, a refugee in Rome from the invading armies of Islam, chosen by the pope to lead the newest and most westerly province in Christendom, Theodore stood for the unity of the whole Christian world. Theodore's career might therefore seem to contradict all the gloomy prognostications suggested by the death of the Emperor Constans II.

But there was a jarring element in this scene of unity. In dispatching Theodore to England the pope sent with him the abbot of a monastery near Naples, an African by origin called Hadrian, to see that Theodore 'introduced no Greek customs contrary to the true Faith into England'. The precaution was not unreasonable, but it is a sign of a growing unease. Greeks and Romans were already divided by an impenetrable wall of divergent habits, most of them insignificant, but deeply disturbing to orderly minds.

The records of Theodore's own teaching at Canterbury show how often these differences exercised his own mind and those of his listeners. When he spoke to his pupils about the outlines of Christian discipline, he reported many differences between the customs of the Greek and Latin churches. He reported that the Romans reconciled penitents within the apse of the church, but the Greeks did not; that the Greeks excommunicated those who failed to receive communion for three successive Sundays, but the Romans did not; that Roman monks had slaves, but Greek monks did not; that the Greeks accepted widows as nuns, but the Romans did not; and so on and so on.[3] In these reports, which stem from a unique range of experience, we can see the widespread diversity of customs in the two branches of the church. Urbane men knew that most of them were of no importance, but urbanity seldom survives long when ecclesiastical customs are discussed. Nothing is more vexing to the temper. If customs differ, how (they ask) is discipline to be preserved? If they differ obstinately, what is this but schism? How can there be unity if men will not renounce their differences? In these questions more than any others lay the seeds of disagreement between the two halves of Christendom.

Moreover there was another far-reaching division. Rome in the late seventh century was cosmopolitan and the popes were more often Greek than Latin. But the West had no interest in a cosmopolitan and half-Greek Rome: it wanted Rome for itself. In the scales of material wealth and culture the Latin West was ludicrously inferior to the Greek East, but in Rome it had one symbol of a latent superiority, and it held on to it with passionate intensity. Kings and princes of the newly founded barbarian kingdom flocked to Rome as to the gate of heaven. Monks and bishops went to Rome in search of authority, learning, and advice. It was disconcerting when they got there to find that they were outsiders in a Greco-Roman court.

This was the experience of St Wilfrid, the greatest papal enthusiast of the century. He arrived at Rome as a litigant in 704, appealing to the pope against the archbishop of Canterbury. He made his speech in Latin and was mortified when the Greek pope turned to talk in a foreign tongue

3. *Poenitentiale Theodori*, ed. A. W. Haddan and W. Stubbs, *Councils and Ecclesiastical Documents relating to Great Britain and Ireland*, 1871, iii, 173–203.

with his advisers, 'who smiled and said many things that
we could not understand'.[4] It was a trivial incident, but it
has a dramatic significance. Men like Wilfrid were the
backbone of papal authority. The countries from which
they came – England in the first place, then Germany and
France – were the only places where papal influence could
be strong because it was strongly desired. This kind of
loyalty and the heroic actions which it inspired made the
linguistic and cultural unity of the Greco-Latin world seem
very thin. As for the political unity, the last threads were
already breaking. The Greek emperor had visited Rome as
the supreme ruler in 663; he never did so again until he
came in the fourteenth century as a suppliant. The pope
visited Constantinople in 710: he has never repeated the
visit. The agreement of Greeks and Latins at the Council
of 680 was soon forgotten in the growing tensions of the
next century.

Political separation

We have seen that at the very beginning of the Middle
Ages there was a great deal of confusion in the relations
between the Greek and Latin churches. On the one hand
there were some impressive displays of the strength of the
ties between Rome and Constantinople, but on a lower
level multitudinous divergences and resentments. The
future lay with the latter tendencies and this was soon made
clear in the eighth century: it is this that makes it one of the
decisive periods in European history. Politics and the
defence of orthodoxy combined to drive the two halves of
Christendom apart.

The immediate need to defend orthodoxy arose from the
iconoclast movement which dominated the church of
Constantinople for sixty years from 726 to 787. In 729 the
Greek emperor sent Pope Gregory II a mandate forbidding
him to place pictures of martyrs and angels in the churches
under his jurisdiction. It was an unwise move. The pope
was already at loggerheads with the emperor over the

4. Eddius Stephanus, *Life of Bishop Wilfrid*, c. 53, ed. B. Colgrave,
1927, p. 112.

payment of taxes, and the mandate raised the controversy from the sordid level of political disobedience, where the pope's legal position was weak, to the more elevated one of orthodoxy where he was strong. His reply showed a remarkable insight into the real basis of his strength. He turned for support to the new nations of the West:

> The whole West has its eyes on us, unworthy though we are. It relies on us and on St Peter, the Prince of the Apostles, whose image you wish to destroy, but whom all the kingdoms of the West honour as if he were God himself on earth.

The pope had never visited these new kingdoms of the West. Hitherto almost the only road he had taken outside Rome had been the road to Constantinople, but now he declared:

> We are going to the most distant parts of the West to seek those who desire baptism. Although we have sent bishops and clergy of our holy church to them, their princes have not yet received baptism, for they wish to receive it from ourselves alone.[5]

These words led to no immediate result, but they mark a turning point. We see the pope cutting himself loose from his ancient anchorage in the Greco-Roman world, from which he had no longer anything to fear or hope, and turning to the new lands where his future strength lay. The English missionaries to Germany, St Willibrord and St Boniface, had pioneered this path for the papacy. The pope had only to follow in the footsteps of these explorers of the new West.

It was another twenty-five years before a pope took the westward road which Gregory II had promised to take, and then it was taken not in order to baptize the Germans, but to cement a new political alliance. Until 754 the pope ruled the duchy of Rome nominally as an official of the emperor at Constantinople. But by this time, imperial

---

5. *P.L.* 89, col. 520, 524. For the authenticity of these letters see E. Caspar, 'Gregor II und der Bildenstreit', *Zeitschrift f. Kirchengeschichte*, 1933, lii, 29–70; against, see J. Haller, *Das Papsttum*, 1950–3, i. 548. I am persuaded by Caspar, but the main point is unaffected by the issue.

power in Italy was rapidly breaking up under the attacks of the Lombards. The pope was not sorry to see the retreat of an imperial authority which he had long ceased to respect or obey; but its disappearance left him in a very exposed position. In December 753, therefore, Pope Stephen II crossed the Alps to explore the possibility of a new western political basis for papal sovereignty. As a result of the exploration he made an alliance with the new Carolingian king, Pepin, with consequences that lasted almost as long as the Middle Ages themselves. Under the terms of this agreement political power in Italy was divided between the pope and the Carolingian dynasty. The Carolingian stepped into the shoes of the Greek emperor in Italy; but he came, not as the pope's political superior, but as his client. He was not yet an emperor in his own right; but he was already an emperor *in petto* to be produced as and when the papacy required him. The ceremonial with which Pepin greeted Pope Stephen II when he approached his palace seems to have been based on that with which emperors had greeted popes in the past. In this transference of power and ceremonial the foundations of the medieval Empire and Papacy were laid.[6]

The long drawn-out consequences of this realignment for both the unity and disunity of Christendom were enormous. For the first time in history the pope had acted as a supreme political authority in authorizing the transfer of power in the Frankish kingdom, and he had emphasized his own political rôle as successor to the emperors by disposing of imperial lands in Italy. These were steps of the highest importance for the future. They were moreover highly treasonable. The pope had passed from mere neglect of his duty of political obedience to the Greek emperor to the downright seizure of political power. The coronation of Charlemagne in 800 was the practical outcome of the policy adopted fifty years earlier. It was at once the symbol

6. For the details of the pope's journey see L. Duchesne, *Liber Pontificalis*, 1886, i, 446–8, and 457–8, where the other authorities are quoted. There are further bibliographical references in the supplementary volume of this work, ed. C. Vogel, 1957, pp. 102–3.

of the political liberation of the West, and of the political –
and ultimately therefore religious – disruption of Christendom.

We have become so accustomed to thinking of Christendom as an ideal body detached from all ties of political loyalty that it is well to be reminded that from the time of Constantine religious unity had stemmed in the first place from political unity. Religious unity could scarcely be thought of apart from political unity, if only because religious unity depended on some ultimate power of coercion. Hence all future medieval plans for the reunification of Christendom are fundamentally plans for political reintegration.

After the end of the eighth century Christendom was no longer politically united even in the most shadowy way. Political disunity was added to those other sources of discord between Greeks and Latins that have already been mentioned, and it was more important than any of them. It now only remained to add differences about doctrine and ecclesiastical authority to make the division between the Greek and Latin churches complete.

Doctrinal differences

Despite the tensions of the eighth century, doctrinal differences were not yet acute when it ended. The dispute about images had been healed and the popes were not eager to widen the breach that had been opened by their political actions. Quite the contrary. Even after the political breach, the popes continued to have a closer intellectual affinity to the Greeks than to their German allies. The East was still the most numerous, the best educated, and the richest part of Christendom. It was still the source of learning and civilization; and it continued to be the scene of the most important definitions of Christian orthodoxy. After all the discord of the eighth century the pope still sent his legates to the Council of Nicaea in 787. This was the last universally acknowledged ecumenical council of the undivided church. It was presided over by a patriarch of Constantinople, and

it drew up a definition of the place of images in Christian
worship which had the approval of papal legates and bore
the signature of the Greek emperor. Like so many other
events in this time of the breaking of ancient bonds it was
the last event of its kind.

For a time it seemed that the intellectual and spiritual
unity of Christendom might survive its political disintegration. Yet, in the long run, this exalted unity of mind and
spirit had little chance of surviving when it was cut off
from the natural strength that springs from political and
social cohesion. The men of the West who provided the
only solid support for the papacy despised and hated the
Greeks, and the popes could not dissociate themselves from
their supporters. Although the minds of the popes were
turned to Constantinople, their interests drew them west-
wards.

There is a striking example of this in the aftermath of the
Council of Nicaea in 787. Although it was an ecumenical
council attended by papal legates to settle the important
question of the place of images in Christian worship, no
representatives of the western churches were present.
Neither the pope nor the Council thought that western
theologians could have anything to contribute to the discussion. But Charlemagne, who had been encouraged to
think of himself as the defender of the churches in the
dominions, felt slighted. As soon as he had obtained a
translation of the decrees of the Council he caused a scathing
attack to be launched on its decisions. He and his scholars
described the proceedings of the Council as stupid and
arrogant, and its decrees as erroneous, criminal, schis-
matical, and lacking in all sense or eloquence.[7] The fact
that their translation of the decrees was a bad one did not

7. The *Libri Carolini*, from which these and the following phrases are
quoted, are printed in *M.G.H. Concilia*, ii. For the origin of the work see
W. v. den Steinen, 'Entstehungsgeschichte der Libri Carolini', *Quellen
u. Forschungen aus Ital. Archiven u. Bibliotheken*, 1929–30, xxi, 1–93; also
A. Freeman, 'Theodulf of Orleans and the Libri Carolini', *Speculum*, 1957,
xxxii, 663–705. H. Fichtenau has cast doubt on Charlemagne's personal
presence at the discussions (*Mitteilungen des Institut f. Oesterreichischen
Geschichte*, 1953, lxi, 208–87).

deter these critics. The Greek church was the source of all
the evils of the Council: 'it is not surprising that streams
which spring up in boastfulness and vainglory should come
together in one filthy pond of hell'. On behalf of the despised
churches of the West the Frankish ruler stood forth as the
defender of the true Faith: 'we are compelled to unite
against these errors, in the hope that the spineless enemy
from the East may be repelled in the West'. The long theological treatise which followed this broadside was a warning
to the Greeks not to presume to speak on behalf of the whole
church. It was also a warning to the pope that his real
strength lay in the West: he had been caught fraternizing,
so to speak, with the enemy.[8]

Of course this attitude of the western ruler was as unacceptable to the pope as it was to the Greeks, but for
different reasons. To the Greeks, it was absurd that a man
like Charlemagne, who could not read, should preside over
a council of insignificant bishops and lay down the law on
difficult doctrinal issues. Such matters should be left to the
learned emperor and bishops of the East. The popes were
equally aware of the absurdity: they had no intention of
setting up an ignorant western ruler in place of a learned
Greek emperor in order to make him an arbiter of doctrine.
In the unlettered West, these were matters for the clergy,
and especially for the clergy of the unwaveringly orthodox
church of Rome. The difference between the two points of
view was a measure of the distance that separated the
societies of East and West.

The pope had no intention of allowing his physical
dependence on the West to limit his doctrinal freedom.
Nevertheless the influence of the lay ruler was very pervasive. Although Charlemagne's onslaught on the Council of
Nicaea could be quietly ignored, on a more important
matter he had a powerful influence in widening the gap

8. There is another example of a warning to the pope not to allow
himself to fraternize with the Greeks in a letter from William of St
Benigne to John XIX in 1024 when the pope was thought to be considering a division of authority with the patriarch of Constantinople (Raoul
Glaber, *Historiae*, ed. M. Prou, 1886, p. 93).

between East and West. This was the matter of the Nicaean Creed, and since it provided the grounds for the first permanent doctrinal dispute between East and West, it requires a little elaboration.

In 381 a definitive statement of belief had been issued by the Council of Constantinople, which came to be known as the Nicaean Creed. This Creed, which was accepted by the whole church, both eastern and western, contained the statement that the Holy Spirit comes 'from the Father'. To this statement the word *Filioque*, 'and the Son', was unofficially added by some unknown person or community in the West, perhaps in Spain in the seventh century. This might have remained a purely local peculiarity if some of Charlemagne's advisers had not come from Spain. Under their influence the additional words were added to the text of the Creed as used at Mass in Charlemagne's chapel. From this moment the addition became a matter of much more than local importance. Charlemagne and his advisers had a passion for uniformity, and they had the power and will to make their views prevail over much of the western church. Whatever formula was adopted in Charlemagne's court was bound to have a widespread influence. The one obstacle was the papacy. Here, as in other matters, the pope still found the Greeks better company than the Franks. Pope Leo III advised Charlemagne to drop the addition, but his advice had no effect, and gradually the addition became universal in the western church except at Rome. At Rome, as it happened, there was no need for the pope to decide about the addition, because an ancient form of the Mass was used which omitted the Creed altogether. At the beginning of the eleventh century therefore, when the whole of the western church had come to use the interpolated form of the Creed in the Mass, the pope had not yet committed himself to maintaining the new use.

The papal chapel first succumbed to the prevailing western fashion in the early eleventh century. It did so, according to an almost contemporary report, at the request of Emperor Henry II.[9] Certainly by this time the mainten-

9. Berno of Reichenau, *De Officio Missae*, P.L. 142, 1060–61.

ance of the older fashion at Rome was anomalous, but the manner of the change is a good example of the way in which western pressure slowly moulded the papacy. There was no formal consultation, no explicit decision. Even the moment of change is uncertain. But by about 1030 a formula that had slowly spread through the western church without papal authorization was installed at the centre of Latin Christendom. For the first time it was possible to point to a distinct point of doctrinal difference between Rome and Constantinople. It had not burst on the world like a thunder-clap as did the short-lived iconoclasm of the East in the eighth century. It had grown silently and secretly from small beginnings –

> *crevit, occulto velut arbor aevo*

– a tree with poisoned fruit.

Probably no one realized at the time that an important step had been taken. It had simply become inevitable that, once the papacy was cut off from the Greeks and aligned with the barbarian West, the popes should express a point of view that was increasingly western. The change of out-look had been accelerated by a change in the background of the popes themselves. We have already remarked on the strong Greek element in the line of popes between 654 and 752. The last of this line of Greek popes was Zacharias, who signalized his allegiance to an undivided Greco-Latin church by translating into Greek the *Dialogues* of his predecessor Gregory I.[10] His successor, Stephen II, was the first of the line of purely Latin popes. There was not another pope of Greek origin until the fifteenth century. From 752 to 1054 the succession of popes tells its own story: forty-four Romans, eleven Italians, four Germans, one Frenchman, and one Sicilian. The identification of the papacy with the West could hardly be more emphatically illustrated.

10. See his contemporary biography in the *Liber Pontificalis*, ed. L. Duchesne, 1886, i, 432–5. Among the last echoes of the ancient unity of the Greco-Latin world the biographer records the gift made by the Greek emperor to the pope of two important estates near Rome, perhaps in compensation for the loss of the papal estates in Sicily and Calabria.

During these three hundred years the relations between the Greek and Latin churches did not fundamentally alter. No one was anxious to push the division further than was necessary. The strength of the East during these centuries kept alive the possibility of a final conquest of the lost territories in the West which would restore the bonds of unity. The weakness of the West discouraged gestures of independence on its side, and arrested the progress of disunity. Throughout these centuries the balance of power and prestige was tilted even more decisively towards the East than hitherto. In the range of their ideas and experience, the scholars and statesmen of the West with very few exceptions were small men, whose strength lay in not knowing how small they were. They knew just enough about the thoughts of the Greeks to think that they were contemptible, and they knew nothing at all about the thoughts of their contemporaries in Islam. In this ignorance the West was able to develop a measure of confidence, however misplaced it might be.

The threads which had been broken in the eighth century were never replaced. This is the ultimate secret of the division of Christendom. Nothing that happened ever seemed irremediable, but from the eighth century onwards every impulse to disunity had a disproportionate effect because the political and social situation allowed no contrary impulses to survive. By the middle of the eleventh century Christendom was held together only by the force of inertia. The West still lacked coherent power. The East was strong within very wide limits, but these limits stopped short – as several fruitless efforts had proved – at the ports of Italy. Except for the *Filioque* question the area of disagreement had not greatly changed in the last few centuries. On this question both sides in their cooler moments agreed that either formula, correctly interpreted, was admissible. As late as 1050 Pope Leo IX defended the orthodoxy of both statements with an illustration: a fruit (he said) may be said to come from the trunk of a tree, or from the branch, or from the trunk through the branch; so the Spirit may be said to come from the Father, or from the Son, or from the

Father through the Son. The illustration is an example of a persistent desire of the popes till this time not to press the division further than need be. But the moment had now come for this and every other point in dispute to take a sharper edge.

II. THE TWO CHURCHES

It has long been held that the year 1054 was the year of the great confrontation between the two churches when, in the words of Gibbon,

> The rising majesty of Rome could no longer brook the insolence of a rebel; and Michael Cerularius (the Patriarch of Constantinople) was excommunicated in the heart of Constantinople by the pope's legates.

It is true, Gibbon adds, that

> according to the emergencies of the church and state a friendly correspondence was sometimes resumed; the language of charity and concord was sometimes affected; but the Greeks have never recanted their errors; and from this thunderbolt we may date the consummation of the schism.[11]

Recent historians have had their doubts about this interpretation of the events of 1054. They have pointed out that the thunderbolt was not noticed by contemporaries nor remembered by their successors, that the authority of the legates had expired before the anathema was delivered, and that everything went on as if nothing had happened. And certainly if we grade events with reference to the number of further events which they cause, the confrontation of 1054 will take a very lowly place. But if we look at events to discover the characteristics of an age Gibbon's judgement will be found to be substantially right. It was in 1054 that all the elements of disunity which had come to

---

11. *Decline and Fall of the Roman Empire*, ch. lx (World's Classics, vi, 401). For a recent interpretation of the incident, see S. Runciman, *The Eastern Schism: a Study of the Papacy and the Eastern Churches during the Eleventh and Twelfth Centuries*, 1955.

light over the centuries were first concentrated into a
single event.

There was nothing new in any single element of this
disunity. The different social and ecclesiastical habits, the
disagreements about ecclesiastical and political authority,
the disagreement about doctrine, the dispute about areas
of jurisdiction – they were all old. But in 1054 they were
all brought together, and they were brought together
without any of the reluctance that the popes had so far
shown in enlarging the area of disagreement. The papal
documents of this year enlarged the differences with all
possible clarity and emphasis; and they did so although –
almost one may say because – their immediate purpose was
to bring about a reunion of Christendom.

It seemed indeed that the moment for reconciliation had
come. The pope and the Greek emperor had now a common enemy against whom they could unite: the Normans
of southern Italy. This was the only part of western Europe
where the government in Constantinople still retained a
shaky political and ecclesiastical control. Politically it had
always been part of the Byzantine empire; but ecclesiastically it had been subject to Rome until the eighth century
when – in retaliation for the pope's political betrayal – the
Greek emperor transferred the area to the patriarch of
Constantinople.[12] The pope was anxious to re-establish his
ecclesiastical authority, while the emperor was eager to
restore his political control. The interests of both of them
were threatened by the Normans, who – in the words of
Leo IX –

everywhere destroy the churches with more than pagan brutality,
murdering Christians and torturing them to death with new and

12. For the removal of the provinces of Sicily and Calabria from papal
authority and their subjection to the patriarch of Constantinople in the
time of the Emperor Leo III (717–41), see F. Dölger, *Regesten der
Kaiser – Urkunden des Oströmischen Reiches*, 1924, i, no. 301. For an argument
for a later date see V. Grumel, 'L'annexion de l'Illyricum oriental, de la
Sicile et de la Calabre au patriarchat de Constantinople', *Recherches de
sciences religieuses*, 1952, lx, 191–200.

horrible torments. They spare neither young nor old, and they respect neither humanity nor holiness.[13]

In 1053 the pope had followed up these words with a military campaign against the Normans, and he had been defeated and made a prisoner of the Normans. This was the first papal defeat in an area that was to be fought over again and again in the next two hundred years, and it taught a lesson that was never forgotten: without allies success was impossible. The Greek emperor on his side also needed allies. Southern Italy was at the end of his lines of communication, and it could only be held with Italian help. There had never been a moment when collaboration between the two great powers of East and West promised greater dividends. Naturally both sides would have to make concessions: the pope would expect the restoration of his ecclesiastical, the emperor of his political, authority. Neither aim seemed beyond the realm of possibility.

The situation however was complicated by a dispute about ecclesiastical customs. The churches of southern Italy at this time were Greek in discipline and customs, and in 1052 the bishop of Trani in Apulia received a letter from the metropolitan of Bulgaria, defending the Greek use of leavened bread in the Mass and the practice of fasting on Saturdays, and attacking the Latin usages in these and other matters. The bishop of Trani was urged to bring these criticisms to the notice of the pope and the western bishops. By the standards of theological controversy the letter was not particularly violent, but naturally it said some hard things about the Latins who were alleged to have broken the unity of Christendom.[14] The effect of the letter, however, on the impending negotiations between Rome and Constantinople was disastrous. It raised in a most acute form the whole problem of the authority of Rome, and it aroused tempers already eager for fresh inflammation.

It was in these circumstances that the pope sent his

13. Leo IX to the Emperor Constantine Monomachus, *P.L.* 143, 777–81 (Ep. 103).

14. *P.G.* 120, 836–44.

legates to Constantinople in 1054 to begin comprehensive
negotiations with the Greeks. The papal letters which they
carried with them had been written in captivity, and it is
an extraordinary indication of the strength and consistency
of papal policy that the letters show no sign of the weakness
of the pope's position. With consummate skill and passion
they surveyed the whole area of dispute, and enunciated
the papal claims with a new breadth of vision and vigour
of argument. At the same time they initiated a policy which
lasted almost till the end of the Middle Ages.[15]

Briefly the policy was this: to speak fair words to the
emperor and stern ones to the patriarch; to offer friendship
to the emperor and demand obedience from the patriarch;
to treat the patriarch like a delinquent and the emperor
like a son. To the emperor the pope wrote as to a favoured
son who might, if he would, bring peace and concord after
long-drawn-out and ruinous discords. In moderate terms
he urged the need for unity with the Roman church. He
described the obligations of the emperor's great ancestor
Constantine towards Rome, and exhorted him to imitate
his example. He sought cooperation against the Normans,
their common enemy. In this soothing discourse we note
the mixture of firmness and pliancy. Even at this critical
moment, the pope did not fail to safeguard the rights of
Henry III of Germany, the western emperor, 'in his own
sphere'. Then, in the next sentence, he softened the harshness of this reference to an imperial rival by a subtle turn
of phrase that was certainly not fortuitous. In speaking of
Henry III he called him simply *clarissimus*, giving him no
higher dignity than that anciently accorded to consuls or
patricians; then at once he turned to the Greek ruler and
distinguished him with the imperial epithet *serenissimus*.
The writer of the letter must, I think, have smiled as he
added this touch. These verbal dexterities are an essential

15. The letters discussed below in which this policy was adumbrated
are printed in *P.L.* 143, 744–81. They are placed in their setting by
Richard Mayne, 'East and West in 1154', *Cambridge Historical Journal*,
1954, xi, 133–48. For their authorship, see A. Michel, *Humbert und
Kerullarios*, 2 vols., 1924–30.

part of the diplomatic game, and we must not forget that reunion on both sides was an exercise in diplomacy.

When it came to writing to the patriarch the language of diplomacy was abandoned. Two letters were addressed to him, and the longer of them (it is about 17,000 words long) is a masterpiece of comprehensive and passionate argument. It set forth a history of Rome as it appeared through papal eyes – a history of the Church controlled from its earliest days by St Peter and his successors; endowed by Constantine with imperial authority over the West; acknowledged by Councils as standing above all human judgement; opposing an unswerving orthodoxy to the multifarious heresies of Constantinople and the East; standing in the relation of a Mother to her daughter churches of Jerusalem, Antioch, Alexandria, and Constantinople. To this patient, suffering, persecuted Mother, Constantinople was a disobedient, insolent, corrupt daughter

sitting at home in delicate security, in pleasure and lasciviousness, in the dissipation of a long leisure, refusing to take part in the fight waged on her behalf by the pious Mother, repaying her efforts by mocking her Mother's old age and her body worn out by long labours, claiming the Mother's primacy, and with girlish levity offering to feed the Mother with the daughter's milk.[16]

Rome is the Mother and her spouse is God. Any nation which dissented from Rome was nothing but a 'confabulation of heretics, a conventicle of schismatics, a synagogue of Satan'; and to attack the observances of Rome was simply to display to the world the sacrilegious temerity, and filthy, lunatic, Manichaean scurrility of the Greeks. I do not think that language quite like this had ever been used before. Certainly the papal theme had never before been brought so comprehensively before the Greek church, nor had it been expressed with such abundance of illustration and imagery, nor with such an emphatic demand for overall obedience.

It has often been regretted that the papal case was stated with such vigour on this occasion, and the blame in recent

16. *P.L.* 143, 761.

years has generally been laid at the door of Cardinal
Humbert, whose hand has been detected in the phrase-
ology of these letters. But whatever Humbert's rôle may
have been it is a mistake to attribute too much to him, and
to speak as if these phrases were simply the result of his
unbridled violence of speech. There is no sign that the
letters were composed in a hurry. There is no sign that they
went an inch beyond what almost the whole western church
would have acclaimed. The letters bore the pope's name,
and he had a long leisure between June 1053, when he was
taken as a prisoner to Benevento, and January 1054, when
he dispatched his legates, to consider every circumstance
of the case. The differences between the letters to the
emperor and the patriarch are sufficient to show how much
care went into their composition, and the policy behind
these differences was not a casual one. Above all, the view
of unity they expressed faithfully reflects the view which became the mainspring of action in the following centuries.

Until this time East and West had simply fallen apart,
and such unity as there was came not from common activity
but from inactivity and lack of contact. But all this was
changing. The Mediterranean was again coming into its
own as a main highway for western Europe. The relations
with Constantinople were bound to become closer. As
relations became closer differences became more acute,
and the needs for a real as opposed to a nominal unity
became more urgent. From now on, unity was seen (at
least in the West) in terms of discipline, obedience, and
uniformity. This was the main contribution of the Latin
Middle Ages to the problem of Christian unity. Perhaps
it was a great mistake. It certainly wrenched further apart
whatever could not be more tightly pressed together. But
it meant the beginning of serious thought about reunion
and the means of achieving it.

III. THE SEARCH FOR REUNION

Roughly speaking there were three methods of uniting
Christendom which received serious attention after 1054.

They were the method of military conquest, the method of political negotiation along the lines of what would now be called a package deal, and lastly the method of religious conciliation. The first is purely western; the second is the joint product of papal diplomacy and Greek imperial necessity. As to the third, in the end both East and West made a contribution characteristic of the two communities. It is only the last that is of any practical interest today, but it is important to remember the military and political solutions, for they were the only ones which offered much chance of success in the Middle Ages, and it was out of their failure that the third emerged.

The military way

There can be no doubt that the military method offered by far the best chance of success. Many people recognized this at the time, and they were right. If only a fraction of the effort lavished on the Crusade between 1095 and 1261 had been devoted to the task of defeating and taking over the Greek empire, not only would Christendom in all probability have been reunited, but even the Crusade against Islam would have had a far better prospect of success. We shudder at the thought. But if we accept the presuppositions of medieval western thought it is hard to see what could be urged against this method of solving the problem. An attack on the schismatic and probably heretical Greeks was much easier to justify than an attack on Islam. The West was never very happy in its justification of the Islamic Crusade. The violence of its advocates covered some very weak points in their arguments. There was a much stronger theoretical case for the use of the secular arm against heresy and schism. Why then was this method not used except in 1204, when confused aims and papal disapprobation robbed the enterprise of half its force?

I think there were three main reasons for the reluctance to settle the question by the sword. Firstly, the weakness of the Greeks was not appreciated until the Crusades were launched in a direction from which it was impossible to recall them. Secondly, people became adjusted to habitual modes of action, and there was a natural reluctance to settle by violence a problem which had grown from imperceptible beginnings until it had almost become part of the normal life of the church. Thirdly, and most important, the political dangers to the papacy of a successful military action against Constantinople were very great. The obvious leader of such an action was either a Hohenstaufen or, later, an Angevin, and no pope could contemplate an extension of the power of either of these two families. Politically these fears were well-founded, for only a western ruler already too strong for papal political safety could have held the East by military force. Consequently the papal curia always preferred political negotiation to military action.

The political package deal

A political solution in practice meant papal support for a Greek emperor in return for the obedience of the Greek church to the pope. This was a solution which had so much to offer both the Greek emperor and the pope that it was never far from their counsels. As we have seen, it was the policy already adumbrated in the abortive negotiations of 1054. At that time the *point d'appui* for the policy of co-operation lay in South Italy; but the policy survived the Byzantine collapse in this area, and it was revived as a counter-weight to Hohenstaufen and Norman power in the twelfth century. Again it survived the collapse of the Hohenstaufen; and was revived by the threat of Angevin ambitions. Momentarily in 1274, it succeeded. The policy had the simplicity of a great idea. Hence its persistence.

Nothing could be simpler. In return for ecclesiastical obedience, the Greek emperor would obtain relative security from western attack and the possibility of help against Islam. The pope would have an emperor without Italian entanglements. He might even again contemplate a single emperor at Constantinople. The Crusade would have a new hope. It was a vision of peace and unity to attract at once the idealist and the practical man. Pope Clement IV, who combined both these qualities, put the plan in its clearest terms when he wrote to Michael VIII Palaeologus in 1267:

> The Crusade is being prepared, and the whole of Europe is rising at our bidding. If you will attack the Moslems on one side while the Crusaders attack them on the other, we shall see an end of their damnable religion for ever. And if you say you are afraid the Latins will attack *you* while your troops are engaged on your other frontier, the answer is simple: return to the unity of the Roman church and all fears of this kind can be put aside for ever.[17]

This passage outlines with all possible clarity the plan which successive popes had followed with growing conviction and intensity. It is the culmination of all that had happened since 1054. If we are alienated by its frankly political message, we must remember that it was a policy full of brilliant promise for the unity of Christendom. It was still plausible in 1267. The pope had not yet lost the power of directing a sizeable proportion of the military resources of the West; he could still hope that this proportion would grow; and, given a firm political base in the eastern empire, the Crusade against Islam was not yet hopeless. The policy enunciated by the pope had the essential characteristic of all great political plans of combining idealism and self-interest in nicely balanced proportions. All in all it was the grandest and most carefully elaborated of all the plans of medieval statesmanship.

There was, however, a snag. The plan depended on the willingness of large numbers of people, lay and ecclesiastic, to accept what their leaders had agreed. The Greek emperor probably always had doubts about this, but if he were to negotiate at all he had to act as if the doubts did not exist. As for the pope and his advisers, there was every reason why they should long remain blind to this difficulty. In the first place they exaggerated the extent to which the emperor was the effective head of the Greek church. They saw

17. A. Potthast, *Regesta Pontificum Romanorum*, 1874–5, no. 20012; Martène and Durand, *Veterum Scriptorum Amplissimo Collectio*, 1724, ii, 469–70.

everything in terms of papal power. Just as they imagined that the caliph in Baghdad was a kind of pope in Islam, so they imagined that the emperor was a sort of pope in Constantinople. They knew that he had deposed and set up patriarchs; they did not know, or they forgot, how often the patriarch had humbled the emperor. A most curious illustration of this misunderstanding is to be found in a letter written by Paschal II to the Emperor Alexius I in 1112. Talking about the emperor's proposals for negotiating a settlement he says:

We are in a great difficulty in this business, because owing to their great diversity, *our* peoples cannot easily agree on one opinion. But, by the grace of God, this is easy for you because the opinions of clerks and laymen, prelates and subjects, depend on your decision.[18]

This gives us a fascinating glimpse of the pope's own views of his difficulties, and it presents a surprising contrast to our own view of the situation. Where we are impressed by the ease with which papal declarations of orthodoxy were accepted in the West, Paschal felt the difficulty of obtaining a general assent to his decisions, and he supposed that the Greek emperor had a stronger grip on popular opinion in the East than the pope in the West.

Yet the situation was in fact very different. In the West popular opinion in theological and disciplinary matters did not yet exist, and ecclesiastical opinion was highly amenable to papal authority until at least the end of the thirteenth century. The Greek emperor, even in collaboration with the patriarch, was in a much weaker position: there was an active body of lay theological opinion, an even more active and firmly entrenched monastic opinion, and a profound danger of popular disturbance. In the face of these potential sources of opposition the emperor's power to make ecclesiastical decisions was very limited. He must have known his limitations, but he could not express them without destroying his power of negotiation: he had to talk as if he could enforce whatever settlement he wished.

18. P. Jaffé, *Registrum Pontificum Romanorum*, 2nd ed. by W. Watten-bach, 1885–8, no. 6334.

Politicians must attempt many things which in their hearts they know to be impossible, either because there is no alternative or because the only alternative is one which they refuse to contemplate. As we have seen, the solution by violence had to be ruled out because of its political dangers from a papal point of view. If the political solution were also to be ruled out on grounds of impracticability, the only alternative would be a discussion of the ecclesiastical issues between the two sides on a more or less equal footing.

Neither side was ready for this. In principle the Greeks favoured discussion, but with their long tradition of intellectual superiority they doubted the capacity of the Latins to discuss: they saw them as the barbarians, the intellectual incompetents. The Latins on their side were against discussion on principle. To discuss, as if they were open questions, matters already decided by the popes was to admit a doubt about the papal authority which was the basis of the whole Latin case against the Greeks. To quote once more Paschal II's letter to the Emperor Alexius:

The first step towards unity is that our brother the patriarch of Constantinople should recognize the primacy and dignity of the apostolic see . . . and correct his former obstinacy. The causes of diversity of faith and custom between Greeks and Latins cannot be removed unless the members are first united to the head. For how can questions be discussed between dissenting and antagonistic bodies when one refuses to obey or agree with the other?[19]

In other words debate is futile unless we first agree who is right; and then of course it is unnecessary. It must be said that the few debates between Greeks and Latins which took place in the twelfth and thirteenth centuries tended to confirm this judgement about the futility of discussion when there was no ultimate authority to impose a decision.[20]

19. ibid. The passage is quoted in W. Norden, *Das Papsttum u. Byzanz,* 1903, p. 94n.

20. This is not to belittle the considerable efforts on both sides to make intellectual contact with the other camp: see for example A. Dondaine, 'Hughes Ethorion et Léon Tuscan', *Archives de l'hist. doctrinale et litt. du Moyen Âge,* 1952, xix, 67–134 (for the twelfth century), and (for the thirteenth century), besides the work of Humbert de Romanis mentioned

If both war and debate were ruled out there was nothing left but to resort to that type of negotiation which we now call the package deal – that is to say the kind of negotiation which aims at an exchange of benefits between parties who have no common principles on which to conduct discussion. In 1274 this kind of negotiation achieved a momentary success. After a vast amount of intensive preparation stretching back over nearly quarter of a century a settlement was reached at the Council of Lyons.[21]

The settlement attained all the objectives that Leo IX's legates had so signally failed to reach in 1054. The timing was admirable. Conditions so favourable for this method of reunion could never recur. But it came to nothing. The reason was simple: what the emperor had accepted in Lyons, clergy and people refused to accept in Constantinople. This was the forgotten factor in all these negotiations, and it was fatal. 1274, like 1054, became one of the great years in which nothing happened. In a sense it was the last hopeful year in the Middle Ages. Henceforth the Greeks were engaged in a losing struggle for survival against external attack, and the Latins were beset with the rising difficulties of internal disintegration.

Western leaders did not at once or easily understand the main lesson, that an ecclesiastical union, arranged for political reasons over the heads of clergy and people, could not succeed. They preferred to ascribe the failure to the perfidy of the Greeks. Nevertheless it became clear that something had been lacking in the type of negotiation which led to the fiasco of 1274. It was not clear what it was, and there was little time left for finding out. But circumstances helped to bring home to both sides some elements of the truth.

below (p. 82), A. Dondaine, 'Premiers Écrits polémiques des Dominicains en Orient', *Archivum Fratrum Praedicatorum*, 1931, xxi; M. Roncaglia, *Les Frères mineurs et l'église grecque orthodoxe au xiiie siècle*, 1954. But in all cases the aim was to provide a confutation of the opposing view, and this was doomed to failure from the beginning.

21. On these negotiations see D. J. Geanakoplos, *The Emperor Michael Palaeologus and the West*, 1959; also *Dictionnaire de théologie catholique*, 1409, ix (art. ' Le IIe Concile de Lyon' by F. Vernet and V. Grumel).

The way of understanding

Up to 1274 all plans for reunion had assumed that the ecclesiastical and dogmatic views of the West would prevail without the slightest deviation, and that Greeks would buy political safety at the price of ecclesiastical submission. This view of the way in which reunion might best be achieved never died out, but it was supplemented in various ways in the two centuries after 1274, and the interest of these developments is that on both sides they led – though too little and too late – to something approaching a spirit of sympathy and conciliation.

There are three symptoms of this new spirit. The first is an appreciation of the merits of the other party; the second a spirit of self-criticism; the third a sense of the corporate incompleteness of each side without the other. Before 1274 a sympathetic appreciation of the other side was almost wholly lacking in both camps. As for the spirit of self-criticism, it was widespread in the West but only with regard to individual vices, and it was linked with a compulsive optimism about the self-sufficiency of western institutions and ways of thought. Most important of all, the sense of mutual need existed on the Greek side only as a political need, and on the Latin side only as a theoretical need to complete the papal system of authority. The inadequacy of this basis for reunion was demonstrated in 1274. What more could be done?

MUTUAL APPRECIATION

If we look first for a developing sympathy and understanding of the other side there can be no doubt that the Greeks went much further than the Latins in the last two centuries of the Middle Ages. The sympathy was partly inspired by sheer fright. The Greek empire lived under sentence of death, and it was the first of all public duties for those who loved their church and civilization to try every way of coming to terms with the West. This great need produced a succession of Greek theologians whose efforts at understanding the literature and life of the Latin Middle Ages are one of the glories of the fourteenth-century Byzantine church. These efforts took two main forms: the translation of the classics of medieval Latin theology and an attempt to appreciate them as part of the general life of the church.

The translations into Greek of works by Augustine, Boethius, Anselm, Peter Lombard, and Thomas Aquinas, which were made in the fourteenth century, gave the Byzantine world its first view of what had really been happening in the West since the falling apart of the two halves of Christendom.[22] The *Summa Theologiae* of Thomas Aquinas was especially important, for no writer has ever been better equipped to convey to an alien world the intellectual qualities of his own age. His breadth and lucidity, his orderly rationality and fair-mindedness, and his unshakeable allegiance to the tradition of the western church, have made him the repository of everything that was best in thirteenth-century western thought. His effect on his Greek admirers in the fourteenth century can be compared with his influence in the modern world since 1870. The reason for his profound influence was the same in both cases: he suddenly showed that a previously despised society had virtues that provided a challenge to the growing chaos of the contemporary world. To a generation beset by uncertainty and surrounded by incalculable dangers he offered safety and certainty. To men struggling with confusion he demonstrated the possibility of systematic and clear-cut theological statements. His writings placed the western church in a quite new light. For some of the best minds in the Greek church he became 'the marvellous doctor', 'the most useful of all the doctors of the church', 'the flawless theologian – barring his error about the Holy Spirit'. One nameless Greek reader wrote in the margin of his copy of the *Summa Theologiae*:

Oh Thomas, I would that you had been born in the East and not in the West. Then you would have written as truly about the

22. For the beginnings of this movement in the late thirteenth century, see G. Hoffman, 'Patriarch Johann Bekkos u. die lat. Kultur', *Orientalia Christiana Periodica*, 1945, xi, 141–64.

Procession of the Holy Spirit as about all the other questions which you here treat so well.[23]

The same vision of order and discipline, which was presented by the works of St Thomas, was also experienced by some of those many Greeks who found their way to the papal court in the course of the interminable negotiations from about 1330 onwards. Among these the outstanding man was a Calabrian monk of Greek parentage called Barlaam. In the end he became a convinced supporter of the papal primacy, and for the Greeks he came to represent the type of those whose Latin sympathies had turned them from their native ecclesiastical obedience. The stages by which he reached this position would make a fascinating study. Barlaam was in many ways the Newman of the fourteenth-century ortho-dox revival. He wrote no *Apologia pro vita sua*, so it is impossible to define at all accurately the influences which dislodged him from his Byzantine allegiance. But in a letter to his friends after his conversion he gives a vivid account of the impression which the western church had made on him. When he looked round in the West he saw (or thought he saw) a wonderful scene of order and integration. Every-thing had its proper place:

> The whole people is ruled by laws. Even the smallest matters are subject to regulation and orderly administration. All ranks of society are taught how to behave towards each other. They know how sins are punished and good deeds rewarded and conduct examined: all these things and everything else that is useful for preserving society in peace is defined and guarded by law.[24]

He declared that he had found western society well instructed in the faith and full of reverence for papal decisions, which were accepted as the ordinances of Christ himself. In contrast to this scene of supernatural virtue, he saw among the Greeks nothing but confusion: church and state in decline, law at the whim of the mighty, learn-ing debased, many conversions to Islam. It is in these

23. Quoted by M. Jugie, 'Demetrios Cidones et la théologie latine à Byzance aux xive et xve siècles', *Échos d'Orient*, 1928, xxvii, 385–402.
24. *P.G.* 151, 1255–83.

sentences that we seem to hear the voice of Newman, and it
is ironical that we should hear them from a Greek at the
moment when the Latins were beginning to be filled with
doubt and despair at their failure to create the order which
Barlaam thought he saw in the West.

The West never discovered the Byzantine church as the
Greeks discovered the Latin church in the fourteenth
century. There were Greek theologians like John of Damas-
cus and the Pseudo-Denys whose works had long held an
honourable place in western thought; but they belonged to
a remote age before the separation of the churches. They
stimulated no interest in the Byzantine church or the Greeks
of the present day.

It is one of the curious limitations of the West that, with
all its intellectual vigour and curiosity and despite its vast
debt to Greek science, it had no interest in the modern
Greek world. The men who were enthusiasts for Greek
science looked right through the Byzantine Greeks without
noticing their existence. They inspired neither emulation
nor fear in western minds; hence there was no incentive
– as to some extent there was with Islam – to understand
them. The superficial and often erroneous impressions of
Greek religion which reached the West discouraged any
closer acquaintance. As Humbert de Romanis, the adviser
of Pope Gregory X on reunion, told the pope, the great
sin of the Latins in this matter was that they did not care.[25]

This attitude has run through western history with
astonishing consistency. When Pope Pius II heard of the
fall of Constantinople in 1453, he shed a tear over the
second, symbolic, death of Plato and Homer, but he saw
the destruction of the Greek church only as a fresh opportunity for the display of his literary and diplomatic skill.
And three hundred years later, Gibbon took his 'ever-
lasting farewell of the Greek empire', on which he had

25. This remark occurs in the course of a searching analysis of the
causes of the schism, in preparation for the Council of Lyons in 1274.
See K. Michel, *Das Opus Tripartitum des Humbertus de Romanis O.P.: ein
Beitrag zur Geschichte der Kreuzzugsidee u. der kirchlichen Unionsbewegungen,*
1926.

lavished all his genius, without a word of sympathy for the vanquished, but with a eulogy on the 'lofty genius' of the conqueror Mahomet II. Both the pope and the historian were the unconscious legatees of a medieval tradition of indifference to Byzantine virtues.

SELF-CRITICISM

Yet the West did not quite stand still in its attitude to the Greek church, though the change came less from a deepening observation or sympathy for the Greeks than from a deepening introspection and self-criticism. The growing criticism of the institutions and habits of the West, beginning with the rather flimsy satires of the twelfth century and ending with the tremendous indictments of the later Middle Ages, is one of the greatest themes in medieval history. It began to affect the Latin attitude towards the Greeks at the time of the occupation of Constantinople after 1204. The friars in the occupied city were the first who realized the extent to which western vices were a cause, if not of the schism itself, at least of its continuance. In 1252 the Dominicans in Constantinople reported that the ostentation and exactions of the papal legates were alleged by Greeks to be one of the causes of the continuance of the schism; and Matthew Paris, who had a finger on every pulse, took up this cry in his own fashion and made the remarkable discovery that the schism had originated quite recently in the rapacious exactions of the Roman church under Gregory IX.[26] The story he told to justify this assertion illustrates the vast ignorance of otherwise well-informed westerners about the state of the Greek church; but it also shows the beginning of a tendency for western writers to attribute the schism to their own shortcomings.

Unluckily there was nothing that could be done about these shortcomings except deplore them. The recognition that there were faults on both sides was something new and important; but those who insisted most strongly upon these faults were more concerned to belabour their enemies at home than to help or understand the Greeks abroad.

26. *Chronica Majora* (A.D. 1237), iii, 448–69; see also v, 191; vi, 336–7.

Wycliffe took to its furthest limit the line of thought initiated in England by Matthew Paris. He argued that the schism had been caused by the pride and cupidity of the Roman pontiff, and that the Greeks alone were faithful to Christ.[27] But he did the Greeks very little good. The western establishment had become by this time very resistant to domestic criticism. Nevertheless the idea that western pride and ambition had contributed to the state of schism became part of the mental equipment of many moderate men, and it helped to soften the asperity of earlier attitudes towards the Greeks.[28]

THE NEED OF ONE FOR THE OTHER

This movement of self-criticism in the West brought the two sides slightly nearer together. But there were two developments which did more. The first of these was the evident decline and impending dissolution of the Greek empire; the second was the Conciliar movement. The first touched the hearts of men of goodwill in the West. Goodwill towards the Greeks rose as the collapse of their church and civilization became ever more imminent. The visit of the Greek emperor, Manuel Palaeologus, to Paris and London during the years 1400 to 1403 gave an opportunity for this generous spirit to show itself among the people of the great cities and the nobility of two kingdoms. The open celebration of the Greek rites in Paris and the presence of the schismatic Greeks at great ecclesiastical ceremonies scandalized the disciplinarians; but rulers and people vied with each other

27. *De Christo et Antichristo*, ii, 8 (*John Wiclif's Polemical Works in Latin*, ed. R. Buddensieg, 1883, ii, p. 672).

28. Besides Matthew Paris and Wycliffe, many other western writers after 1250 mention the pride and avarice of papal legates and of the whole Latin church as an important cause of the schism, e.g. the report of the Dominicans in Constantinople in 1252, *P.G.* 140, 540; Cardinal Simon of Gramaud in a letter to the archbishop of Canterbury c. 1400, Martène and Durand, *Thesaurus Novus Anecdotorum*, 1771, ii, 1235; Boniface Ferrier, General of the Carthusians 1402–10, ibid., ii, 1450; Thomas Gascoigne, *Loci e libro Veritatum*, ed. J. E. Thorold Rogers, 1881, p. 102–3.

in offering tokens of sympathy and friendship.[29] The mood throughout these proceedings was one of chivalrous understanding in the face of a common enemy. But it went no further. Manuel Palaeologus returned as poor as he had come, and he owed the survival of his empire not to the chivalry of France and England, soon to be otherwise employed, but to the ravages of the bloodthirsty Tamberlaine among his enemies.

Yet the spirit of goodwill persisted. It got practical and intellectual support from the outburst of Conciliar activity in the West. This long dormant strain in western thought got sudden strength from the growing conviction that, whatever might be true of the Greek schism, the schism in the papacy could only be solved by invoking the authority of a General Council. This was what the Greeks had consistently demanded as the only method for settling the points at issue between Rome and Constantinople. If it were now to prove the only means of saving the unity of the Roman church, the reunion of Greeks and Latins would be within sight.

The noblest expression of these hopes and plans is to be found in a sermon preached by Jean Gerson, chancellor of the University of Paris, before the king of France in 1410.[30] Gerson's sermon marks the furthest limit to which a combination of liberality and orthodoxy in the West could go in seeking an accommodation with the Greeks. Gerson indeed insisted on the necessity for the papal primacy, but this in itself was not unacceptable to the Greeks. The real issue arose over the source and scope of this primacy: did it derive from the authority of the church expressed in the decisions of General Councils, or from Christ's original mandate to St Peter; and how far did it extend? On the first point, Gerson was silent; but he went very far in meeting the Greeks everywhere else. No papal decision even in a General Council was binding (he declared) except on matters directly affecting the truth of the Faith and the

29. See G. Schlumberger, 'Un Empereur de Byzanz à Paris et à Londres', *Revue des deux mondes*, 1915, xxx, 786.

30. J. Gerson, *Opera Omnia*, ed. du Pin, 1706, ii, 141–53.

Gospel. All those matters of local usages which had caused so much trouble – the use of leavened bread in the Mass, the marriage of priests, the differing practices with regard to confession, and so on – lay outside the scope of papal authority. As for the General Council, the Greek demand was justifiable, and their claim to proper representation was fair. In a word, the moment for unity was at hand, and there was no agent so suitable as the king of France – whose patron was the Greek saint, Denis, the Apostle of France – acting in conjunction with the pope, Alexander V, who was the first pope of Greek birth since Zacharias in the middle of the eighth century. A Greek pope and a French king with a Greek patron saint seemed to be instruments divinely fashioned for the cause of unity.

For a brief moment it looked as if the search for unity might take a new direction, guided no longer by the political and ecclesiastical assumptions of an earlier age, but by the melancholy and enlightening experiences of the last hundred years. As Jean Gerson surveyed the limitless disorders of the West, and contrasted them with the western claim to impose peace on the whole world, he began to understand something of the Greeks' point of view. He supported their refusal to be bound by decisions of Councils at which they were not represented; he foresaw the possibility and wisdom of recognizing wide areas of local autonomy in ecclesiastical usage; he looked without horror at leavened bread, married clergy, and a whole range of customs that had long been anathema in the West. These were hopeful signs. But the Greek pope soon died, the French king soon forgot his Greek patron in the midst of more immediate struggles with England, and the whole Conciliar idea was soon to sink into discord and impotence. The sermon of Gerson, and the whole line of thought that it represented, remained – like the chivalrous reception of Manuel Palaeologus – without effect.

Regression

Time was now running out. From the middle of the four-teenth century the Greeks were not so much declining as doomed. It was evident to everyone that unless unity came quickly there would be nothing left to unite. In some chivalrous hearts this appalling prospect inspired a desire to give the Greeks more than their strength could have exacted. But in others – and they were the majority – it simply made it seem more than ever foolish to give anything at all. Moreover, as time went on, the whole corporate theory of ecclesiastical government ran into insuperable difficulties. These difficulties were partly the result of the chaotic conditions of the Councils which embodied the corporate being of the church, and partly they arose from the inability of popes – even when they had themselves been adherents of Conciliar principles – to renounce any part of the authority that had been claimed for them in the past. The machinery of papal government was too strong for the exercise of papal liberality. In the midst of all these doubts and difficulties the spirit of generosity was choked.

Moreover the opportunity for its exercise was slipping rapidly away. The Greeks were in a position of great perplexity. Faced with the certainty of total destruction unless help came from the West, denied help because of ancient disagreements which seemed to many of their leaders irrelevant, confused by promises which no one could dismiss as certainly illusory, they were pressed on every side.

In 1422 Pope Martin V wrote words to the Emperor Manuel Palaeologus which take us right back to the letter of Clement IV to Michael Palaeologus nearly two hundred years earlier:

> The Turks will fear to attack you if they know you are united to the rest of Christendom, and Christians will come to your help with more eagerness if they know that you are in full agreement with them.[31]

These were the terms: submit or be destroyed. In the thirteenth century these terms were still backed by the possibility of effective papal action; now they were empty words. But no one, not even the pope, could be quite sure

31. O. Raynaldus, *Annales Ecclesiastici*, 1752, viii, p. 545.

that they were nonsense. In the end, in 1439, the Greek delegates at Florence, led by their emperor and weakened by deaths, desertions, and sheer fatigue, agreed to submit. They subscribed to the doctrine that the Holy Spirit had 'His essence and substantial being equally from the Father and the Son', that 'the word *Filioque* had been lawfully and reasonably added to the Creed', and that the pope was 'the true vicar of Christ with full power given him by our Lord Jesus Christ in St Peter to nourish, rule, and govern the universal church'.[32] These phrases – although accompanied by some ambiguities which gave some of the Greeks the illusion of safeguarding their ancient position – were an uncompromising statement of the Latin claims and a denial of all the main points that the Greeks had consistently asserted.

Opinions about this agreement and the way in which it was obtained will perhaps always differ. But it is impossible not to feel indignation at the spectacle of western Christians offering to those of the East a salvation which they were unable to provide, in return for a submission which the Greeks could not conscientiously make. It was left to the clergy and people of Constantinople – no doubt for the wrong reasons and under the influence of ancient hatred and ignorant confidence – to refuse to give up what they had long held to be the truth in exchange for help that could never come. Their steady opposition brought the union almost to a standstill. Although it was at last proclaimed in St Sophia on 12 December 1452, it had been too long delayed and it was too little accepted to leave any mark on the Greek church. Within six months the city and empire fell. By that time the unionist patriarch had fled to Rome, and the last of the emperors perished on 29 May

32. The terms of union were declared in a document of Pope Eugenius III, 6 July 1439 (*Conciliorum Oecumenicorum Decreta*, ed. J. Alberigo and others, 1962, 499–504). For an account of the last phase of the negotiations, see J. Gill, *The Council of Florence*, 1959, 270–304. It should be added that although the Greeks were obliged to submit on the main points, they obtained a declaration of the legitimacy of their use of leavened bread in the Eucharist. Three centuries earlier this stood high on the list of Greek errors.

1453 at the breach in the walls on the last day of the siege. The problem of the rival patriarchate was solved, as that of Jerusalem, Antioch, and Alexandria had been eight hundred years earlier, by Islam.

Rome had now no rival. Pope Pius II hastened to address the conqueror, offering to make him emperor of the Greeks in return for baptism:

> Be baptized and no prince in the world will be your equal in glory and power. We will call you Emperor of the Greeks and of the Orient, and what you now possess by force and injury, you will hold by right. All Christians will venerate you, and make you the judge of their disputes. . . . The see of Rome will love you like any Christian king, and so much the more as your position will be greater than theirs.[33]

This was the last expression of that vision of a politically and ecclesiastically united Christendom, based on the twin foundations of papal authority in Rome and imperial power in Constantinople guaranteed by the pope, which had given an intermittent direction to the larger policies of the papacy since 1054. If at this moment the miracle of the conversion of Constantine and Clovis had been repeated, the vision might yet have become a reality. But it was not to be. What actually happened was something that seemed even more unlikely in 1453 – the destruction from within of that undivided papal supremacy that had been so clearly established in the eyes of the world by the destruction of the Greek church and empire.

The historian, however, in looking forward sees too much. In 1453 the papal view of Christendom had triumphed. More than any other force it had been responsible for giving western Christendom an independent existence in the eighth century, and for providing a doctrinal basis for western supremacy from the eleventh century onwards. The movement towards Conciliar government in the church, which might have offered a new path to unity, had in the end collapsed, not least because of the strength

33. Letter of Pius II to Mahomet II, ed. G. Toffanin, 1953, pp. 113–14.

of the papacy. So, from the point of view of Christendom as a whole, the papacy was the great divisive force throughout the Middle Ages. But, from the point of view of the West, it was the source of unity and the symptom of strength. To this aspect of the papacy we must now turn.

4

The Papacy

To write briefly about the medieval papacy without being superficial requires a strict limitation of the questions to be discussed. Even then it will not be easy. The splendour and overwhelming authority of the papal position during most of our period, the wealth of documents, and the ramifications of papal activity into every corner of Europe and into every branch of European life make limitation difficult. The thirteenth-century formula *Papa qui et ecclesia dici potest*: 'the Pope who also can be called the Church' has sufficient truth in it to make it hazardous to treat the papacy as an institution apart from the body which it animated. We may however introduce a certain degree of simplification by concentrating on the following questions. What power did the popes at various periods of the Middle Ages actually possess? What relation had this practical power to the authority which they theoretically claimed, or which was claimed on their behalf? Why was this power, great as it was, not greater?

These are the questions, and in discussing them it will be convenient to observe the division of periods which has been sketched above.

I. THE PRIMITIVE AGE,
c. 700–c. 1050

A convenient starting point for considering the claims and powers of the papacy in this period, and indeed throughout the Middle Ages, is provided by a famous document that has already been mentioned – the *Donation of Constantine*.[1]

---

1. The latest and most valuable edition is H. Fuhrmann, *Das Constitutum Constantini* (*M.G.H. Fontes Iuris Germanici Antiqui*, vol. x), 1968. The history of the document down to the fourteenth century is discussed in F. Laehr, *Die Konstantinische Schenkung in der abendländischen Lit. des Mittelalters bis zur Mitte des XIV Jhts.*, 1926 (*Hist. Studien*, vol. 166).

Like many early title deeds it is a forgery. Although it
purports to be a letter from the Emperor Constantine to
Pope Silvester I written on 30 March 315, everyone would
now agree that it was not written until the eighth century
or even later. There have been various suggestions about
the date of its composition, but the most likely explanation
is that it was written shortly after 750, partly to justify the
papal breach with the Byzantine emperor and partly to
prove to the Franks that the pope was legally entitled to
offer them large areas of former Byzantine territory in
Italy. But whatever may have been the exact purpose of
the document, it certainly offers a very clear and complete
view of papal power as seen by its best friends in the late
eighth century. A brief account of its contents will put us
in a position to compare the ideal and the actuality, and to
see how both of them differ from what comes later.

Before describing the document it may be well to deal
with a difficulty. It may seem odd, and even repellent, to
begin a discussion of the greatest of all ecclesiastical institutions with a forgery. To put this matter in perspective it is
important to understand the importance of forgeries as
vehicles of ideas in this early period. They did not have the
vulgar associations of modern forgeries. The primitive age
had few records, but it had clear ideas of the past. These
ideas were based on accumulated traditions, legends,
pious fabrications, and above all on a reluctance to believe
that the past is largely unknowable. Hence even learned
and critical men easily believed that the past was like the
present, only better; in a word that it was an idealized
present. Documents were therefore drawn up in which the
theories of the present were represented as the facts of the
past. These documents were inspired by a strong fear of
losing any possession that the saints, whose dominion embraced every church in Christendom, could claim as their
own. Everyone felt that it was safer to overstate a case and
to give their church the benefit of every doubt, rather than
lose something that could justly be claimed. Every church
had claims to lands and privileges for which the evidence
was slight. But the transitory officials of these churches

fought for their disputed claims with passionate conviction as for inalienable rights. The forgeries, which are a conspicuous feature of the age, provided documentary proofs for claims which, in the minds of those who made them, scarcely needed to be justified. The pen corrected the corruptions of nature and restored the gross imperfections and injustices of the world to a primitive excellence. The falsehoods implicit in these documents did indeed raise moral problems of which contemporaries were not unaware, but the authors believed that they enforced truths which could not be abandoned without grave danger to their souls. Forgeries, like art, brought order into the confusions and deficiencies of the present. Such, among very many other documents of less importance, was the *Donation of Constantine*.

The document begins with a long account of Constantine's conversion, baptism, and cure from leprosy at the intercession of Pope Silvester. It then goes on to record the emperor's gifts to the Vicar of St Peter: the grant of pre-eminence over the patriarchal sees of Antioch, Alexandria, Jerusalem, and Constantinople, and all other churches; the gift of the imperial insignia, together with the Lateran palace in Rome; and finally the transfer to the pope of the imperial power in Rome, Italy, and all the provinces of the West. As a guarantee of the inviolability of these gifts Constantine is described as placing the document of donation on the body of St Peter, for whom the gifts were personally intended.

All this of course is not history – it is theory masquerading as history. But it deserves no less attention on that account, for the writer of this document has put into the mouth of the first Christian emperor all the basic ideas of the medieval papacy. The pope is portrayed as the 'universal bishop'; the teacher, preserver, and godfather of the emperor; the vicar through whom St Peter displayed his power; and finally, as a result of the Donation, he was the supreme temporal lord of the West. How did these claims work out in practice?

The Vicar of St Peter

We start with the pope as Vicar of St Peter because, whatever else might be denied, no one in the West denied that the
pope possessed all the authority of St Peter over the church.
The derivation of the pope's authority seemed one of the
clearest facts of history. The descent of this authority could
be traced step by step from the earliest days without any of
the shadows of ambiguity or ignorance that trouble a
modern observer: in A.D. 34 St Peter became bishop of
Antioch; in 40 he moved his see to Rome; in 57 he instituted
the fasts of Advent and Lent; in 59 he consecrated Linus
and Cletus, his successors. There were no awkward gaps.
From the beginning St Peter and his successors could be
seen at work directing the church, instituting ceremonies,
defining discipline, founding bishoprics. This scheme of
things had the same unambiguous clarity as the generations
of mankind from Adam.

Besides this historical certainty there was the unambiguous bodily presence in Rome. For the western church from
the seventh to the eleventh century the existence of the tomb
of St Peter was the most significant fact in Christendom.
The body within the tomb, which would one day clothe
the door-keeper of heaven, was the link between the presence
in heaven and the church on earth. It was pre-eminently
through his continuing physical presence that St Peter
continued to bless and to curse, to cure and to guarantee.
Men thought of him as being there, in Rome. When Ceolfrid,
abbot of Jarrow, set out for Rome in 716, he carried a Bible
with an inscription dedicating the book, not to the pope,
but to the body of St Peter.[2] Similarly the *Donation of
Constantine* described the emperor swearing an oath to St
Peter to uphold the gift which he placed on the Apostle's
body. In 731 the Council that met in Rome assembled
'before the most holy burial place of the most blessed body
of St Peter', and this physical contact between Councils
and the source of their authority is something that is

2. The text of the inscription (now mutilated) has been preserved by
Bede, *Opera Historica*, ed. C. Plummer, 1896, i, 402.

frequently recalled. The rulers and pilgrims from the newly converted peoples of Europe, who came to Rome to be baptized and if possible to die in the presence of the Apostle, were not drawn by any sophisticated theories of papal authority but by the conviction that they could nowhere find such safety as in the physical presence of the keeper of the keys of heaven.

St Peter still worked in the tomb, but his *persona* on earth was entrusted to the pope. Therefore, though men came to Rome in the first place to visit the Apostle, they prostrated themselves before the pope. The hands might be those of Gregory or Leo, but the voice was that of St Peter. The papal documents of this period were never tired of reiterating the name of St Peter. When the papal legates journeyed to Constantinople for the council in 680, they went 'in the company of St Peter'. When the archbishop of Ravenna was blinded by the emperor in 710 for rebellion against the imperial official in Rome, who happened to be the pope, this punishment appeared to the Roman writer as a sentence pronounced by St Peter for disobedience to *his* vicar.[3] Disobedience to the pope even in temporal affairs was synonymous with disobedience to St Peter. All the more, therefore, was this true of ecclesiastical affairs. The argument that weighed most strongly with the English in abandoning the Irish for the Roman ecclesiastical calendar was the simple calculation that St Peter had more power than St Columba:

'Was any similar power given to your St Columba?' 'None.' 'Then I tell you, I have no wish to contradict that door-keeper; lest when I come to the gates of heaven, the bearer of the keys is my enemy and there is no one to open.'[4]

It was an unanswerable argument. Likewise the English missionaries, who transformed the position of the papacy in the western church by going to Rome for authority in their

---

3. For these and similar details see *Liber Pontificalis*, ed. L. Duchesne, 1886, i, pp. 351, 352, 389, 416.
4. Bede, op. cit., i, 188–9.

mission to Germany, were not thinking of the authority of
the papacy but of St Peter. The commands which Boniface
promised to obey in Germany were those of St Peter himself, and the oath which he took was taken directly 'to you
St Peter and to your vicar'.[5] The pallium, which he and
other archbishops received as a sign of their authority, had
lain on the tomb of St Peter; it brought with it the touch
of the Apostle himself.

The examples could be multiplied indefinitely, but what
they all make clear is the fact that from the eighth to the
eleventh centuries, more emphatically than at any other
time before or since, the active force in Rome was seen as
St Peter himself. It was into his presence that men came,
and from him they received commands.[6] They did not
ignore the pope but they quite simply looked through
him to the first occupant of his throne. It was possible to
say in a quite practical way, without any thought of
metaphor, that men met in Rome 'in the presence of St
Peter'. This presence was the source of western unity during
these centuries.

It was a unity compatible with the very slightest exercise
of administrative authority. The affairs of the church
received little direction from Rome. Monasteries and
bishoprics were founded, and bishops and abbots were
appointed by lay rulers without hindrance or objection;
councils were summoned by kings; kings and bishops
legislated for their local churches about tithes, ordeals,
Sunday observance, penance; saints were raised to the
altars – all without reference to Rome. Each bishop acted
as an independent repository of faith and discipline. They
sought whatever advice was available from scholars and
neighbouring bishops, but in the last resort they had to
act on their own initiative. The legal compilations which
were made for their guidance were the work of local

5. *S. Bonifatii et Lullii Epistolae* (*M.G.H. Epistolae Selectae*, i), ed. M.
Tangl, pp. 28–9.

6. There is an interesting study of the place of the Roman pilgrimage
in the early Middle Ages in W. J. Moore, *The Saxon Pilgrims to Rome and
the Schola Saxonum*, 1937.

compilers. The majority of papal letters during this period simply confirmed and approved what others had done.

Western Christian unity was centred on Rome, but it was created less by papal activity than by the spontaneous impulses which led men to St Peter. So far as it came from papal action, this unity involved a conscious rejection of Byzantine political and ecclesiastical claims. But so far as it came from popular impulses it represented a simple gravitation towards the visible source of supernatural power.

It is obvious, however, that though spontaneous devotion was enough to keep the papacy alive during these centuries, the author of the *Donation of Constantine* had larger aims in view. The pope would never be the 'universal bishop' and supreme temporal lord of the West simply by listening to those who came to him and approving what they proposed. The writer of the *Donation* had inherited classical and imperial notions of government, and he saw the pope as an active and independent ruler in a practical world, not merely as a living icon. This vigorous tradition of government did not die. Several of the popes of the ninth, tenth, and early eleventh centuries were men with a firm grasp of politics: it was only circumstances that made them weak. Nevertheless the circumstances which made strong and consistent government impossible showed no signs of changing, and those parts of the *Donation* which spoke of the pope's spiritual and temporal jurisdiction were no more than a distant and (as it seemed) receding ideal.

The only permanent links between the pope and the local churches were the archbishops. It seems to have been in England in the seventh century that the idea first took root that no archbishop could exercise his metropolitan functions until he had received a pallium from Rome.[7] But whatever the origin of the practice, it soon became universal in the provinces of the western church. Before receiving his pallium a new archbishop was required to make a written statement of his orthodox faith, and this requirement established the pope as the judge of orthodoxy at the

7. See W. Levison, *England and the Continent in the Eighth Century*, 1946, pp. 19–21.

highest provincial level of the ecclesiastical hierarchy. Moreover, in some provinces, the archbishop required a similar
profession of faith from his suffragan bishops. So there was
established a single chain of profession and obedience
throughout the western church.

However slight the practical effects of this system might
be, the principle of a supreme arbiter of the faith was
maintained by this slender chain of authority at a time
when papal legates were very infrequent, when there were
no General Councils in the West, when papal letters seldom
conveyed commands, and when papal commands anyhow
could not be enforced. This practical ineffectiveness was
intensely irksome to popes who still had some idea of government. In Rome there survived archives, an official hierarchy,
and the outlines of a business routine which reminded them
of what the papacy might be. The popes worked among
relics of an older conception of government, and some of
them understood that there had once been government
where there were now only ruins. They felt the frustration of
impotence. Pope Nicholas I wrote in 867 that he would like
to call the archbishops of the West to Rome to confer
about the Greek opposition 'to every church that uses the
Latin language, and especially our own', but the evils of
the time made a meeting impossible. The pope was therefore reduced to asking the archbishop to circulate his letter
appealing for western solidarity against the deviationists of
Constantinople:

I cannot remember that the western countries – to speak of no
others – have ever disagreed with the See of St Peter in questions
of this kind.[8]

This was the old appeal to the barbarian West, and it
was not made in vain. But it was no substitute for active
government.

The supreme temporal lord

The position of the pope as 'universal bishop' and 'Vicar
of St Peter' was thus limited by the physical condition of
western Europe. With regard to the other great claim of

8. *M.G.H. Epp.* vi, no. 100, pp. 603–5.

the *Donation of Constantine* – to supreme temporal lordship in the West – the limitations were even more severe, for here the pope could not confidently appeal to the sentiment of western solidarity. It seems very likely that the papal coronation of Charlemagne as emperor was intended to show that the pope could delegate imperial authority in the West to whom he would, in accordance with the terms of Constantine's gift. But it is certain that Charlemagne did not acquiesce in this view of his position.

Indeed it is evident that the idea of a western empire as a means of extending papal authority was a mistake from beginning to end. It was a mistake primarily because in creating an emperor the pope created not a deputy, but a rival or even a master. The theoretical supremacy implied in the act of creation could never be translated into practical obedience to orders given and received. Hence the pope's practical supremacy over his emperor came to an end at the moment of coronation. It is not surprising that the popes of the later Middle Ages sought to exercise their supreme temporal lordship through other channels than the empire, which Pope Leo III had rashly created for this purpose on Christmas Day 800. This action was the greatest mistake the medieval popes ever made in their efforts to translate theory into practice.

Quite apart from the inherent unlikelihood of obedience, there was another reason for the failure of this papal initiative. Although the pope could always rely on an appeal to western resentment against the Greeks, he could not prevent western emperors learning something from rulers who greatly outshone them in power and prestige. Among other things, they learned to look on themselves not only as the protectors of the papacy, but as its arbiters and overseers. This point of view is very clearly expressed in the great Donation of 962 in which Otto I confirmed the popes in their Italian possessions 'saving in all things our own power and that of our successors'.[9] For Otto, the

---

9. *M.G.H. Diplomata*, i, no. 235 (13 Feb. 962): like the oath of Boniface already mentioned, this document also was couched in the form of a promise to St Peter 'et per te vicario tuo'.

imperial power included the right of ensuring that papal elections were justly and canonically carried out – ensuring in fact that no election was made contrary to the emperor's wishes. Further, the emperor laid it down that he was to receive annual reports on the administration of justice in the papal lands. It has been argued that these clauses form a slightly later addition to the original document, but they certainly express the attitude of Otto and most of his successors. They saw themselves standing to the pope as the Greek emperor to the patriarch of Constantinople. For over a century this vision was not unrealistic. The emperor's responsibility for the pope's good conduct had both practical and theoretical significance at a time when the temporal lordship of the pope in the West was a meaningless phrase. Before 1050 there was nothing to suggest that it could ever be more than this.

II. THE AGE OF GROWTH,
c.1050–c.1300

When we turn to consider the great change in papal pretensions after 1050, the personality of Leo IX, who was pope from 1049 to 1054, must first attract our attention. He was a quieter and much less controversial character than Gregory VII, but nearly everything that we associate with the papacy in its most expansive period can be traced back to his initiative: the political alliance with the Normans; the exacerbation of relations with the Greeks; the reform of papal administrative machinery; the beginnings of a consistent plan of government through legates, councils, and a vastly increased correspondence. These were the foundations of the reactivated papacy, and they were laid by Leo IX – or rather they were laid by the men whom he attracted to Rome. Leo was a great chooser of men, and he brought to the service of the papacy men who had the energy and courage to give practical effect to the long dormant programme of the papal monarchy.

The minds of these men turned back to a happier period

of papal enterprise. They dedicated themselves to the task
of restoring the papacy to the position which it had held
in a remote past and ought to hold again. Above all they
wished to restore the papacy to the controlling and directing
rôle in the church that (as they thought) it had once had,
and they wished to make the pope's temporal lordship an
unambiguous force in European politics. As their minds
travelled back into the past they saw traces of a former
greatness which had been worn away by centuries of German
tyranny, and among these ancient monuments of greatness
the *Donation of Constantine* held a conspicuous place.

We can easily see why the document appealed to them.
In the first place it was very ancient. It showed the first
Christian emperor resigning to the pope his imperial position
in the West and recognizing his ecclesiastical supremacy
everywhere; it spoke, or seemed to speak, of a time when
papal power really meant something. This was a part of
the past that the idealists at the court of Leo IX and his
successors wished to hear about, and none more so than the
greatest among them, the monk Hildebrand who became
Pope Gregory VII in 1073. Under his influence and that
of Cardinal Humbert the central passages in the *Donation
of Constantine* were included in the new collections of canon
law and became part of the official armoury of the popes.

Nevertheless, satisfactory though it was in its general
tenor, the document did not in all respects meet the views
of Hildebrand and his fellow-workers. A close study of its
terms suggested that already in the fourth century the pure
ideal of papal rule had been corrupted. The document
represented the emperor as *giving* the pope authority over
the other churches, and as himself *placing* on the pope's
head the imperial crown. It was not thus that Gregory VII
saw his position. For him and for all his successors, the
primacy was the gift of Christ himself, and the papal authority
over kings and emperors came from no human transference
of imperial authority but from God alone.

Hence, although we start this period of papal history
with a rehabilitation of the *Donation,* and although it
continued for centuries to be used as a papal title-deed in

appropriate cases, it was already out of date by the end of
the eleventh century. It was not only out of date; it was
potentially dangerous, for it was capable of an imperialist
interpretation. Moreover its use clashed with a principle
of the new generation of papal lawyers, that no document
of secular origin should be quoted as authoritative. For
most purposes, therefore, the *Donation* was superseded by
texts which took the papal claims to a deeper level. There
are no words which convey the spirit of the medieval papacy
so brilliantly as the trenchant statements of the papal
position inserted in the volume of Gregory VII's letters,
probably on the instructions of the pope himself. Among
these statements we find the following:

the pope can be judged by no one;
the Roman church has never erred and never will err till the end
   of time;
the Roman church was founded by Christ alone;
the pope alone can depose and restore bishops;
he alone can make new laws, set up new bishoprics, and divide
   old ones;
he alone can translate bishops;
he alone can call general councils and authorize canon law;
he alone can revise his own judgements;
he alone can use the imperial insignia;
he can depose emperors;
he can absolve subjects from their allegiance;
all princes should kiss his feet;
his legates, even though in inferior orders, have precedence over
   all bishops;
an appeal to the papal court inhibits judgement by all inferior
   courts;
a duly ordained pope is undoubtedly made a saint by the merits of
   St Peter.[10]

Taken as a whole these statements comprise a complete
programme of action. They imply nothing less than a
total papal sovereignty in all the affairs of the Christian
community, and it is a measure of the greatness of the man
who caused these statements to be brought together that

10. *Gregorii VII Registrum, M.G.H. Epistolae Selectae*, ii, ed. E. Caspar,
pp. 201–8.

not one (except perhaps the last) is an idle boast. With this exception, each one of them became a practical force in European life within an astonishingly short space of time. When we compare these statements with other great programmes of action – Magna Carta, the Bill of Rights, the American Constitution, the Communist Manifesto – we may think that only the latest of these documents has had so profound and detailed an effect on the practical affairs of many nations.

Among all these visionary yet intensely practical claims there is one which stands out like a monument to some different mode of thought. Since exceptions often provide a clue to the system from which they diverge, it is worth pausing for a moment over the words 'a duly appointed pope is undoubtedly made a saint by the merits of St Peter'. This is one of the least well documented of Gregory VII's principles of action, and we may ask what he meant. We have already noticed the extent to which the popes of the earlier period were, so to speak, swallowed up in the personality of St Peter and were regarded simply as the mouthpiece of the Apostle. Gregory VII, a child of the Roman church from infancy, shared this point of view. In 1076, at the most dangerous moment in his career, when he took the plunge and excommunicated Henry IV, the heir to the western Empire, he prefaced the act of excommunication with a passionate address to St Peter:

Blessed Peter, prince of the apostles, incline your merciful ear and hear me, your servant, whom you have nourished from childhood. Until this day you have delivered me from the hands of wicked men who hate me for my fidelity to you. You are my witness, together with my Lady the Mother of God and your brother Paul among the saints, that your holy Roman church constrained me unwillingly to govern it . . . and therefore as I believe, it is your good pleasure that the Christian people, who have been committed to you, should specially obey me because you have given me your authority.[11]

These words belonged to an old tradition of personal dependence on St Peter, and it would perhaps be true to

11. ibid., p. 270.

say that no later pope could have expressed so complete an immersion in the personality of the Apostle as Gregory VII. As we shall see the papal emphasis was soon to shift from the Apostle to Christ himself. Gregory's words at this crisis in his life show that he regarded his whole life, and above all his crowning act of political defiance, as especially dedicated to the service of St Peter in person. It was a moment of decision. In the eighth century the popes had turned from the Byzantine emperor and committed their future to the new Carolingian family in the West. Now Gregory VII turned from the successor of the Carolingians and stood alone against the world. As he looked back over the long list – it can never have been far from his mind – of nearly a hundred popes venerated as saints, he seems to have concluded that their personal sanctity and salvation were guaranteed by St Peter himself. With this conclusion we reach the summit of the vicariate of St Peter. It was impossible to go further, and Gregory's successors did not go so far. They took a different path.

The Vicar of Christ

After Gregory VII the papal emphasis on St Peter diminished. The overwhelming dependence on the Apostle belonged to the days when Rome had been a city of shrines and pilgrims with little power of practical direction. As this situation changed the title 'Vicar of St Peter' gradually fell out of use, and was replaced by another which suggested a higher authority and more extensive field of activity. From about the middle of the twelfth century, the popes began for the first time to take the title 'Vicar of Christ' and to claim it for themselves alone.[12] In the past, kings and priests had called themselves 'Vicars of Christ'; but not the pope. For him the title was too vague. He was pre-eminently the 'Vicar of St Peter': in a world dominated by saints and relics, this title alone could express the uniqueness of the pope's position. But now the struggle

12. On this subject see M. Maccarrone, *Vicarius Christi: storia del titolo papale (Lateranum, nova series,* xviii, 1952).

was for jurisdiction and sovereignty, and the popes needed a title that could support a universal authority without ambiguity.

The title 'Vicar of Christ' supplied what was needed. It met the need widely shared by all twelfth-century governments, to trace claims back to their source. It met the need, shared by all theologians and philosophers of the time, to give theories their most general form. Interpreted in the spirit of the new scholasticism it made a precise claim to universal sovereignty. The new formula showed that the popes no longer looked backwards, and were no longer primarily concerned to preserve an ancient tradition as the trustees of St Peter on earth. They were the deputies of Christ in all the fullness of His power. By the end of the twelfth century Innocent III could deliberately sweep aside the limitations implied in the old title:

> We are the successor of the Prince of the Apostles, but we are not his vicar, nor the vicar of any man or Apostle, but the vicar of Jesus Christ himself.[13]

Armed with this new title, precisely interpreted, the way was clear for the full exercise of power in the name of the 'King of Kings and Lord of Lords to whom every knee shall bow, of things in heaven and things in earth'. Phrases such as this are liberally scattered through the letters of Innocent III. It only remains to ask what, in practice, they meant.

The growth of business

The theory of papal supremacy is certainly one of the grandest, most integrated, and best developed systems that has ever been devised for the conduct of human life. But in the end what matters is its practical application. If the claims succinctly expressed by Gregory VII and elaborated by his successors had not been capable of being translated into action, they would have been no more than a historical curiosity.

Like many men who are irked by a lack of resolution in others Gregory VII was very impatient for results. He

13. *P.L.* 214, 292.

demanded an instant obedience. On one occasion he sent legates to northern Germany with large powers to put everything in order. The legates demanded that the archbishop of Bremen should assist them to hold a council in his province. He resisted, and the legates ordered him to present himself in Rome without delay. He failed to appear. At once the pope suspended him from his office and required his attendance at the next council in Rome. When the archbishop got the letter, there were only four weeks before the meeting of the council. The journey from Bremen would have taken six or seven weeks, and the archbishop was absent. He was at once suspended and excommunicated 'for pride and disobedience'.[14]

These peremptory proceedings were not simply an expression of Gregory VII's temperament; they were characteristic of the first chaotic phase of renewed papal activity. But it was not by slap-dash methods such as these that the general theory of papal power became the most successful plan of action in western Europe during the next two centuries. It was by the steady elaboration of a machinery of government, by the multiplication of papal agents, and above all by the pressure of litigants striving at all costs to reach the papal court. We must therefore try to understand the ways in which these factors combined to make papal government the central force in Europe in the twelfth and thirteenth centuries.

THE TOOLS OF GOVERNMENT

The easiest part of our task is to trace the growth in the machinery and agents of papal government. The difficulty here lies not in any obscurity or lack of evidence, but in the multiplicity and complexity of the details. It is impossible to work on any body of medieval documents without being quickly aware of the quickening of papal activity after 1050 and its consuming growth after about 1130. The mere

14. *Gregorii VII Registrum*, pp. 160, 196. The facts were elucidated by M. Tangl, in *Abhandlungen des Preuss. Ak. der Wissenschaften*, 1919, reprinted in his collected papers, *Das Mittelalter in Quellenkunde u. Diplomatik*, 1966, i, 255.

figures are impressive enough. If we classify the main instruments of papal policy as Councils, legates, and letters, the story of papal expansion can be told in the following brief statistics.

The Councils which the western church reckons as ecumenical may be plotted along a chronological line from 680 to 1312 as follows:

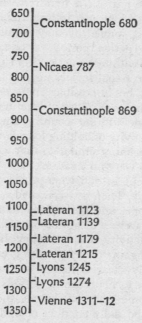

650
    — Constantinople 680
700

750
    — Nicaea 787
800

850
    — Constantinople 869
900

950

1000

1050

1100
    — Lateran 1123
1150 — Lateran 1139
    — Lateran 1179
1200
    — Lateran 1215
1250 — Lyons 1245
    — Lyons 1274
1300
    — Vienne 1311–12
1350

COUNCILS IN EAST AND WEST, 680–1312

The conclusions to be drawn from this brief chart are very clear. Between the seventh century and the early twelfth the Councils are few and, from a western point of view, insignificant. They were all held in Byzantine territory, and there were no representatives from the West except the papal legates, who played a minor rôle in the proceedings. The whole picture therefore is one of western inertia and papal impotence. Then for two centuries after 1123 the position is dramatically altered. There are no less than seven General Councils culminating in the huge Council of Vienne in 1311–12. All of them were summoned by the pope, who presided and was responsible for the decrees that were issued; all were held in the West; they were almost purely Latin; and the proceedings were of central importance in many fields of doctrine, government, and politics. They were all essentially constructive. Then after 1312 there was a gap for a hundred years until the new series of Councils which met in disharmony and crisis from 1414 to 1445. So, judged by the evidence of the Councils alone, the constructive period of papal government is precisely defined within the period from 1123 to 1312.

With regard to papal legates no simple statistics can be given. It would be impossible on a brief view to take account of the many varieties of legatine commission. But if we limit our view to one country, England, and to the single legatine activity of holding local councils, the pattern of events is remarkably similar to that which we have just examined. There were no legatine councils held in England before 1070 except in 786 when two legates of Adrian I visited the country. Then between 1070 and 1312 there were at least twenty-one, and perhaps as many as thirty. Then after 1312 there were no legatine councils till we get a last short burst of activity under Wolsey between 1519 and 1523.[15] Here again therefore the great age of papal initiative is fairly clearly defined within the two and a half centuries that form the central period of the Middle Ages.

Finally we come to papal letters, the most important instrument for the daily conduct of business. In this field new discoveries are constantly being made, but we may for our present purpose confine our attention to the last general survey of papal letters made some eighty years ago. The average number of surviving letters for each year under successive popes will give some indication of the rise or decline in the volume of business. What we find is that the annual average of surviving papal letters falls in the first half of the eleventh century from ten a year under

15. See the list in *Handbook of British Chronology*, ed. F. M. Powicke and E.B. Fryde (*Royal Historical Society Handbook*, no. 2), 1961, pp. 545–65.

Silvester II (999–1003) to only one a year under Benedict IX (1033–1046). Then the average rises under Leo IX to thirty-five and remains around this level until about 1130. Thereafter a swift and prolonged increase begins: an annual average of seventy-two under Innocent II (1130–1143), 130 under Adrian IV (1154–1159), 179 under Alexander III (1159–81), 280 under Innocent III (1198–1215), 730 under Innocent IV (1243–54), rising to 3,646 a year under John XXII (1316–24).

These figures are certainly very crude and their interpretation is subject to every kind of qualification, but it is quite unlikely that they exaggerate the rate of growth after 1050. Crude and incomplete though these figures are they provide a concrete illustration of the modest expansion of business under Leo IX and his immediate successors; and then of the rapid strides after the middle years of the twelfth century when the machinery of papal justice and administration began to reach its full development.

We must of course be on our guard against isolating the growth of papal business from the growth of business in every department of European life. These figures must be read against the background of a rapidly expanding society, and it is well known that in a period of general growth almost any organization, however backward and insignificant, will tend to grow. Judged simply by the number of official letters that have been preserved, the royal governments of France, England, and even Germany all show a similar trend. But there can be little doubt that the papal organization had the highest rate of growth of any organization in this period.

THE PRESSURE OF BUSINESS

Growth of business however does not necessarily mean that the policies which stimulate growth are succeeding. It is very clear that papal policy after the time of Leo IX helped to create business for the papal court. But the business grew, not mainly because the popes desired it, but because others could satisfy their own purposes at the papal court.

The eleventh-century popes cannot have foreseen the consequences of the litigious thirst that took possession of Europe in the twelfth century. Gregory VII certainly wanted to see archbishops, bishops, and litigants coming to Rome. But this was only a detail in his dream of a great Christian society bound together by loyalty to St Peter, with kings, princes, bishops, and monks working together under a single leader for a single end, and the leader the pope. He thought that he might himself lead a liberating army to the East.[16] The details eluded him; but he evidently did not yet feel the daily weight of business which disturbed the vision of later popes. In the intervals of conflict he was free to dream. After about 1150 the popes had lost this freedom. They were the busiest men in Europe. Several of the popes who saw the business growing disliked what they saw. But they could do nothing to stop it.

Calixtus II, who was pope from 1119 to 1124, was one of the first to feel the burden imposed by the new condition of the papacy:

I know [he told the canons of York who congratulated him on his election] that the see of Rome is a greater honour than any other, but its glory is misery and tribulation to me. When I am in Rome I have as many lords as I have cardinals and as many masters as I have citizens – I know them![17]

As he said this he kept glancing round to see that none of his new masters could hear him. He could not forget his happy days as archbishop of Vienne when he had been a *grand seigneur*: 'Wherever I went there was almost no one of note who was not my nephew or cousin or neighbour or vassal.'

These words were spoken in 1119. A hundred years earlier the popes had been *grands seigneurs*, but now they were increasingly the prisoners of the machine, and by an instinct of self-preservation a new type of pope was evolved

16. See his letters of December 1074 in P. Jaffé, *Regesta Pontificum Romanorum*, ed. W. Wattenbach, 1885, i, nos. 4904 (7 Dec.), 4910 and 4911 (16 Dec.).

17. *Historians of the Church of York*, ed. J. Raine, *Rolls Series*, ii, 163.

to fit the machine. Many intelligent men watched the process with amusement, cynicism, or anger according to their temperaments. St Bernard watched it with alarm and indignation. In 1150 he wrote to warn his protégé Eugenius III against the machine:

> Where shall I begin? Let me begin with the pressure of business. If you hate it, I sympathize with you. If you don't, I mourn all the more, because the unconscious patient is in the greater danger. . . . See where all this damnable business is leading you! You are wasting your time! I will speak to you as Jethro spoke to Moses and say, 'What is this thing that you are doing to the people? Why do you sit from morning till evening listening to litigants?' What fruit is there in these things? They can only create cobwebs.[18]

Eugenius would perhaps have liked to arrest the papal descent into a vast ocean of litigation, but he had neither the knowledge nor the strength to do so. Among his successors Adrian IV accepted the situation with his habitual good humour and competence, and Alexander III plunged into the intricacies of legal business with incomparable skill and zest. By the time of his death in 1181 the pattern of papal activity was fixed for the rest of the Middle Ages.

It was not the pattern that St Bernard desired. He wanted the pope to stand like Moses, in the words of Jethro, 'for the people to God-ward', 'to teach them ordinances and laws and the way wherein they must walk', but not to judge between one man and another 'in every small matter'. But leadership could only be obtained on the terms that were available at the time. Leadership meant lordship, and the popes descended into the arena where lordship was to be won. It could only be won in the fashion of every other medieval ruler, in the ceaseless petty round of business and litigation.

THE SOURCES OF BUSINESS

The two main characteristics of medieval government, whether secular or ecclesiastical, were these: the ruler was a dispenser of benefits, and he was a dispenser of justice. He

18. *De Consideratione*, I, i–ii (*P.L.* 182, 727–31).

was a dispenser of benefits in the first place because it was the chief way in which a ruler could attract loyalty; generosity was what men expected of the great, and they responded to it. This was the great rule of government from the earliest days when the ruler had been known as the 'giver of rings' and men had been glad to die thinking of the benefits their lord had bestowed on them. In the thirteenth century Henry III of England was so impressed by the importance of this piece of political wisdom that he inscribed on the walls of his palaces and on the border of his chess-board the motto 'He who does not give what he has, will not get what he wants.'[19]

There was nothing shameful in this chain of mutual benefits: it was simply the universal law of life –

> It becometh a king who keepeth a realm
> To give mede to men who serve him meekly,
> To honour aliens and all men with gifts.
> Mede makes men love him and honour his manhood. . . .
> The pope and all prelates give presents,
> And mede makes men maintain their laws.[20]

To be able to give was the first law of political life, and there was a close connexion between this and the most important function of medieval government, the dispensing of justice. If the distribution of benefits was essential to the survival of a government, the dispensing of justice was necessary for the growth of its influence. There were several reasons for this. In the first place, the dispensing of justice vastly enlarged the gifts that a ruler could give; indeed it was the source of most of them. The punishments of the evil-doer provided the rewards of the well-doer; and he who dealt out punishments to his enemies could also remit them for his friends. The records of governments are full of such remissions and rewards for friends drawn from the deep well of judicial supremacy. These rewards and remissions kept the wheels of government turning and the timing of them was a main part of the art of government.

19. H. M. Colvin, *History of the King's Works*, 1963, i, 497, ii, 1011.
20. William Langland, *Piers the Plowman*, B. Text, iii, 208–15.

This was one reason why judicial rights were everywhere the chief growing-point in government at this time, and why nearly all political quarrels resolved themselves into quarrels about jurisdiction. Another reason was that justice was the one form of governmental activity that paid for itself. Once a right to jurisdiction had been established, suitors came of their own accord. They did not come empty-handed. They paid on the nail for everything they got. In every other sphere governments had to struggle to extort obedience, and the effort cost money; but in dispensing justice the business came without prompting, so long as the article was good. The fees of litigants paid for everything.

It would be wrong to think that governments sought jurisdiction mainly for the income it provided, for most of the income was swallowed by the officials who worked the judicial machinery. The real reason why governments sought jurisdiction was because it was the only practical way in which they could enforce their claims to lordship. But once the process had started, the officials who were created by the process had a strong interest in keeping it going.

Benefits, then, and justice went hand in hand, and in both these fields the pope outstripped all other rulers. The benefits he could grant were solid and lasting, and the justice he could give was stronger and better than any other. It lasted for ever and there was no appeal. We may examine the structure of both these activities by taking a few samples from an overwhelming mass of material.

Papal benefits. In the first two generations after 1050, down to about 1130, the majority of papal letters that survive grant benefits of various kinds to monasteries. The great monasteries were the first important class of clients at the papal court. They sought confirmation of their possessions and customs, freedom from episcopal jurisdiction, insignia of honour like the use of an episcopal mitre or sandals. The corporate pride of great religious communities found an outlet in a scramble for honours, dignities, and exemptions; and it was one of the easiest ways for a pope to display his generosity. When the monks of St Albans, for example, learned that Nicholas Breakspear, the son of a member of their community, had been elected pope, they made careful preparations for a flow of reciprocal benefits. They spent a year collecting money and gifts to take to Rome, and their delegation came back laden with every kind of privilege or amenity that a pope, in virtue of his jurisdictional supremacy, could confer on a monastery.[21] Monasteries all over Europe had been doing this kind of thing for a century or more, though few from such a position of strength as St Albans.

At first sight it is hard to know why popes lent themselves and their office to these often pointless monastic ambitions. It cannot often have been in the real interests of monastic discipline to free monasteries from episcopal supervision, or to give them the other privileges that popes had it in their power to grant. Probably the popes, like other rulers, simply gave what they could to those who asked and could pay for what they asked, in return for loyalty and obedience. They followed the line of least resistance, and in doing so they opened up channels along which a growing stream of papal directives could flow. They followed the ordinary laws of medieval government because they knew no others.

We can see this very clearly exemplified at another great English abbey, at Bury St Edmunds. In the later years of the twelfth century Abbot Samson was very successful in getting papal privileges for his abbey. These privileges brought the abbey into a close dependence on the papal court, and it was reasonable to expect that the abbot in return would give benefices in his gift to papal nominees. Abbot Samson's biographer tells us that a papal nominee once brought a letter giving him a claim to one of the abbey's benefices. These were very early days in the history of such papal letters, but Samson already knew all about them. He opened a drawer and showed the applicant

21. *Gesta Abbatum Monasterii Sancti Albani, R.S.,* ii, 125-6; W. Holtzman, *Papsturkunden in England,* iii, nos. 100-13, 117-19 (*Abh. der Gesellschaft der Wissenschaften zu Göttingen,* 1962). For further details see R. W. Southern, *Medieval Humanism and Other Studies,* p. 249.

seven other letters. 'Do you see these papal letters?' he said. 'When I have satisfied those who came first, you shall have your emolument; first come, first served.'[22] The good-humoured worldliness of this scene is a very important element in the ecclesiastical government of the Middle Ages. Until the whole system came under fire, the chain of recipro-cal benefits was impossible to break because it satisfied the greatest possible number of influential people. In many ways it must have contributed to the amenity and expan-siveness of life. It was not very elevating, and many religious movements began by renouncing special papal benefits; but in the end they all succumbed. There was too much common humanity in this exercise of papal power to be long resisted.

It was to monasteries, and later to religious orders as a whole, that the pope could grant the most extensive privileges, but the flow of papal benefits was not confined to this narrow channel. We shall see later some of the manifold ways in which papal benefits made papal government acceptable to men at every level of society. But before we can do this, we must examine the most important develop-ment in papal power in the whole medieval period: the emergence of the papacy as a universal court of first instance in a vast area of litigation.

Papal justice. It was in the decade from 1140 to 1150 that papal jurisdiction emerged as a perceptible fact in every-day European life. In these years we first begin to see it penetrating the lowest strata of the ecclesiastical structure as a matter of ordinary routine.

There is an early illustration of this penetration in a letter which has been preserved from Pope Lucius II to the bishop of Worcester in 1144.[23] The letter instructed the bishop to take the bishop of Hereford as his colleague and settle a dispute about a parish church in the diocese of Lichfield. The canons of Evreux claimed that it belonged to them; they alleged that the earl of Worcester had driven out their

22. *Chronica Jocelini de Brakelonda*, ed. H. E. Butler, p. 56.
23. W. R. Holtzmann, op. cit., 1930, i, no. 29.

vicar and sold the right of future presentation to the archdeacon of Chester. By the time we hear of it the case had already travelled from Normandy to Rome and from Rome to England, and now two English bishops were required to summon representatives of an earl, an arch-deacon, a cathedral chapter, and two or three vicars or ex-vicars from both sides of the Channel, and settle the affair on papal authority. If we reflect on this it is very remarkable. At a time when England was in a state of acute civil war, when relations with Normandy were severed, and when local powers were everywhere supreme, the pope could expect his orders to be carried out two thousand miles from Rome, in a dispute about a property worth perhaps £10 a year.

Not the least remarkable feature of the case is the pertinacity of litigants, and the expense they were willing to incur to gain their ends. The expense of this case must have been many times the value of the income of the parish church. But the litigation of corporate bodies had some of the characteristics of an arms race: it could not be stopped without abandoning some lawful claim, and no one was willing to do this. The rights of corporations are for ever: the expenses of a law-suit are only for today. No one would sacrifice the future for a few pounds. So the flood of litigation rose. In 1144 it was just beginning, but its main lines were already laid down.

This flow of business had one great positive result. It was responsible for tidying up large areas of ordinary life. The papal court protected parish priests against eviction and gave them a minimum income that could not easily be plundered; it gave laymen a discipline that was clear-cut and not very onerous; it laid down rules and conditions for all the main occasions and areas of the Christian life – baptism, confirmation, confession, communion, penance, marriage, religious instruction and religious duties, alms, usury, last wills and testaments, the last rites, burial, graveyards, prayers and masses for the dead. With similar clarity and completeness it dealt with all the incidents of clerical life – dress, education, ordination, duties, status, crimes and punishments. It drew into one intricate but coherent system the vast complex of religious Orders that grew up in the twelfth century. The materials for much of this work lay to hand in the writings of earlier centuries, but the responsibility for bringing these materials into order, for filling the many gaps and meeting the problems presented by a rapidly developing society, lay in the first place with the pope. Without the papal supremacy it is inconceivable that any such comprehensive system of law could ever have been developed. In their response to this responsibility the popes of this period justified the claims of the Roman church to be the mother-church of all the churches – at least in the West. But these beneficent results were only a by-product of the great uncontrollable flow of litigation. It is remarkable how little business the popes initiated in the great days of growth. They had no need to initiate. The business rushed upon them; they had only to invent the rules and reach the decisions.

THE MAKERS OF BUSINESS

The flow of business through the papal court in the twelfth and thirteenth centuries left a golden residue of legal achievement, but there was a price to pay which only became fully payable at a later date. Part of this price had been foreseen by St Bernard in his rôle as Jethro: 'The thing that thou doest is not good: thou wilt surely wear away, both thou and this people that is with thee, for this thing is too heavy for thee.' Litigation at the papal court became an obsessive feature of the religious life, and it is written all over the records of every important religious community.

The monks of Canterbury, for instance, kept a noble record of their activity at the papal court between 1185 and 1201. They were not more litigious than other monks, but like other monks they were determined to have their rights. So when their nominal abbot, the archbishop, proposed to endow a college for canons near Canterbury they at once scented a danger to their own interests and dignity. They opposed the plan with all their strength, and this required incessant litigation at the papal court for fifteen years.

During this period they wrote hundreds of letters to popes, cardinals, kings – to everyone who could possibly bring any influence to bear on the case. A series of popes wrote about seventy letters on the case, and Innocent III, the sixth pope to be involved in it, became rather impatient: 'I have so often had to pile mandate on mandate and letter on letter in this business of the church of Canterbury, that I blush to hear of this mouldy business.'[24] But the monks persevered, and in the end they got what they wanted. They gloried in their sufferings, and treasured the records of the case as a fitting sequel to the martyrdom of Thomas Becket.

The path to Rome was strewn with death and disaster, and money was poured out like water to secure the appointment of favourable judges:

We cannot rival the archbishop's party in the quantity of gifts, but since our cause cannot be conducted without gifts, we prefer to promise what we haven't got, rather than to spare expense and suffer perpetual servitude. It would be lunacy to be careful of the wealth that perishes when we are prepared to lay down our lives in defence of our church.[25]

And when the judges arrived, the wheels of justice still needed careful attention:

The new legate is fairly pious, subtle, taciturn, and modest; so let your words also be circumspect, brief, and modest. Be careful not to offer him any gift. I tried to give him a reliquary ... but because of the silver and precious stones on it, he refused. However, with some difficulty I managed to lend him the prior's horse.[26]

Even the smallest cog needed to be oiled:

24. *Epistolae Cantuarienses* (*Chronicles and Memorials of the Reign of Richard I*, ii, *R.S.*, ed. W. Stubbs), p. 509; the case dragged on for another year, and the pope had to write several more letters, before it was finished.
25. ibid., p. 197.
26. ibid., p. 272.

Show a cheerful face to the legate's clerk and load him with promises. Don't let our present poverty stand in the way: 'Anyone can be rich in promises.'[27]

So from pope to legate and from legate to legate's clerk the stream broadened out. These were heroic days for litigants. They fought like tigers for their rights. Nothing could stop them, not even empty purses, so long as money-lenders were willing to lend. For the popes the open road to Rome had become the proof of their primacy. Secular attempts to check the flow were regarded, perhaps rightly, as concealed attacks on the primacy itself. The resistance of bishops and archbishops in defence of their own juris-diction was brushed aside by the legal logic of the papal court. And even without the aid of logic, all obstructions would have been overcome by the pressure of the litigants themselves. The flow of litigants made it necessary to provide the facilities they needed. Slowly the heroic impro-visations and the hectic canvassing for support illustrated in the letters of the 1180s gives place to a more orderly conduct of business imposed by the rules of the papal curia. By 1225 or thereabouts the papal machine was in very good order.

It would be possible to find countless illustrations of the process whereby the turbulence of twelfth-century litiga-tion gave way, at least on the surface, to a well-ordered sequence of judicial procedures controlled by the papal court. There is a basic similarity about all the examples that have come to our notice, and two final illustrations from Canterbury may stand for them all. They come from the years 1184 and 1228 – from either end, therefore, of the period of consolidation.

In each of these years the archbishopric was vacant, and on both occasions there was a clash of interest between the monks of Canterbury, who were the canonical electors, and the king and bishops of the kingdom. In 1184 the fight between the two sides was confused and uninhibited.[28]

27. ibid., p. 303.
28. For full details see Gervase of Canterbury, *Historical Works*, ed. W. Stubbs, *R.S.*, i, 310–25.

Claims were advanced on all hands, only to be modified or withdrawn later. The king kept everything in confusion by contradictory promises to the monks and the bishops. No one knew how to proceed. The business was protracted by obscure intrigues and arguments about formulas: would (for instance) the claims of the monks be satisfied if their prior announced the election with the words 'the bishops of England, and I the prior, and the monks of Canterbury with the assent of the king, have elected . . .'? Such questions as these were hard to answer. Everyone suspected a trap in every move proposed by the other side. There were terrible emotional scenes. The prior fainted after one angry speech of the king, and the king protested that he had spoken only in jest. It was all very humiliating. After many months of fruitless wrangling, the monks produced documents (one would like to know where they had got them) giving them the right of free election and the first voice in choosing an archbishop. But in the end the king and bishops got the man they wanted, and the monks had only the meagre satisfaction of announcing his election through the mouth of their prior.

Outwardly at least, the contrast with the events during the vacancy of 1228 could not be more complete.[29] From beginning to end there was an outward appearance of cheerful unanimity under the authority of Rome. Everything took place in due order. The monks began the proceedings by putting themselves, their goods, and their liberties under the protection of the pope. The king readily promised them a free election. The monks made an election, carefully observing the rules of canon law and fortifying their action with the necessary documents. Then they sent their chosen candidate to Rome to obtain papal confirmation. Here, however, they found an unexpected difficulty. Messengers from the king and bishops had got there before them and had whispered in the pope's ear. Gravely and deliberately the pope examined the case and quashed the election made by the monks; then he appointed the man

29. The details are fully recorded in the continuation of Gervase, op. cit., ii, 115–24.

recommended by the king. There were no protests, no emotional scenes. A well-oiled machine produced without effort the result that had required an immense expenditure of nervous energy in 1184; but in principle it was the same result.

This was the golden age of government, and especially of papal government, before the system had been choked with the vexations of politics and the complications of over-elaboration. Much that was done had no practical effect. Much that was effected would in any case have happened. Yet, when every allowance has been made, we may still say that the papal machinery of government was as effective as any government could be before the late nineteenth century. The papal curia of the thirteenth century was, by any standards that were applicable before the days of modern mechanical aids and salaried officials, a large and efficient organization. Like any other government it was constantly engaged in war or the preparation of war, in diplomacy, in the management of estates, in the assessment and collection of taxes; but by far the most highly developed part of the organization was that which dealt with the various stages of legal processes. There was a complicated organization for hearing petitions and complaints, for recording decisions, for drafting the documents necessary for carrying them out, and for keeping copies of the letters sent out.[30] The office routine for performing these duties in a systematic way was the subject of a specialized literature. At most times there were probably well over a hundred experts at the papal court engaged in legal work. Every important ecclesiastical and secular person or corporation in Europe had to be familiar with the procedure of the papal curia, and the most important had proctors permanently retained to look after their interests in the labyrinth of papal government.

30. The first serious (and still valuable) sketch of this organization is L. Delisle, 'Mémoire sur les actes d'Innocent III', *Bibliothèque de l'école des chartes*, 1858, 4th ser., vol. iv. 1–73. For a more recent survey with copious bibliography see B. Rusch, *Die Behörden u. Hofbeamten der päpstl. Kurie des xiii Jts.*, 1936.

THE VARIETY OF BUSINESS

Before leaving the papal court at the height of its effectiveness we may survey the scene for a few months in 1244,
just a hundred years after the dispatch of the papal letter
to the bishop of Worcester which we have already noticed.
We choose a quiet time from January to June 1244, when
the routine of government was little disturbed by great
events or pressing business. The rush of business which had
followed the election of a new pope, Innocent IV, in June
1243, had subsided. There was a lull in the conflict with
the Emperor Frederick II, who still hoped that the new
pope would be less intransigent than the last one. The
pope was in Rome thinking about the Council he proposed
to call in the following year. We happen to know that he
was already considering further action against Frederick II,
but on the surface all was peace, and the papal records
present an appearance of humdrum activity.

During these six months the papal clerks kept copies of
about four hundred letters.[31] There must have been many
more, but these preserve a fair selection of the most important business. The letters deal with every side of ecclesiastical administration in nearly every country in Europe.
The privileges of the Cluniacs, Cistercians, and Dominicans
were confirmed. Each Carthusian house was granted the
right to have up to six hundred cows. King Louis IX was
required to burn copies of the Talmud and other books of
the Jews. The theologian Roland of Cremona was directed
to inquire into the heresies of the rebellious Ezelinus de
Romanis. A moratorium was declared on excommunications in the diocese of Toulouse for five years because the
vast number of such sentences had brought them into
contempt. The religious vows of the schoolmaster of Asti,
who had been induced to enter the Dominican Order in a
state of drunkenness, were declared void. Benefits, such as
freedom from excommunication, exemption from interdict,

31. E. Berger, *Les Registres d'Innocent IV*, 4 vols., 1884–1919: the letters
from 1 January to 30 June 1244 are numbered 357 to 747, but there are
a few intrusions from an earlier date in this series.

mitigation of debts to usurers, and a general relaxation of future ecclesiastical sentences, were granted to the king of France, the prince of Antioch, the counts of Provence, Vienne, and Tuscany, the lord of Bourbon, the landgrave of Thuringia, the archbishop of Mainz, among others. Nothing could look more peaceful.

Yet as we look beneath the surface of these letters, we see the shadow of great events which occupied the pope's mind. Europe was at this time divided into two loose associations under the pope and emperor respectively. The papal sphere of influence was centred on the county of Provence, where the kings of France and England were held together by marriage in a loose family concord. The sphere of influence of the emperor, who was also allied to the king of England by marriage, included Sicily, many Italian cities, a large part of Germany, and the county of Toulouse. There were men working on both sides to bring the two sides together, and on 31 March a general treaty of peace between the pope and emperor was concluded at Rome. If this treaty had worked the later history of the medieval church might have been perceptibly altered; but within a month it had broken down.

Many of the papal benefits which were dispensed at this time must be read with this situation in mind. The pope made no secret of the severely practical purpose that prompted his favours. They were intended to encourage his friends, to win over waverers like the count of Toulouse and the landgrave of Thuringia, and to penalize the pope's enemies. In very many of his small and apparently unconnected threats and favours the pope had these objects in mind, and he frankly explained the policy to the king of France:

> It is the practice of the Apostolic See to decorate with honourable privileges those illustrious men whom it has found prompt and fervent in its service.[32]

Papal privileges helped to cement alliances based on common interests, and in these quiet months they were quietly

32. ibid., no. 718.

used to promote the pope's anti-imperialist policy in Italy and Germany.

These political considerations were least obtrusive in the pope's dealings with England, and the seventy-seven letters written to this distant kingdom during the first six months of 1244 provide a good sample of the ordinary routine business of papal government.[33] Nearly all these letters illustrate the work of a supreme judicature. About a third of them were papal directives in ecclesiastical law-suits. In another third the pope exercised the power of a supreme court which is also a supreme legislature in dispensing with its own laws. The dispensations were largely routine matters. Ten bastards were allowed to proceed to Holy Orders despite the barrier of illegitimacy; thirty-one clerks were allowed to hold more than one cure of souls. At a rather higher level, a noble clerk of the house of Clare was given permission to hold as many benefices with the cure of souls as would bring him a revenue of £200 a year; and a papal chaplain, John of Vercelli, was given a similar privilege. Finally there is a batch of twenty-two letters containing confirmations, licences, and exhortations of various kinds. It is in these letters that the unspectacular cooperation of secular and ecclesiastical authorities can best be seen. In one of them, the pope confirmed the conditions of a loan from the king to his father-in-law; in another he confirmed the king's testamentary arrangements for his kingdom and the amount of the queen's dowry; in another he gave authority to the archbishop to absolve the king from any automatic excommunication incurred through his officers having laid violent hands on a clerk; in another he exhorted the king to allow the translation of the bishop of Norwich to Winchester.

Here then we have a cross-section of the papal government of the church during the few months of relative peace in the middle of the thirteenth century. Of course the records of these months cannot illustrate everything that the pope could do, but they show very clearly that the detailed control of all ecclesiastical affairs was not an

33. *C.P.R.*, i, pp. 204–10.

empty dream. Throughout western Europe the papal directives flowed with smooth efficiency and were received with a remarkable absence of opposition. In this area at least, Gregory VII's dream of papal authority seemed to have come true.

The primacy and temporal power

When we turn to the question of papal authority over temporal rulers the evidence of our six months' probe in 1244 is ambiguous. Clearly the pope exercised a far more extensive political influence than had been possible in the eleventh century. His power to depose emperors was about to be put to a final test which, if not conclusively successful, at least destroyed the family of his adversary and virtually destroyed the empire at the same time. But there are signs of a fundamental weakness. The pope's power over princes could only be effective by being over-effective. It was impossible for him to pluck out and destroy an individual without bringing about a general political, and sometimes an ecclesiastical, collapse. As late as 1244 the pope, by forbidding further excommunications in the area of Toulouse, was still trying to tidy up the mess that had been left by the decision to root out the rebellious count of Toulouse thirty years earlier. And thirty years later he would still be left with the mess caused by the destruction of the Hohenstaufen family.

The reason for this disproportion between the results aimed at and the results actually achieved was quite simple: the only weapons under the pope's direct control were interdict and excommunication. These weapons might have been effective if they had commanded unanimous respect and obedience, but they did not. In minor disputes they sometimes worked; but in major ones they either did not work at all, or they unleashed a flood of self-interested violence which destroyed everything within reach, including in the end the authority of the censures which justified this violence.

The operation of this law of disproportionate means and

ends provides one of the most tragic spectacles in European history. The papal claims in temporal affairs could never succeed because the pope lacked the appropriate weapons; but he could never stop trying to succeed with inappropriate weapons so long as there was no effective challenge to the theory of papal supremacy in secular affairs. In the twelfth and thirteenth centuries there was no satisfactory theoretical answer to the proposition that 'it belongs to the spiritual power both to set up the secular power and to judge it'.[34] The old answer, that the secular ruler had an independent spiritual authority derived from God himself, had been blown away. The later answer, which arose from the minute analysis of the nature of spiritual power in the fourteenth century, had not yet appeared. Meanwhile every major effort of the papacy to translate the theory of temporal sovereignty into practice was disastrous. In theory, the power to take kingdoms from unworthy rulers and give them to those whom the pope judged worthy should have been the culmination of the system of papal jurisdiction and benefits. But in practice the Norman kings, who came to England as the pope's protégés, were a greater menace than the Anglo-Saxons whom they displaced; Henry V, whom the pope crowned as emperor, was more dangerous than Henry IV, whom he refused to crown; and not all Innocent III's political acumen could produce an acceptable successor to Henry VI. The popes could 'root out and destroy', but they could not 'build and plant'.[35]

The failure of papal temporal lordship stands in sharp contrast to the success of papal ecclesiastical primacy. But we must not exaggerate the contrast. Even the success of the ecclesiastical primacy followed the same law as the failure of temporal lordship: it succeeded only in so far as it was acceptable to large numbers of influential people. Both success and failure were determined by secular con-

34. Hugh of St Victor, *De Sacramentis*, ii, 2 (*P.L.* 176, 418).
35. For Innocent III these two phrases expressed the totality of papal temporal power: see, for example, C. R. Cheney and W. H. Semple, *Selected Letters of Innocent III concerning England*, pp. 24, 151, 216 and the references there provided.

siderations. Needless to say, many men believed that papal authority in both these spheres was right and ought to suc-ceed. Without this belief no measure of success would have been at all possible. But this belief was never sufficient to ensure success. To understand the limits of papal power, whether ecclesiastical or political, we must look for other causes than theoretical conviction.

The first element in the success of the papacy in the eleventh and twelfth centuries was the support of religious communities who found in papal authority their best safe-guard against the pressures of episcopal discipline and secular depredations. Then, more widely, the papal primacy offered to the clergy everywhere substantial bene-fits: security for their property, freedom from secular punishments, a refuge against violence, and a means of settling intricate disputes. The status of every clerk was enhanced by the papal primacy, which communicated to them all something of the greatness of Rome. I have called the clerical interest in the Middle Ages the greatest of all trade-unions, and the papal primacy would never have become effective if it had not won the support of the ecclesi-astical hierarchy by maintaining the interests of the clergy as a whole. But equally it would never have been effective if lay rulers had not found that, even if it offered them nothing, it took almost nothing from them.

How little in the end, despite their initial fears, lay rulers suffered from the growth of papal authority is well illustrated by one of the papal letters of 1244 which has been briefly mentioned already. The letter is a sharp warning to the king of England to allow the bishop of Norwich to be trans-lated to Winchester.[36] It looks like an easy exercise of papal supremacy; but behind it there lies a story which illustrates the whole strength and weakness of the medieval papal government of the church. It deserves therefore a short explanation.

The bishop on whose behalf the pope intervened was William Raleigh, who was one of the greatest of the king's servants. He has been described as 'the foremost judge in

36. *C.P.R.*, i, p. 206, dated 28 Feb. 1244.

the king's court' and the champion of English secular common law 'against the laws and canons and consensus of Christendom'.[37] As a reward for these services the king had given him a great array of ecclesiastical benefices, and the final reward of a bishopric could not be far off. No doubt the king fully intended that he should have this reward in his own time, but unluckily for Raleigh, when the bishopric of Winchester fell vacant in 1238, the monks had rushed in and elected him without the king's consent. This was a mistake. Winchester was the most desirable bishopric in the kingdom. It had a fine palace, a convenient situation, large revenues, a great political position – all that could be wished. But it was not the king's intention that all this should be lavished on his old servant however meritorious. He intended it for William of Savoy, a member of his wife's family. So he arranged that Raleigh should be elected to Norwich, a humbler see, while William of Savoy got Winchester. This amicable arrangement, however, was no sooner made than William of Savoy died, and the monks of Winchester, unable to learn a lesson, rushed in once more and re-elected Raleigh. The king was distinctly vexed, but he now had a new remedy. Since Raleigh was already bishop of Norwich his translation would require papal approval, and the king employed the best canon lawyer of the day to contest the election at the papal court. He was in no hurry. While the case stood still he enjoyed all the revenues of Winchester, and dispensed all its ecclesiastical patronage. His lawyer, Henry of Susa, who would one day be a cardinal and a very famous canonist, was not in a hurry either. The case brought him experience, as his later writings show, and he grew steadily in fame and wealth.[38] The monks of Winchester had to wait a long time for a bishop, and perhaps they too were in no hurry.

The see was vacant for five years before a papal judge-

---

37. F. Pollock and F. W. Maitland, *History of English Law*, 2nd ed., 1898, i, 189, 196. The course of the disputed election is fully discussed in F. M. Powicke, *Henry III and the Lord Edward*, i, 270–74.

38. See N. Didier, 'Henri de Suse en Angleterre (1236?–1244)', *Studi in onore V. Arangio-Ruiz*, 1952, ii, 333–51.

ment was given in their favour in 1243. Henry of Susa
lodged a last appeal on the ground that the judgement was
contrary to royal rights. This kept the case going for another
six months, but even the best of lawyers had come at last
to the end of his expedients. In January 1244 the pope
wrote to the king with some severity; in February he made
a final appeal to him before proceeding to sterner measures.
The king saw that he had reached the end of the legal
road, and he gave in. Probably, with increasing bitterness
on both sides, he could have kept the case alive for a few
more years, but he knew when to stop. He was some
£20,000 richer as a result of the vacancy. Many of his
servants had obtained benefices they could not otherwise
have got. Henry of Susa emerged as prior of the Hospital
of St Cross, one of the pleasantest places near Winchester.
The king had no grudge against his old servant Raleigh.
He enjoyed the see for six years, and by this time another
member of the royal family was old enough to take over the
bishopric. The pope had the satisfaction of seeing the law
upheld. It had all been very friendly; no one had gone too
far; no one had lost his temper; no one had been excommunicated. Everyone was happy.

In an important ecclesiastical matter, the papal primacy
had been vindicated. No one had denied the pope's right
to settle the question in his own court, by his own law,
following the processes determined by himself; nor had
anyone denied that he could override all local rights and
claims, whether secular or ecclesiastical. To this extent the
case was a triumphant display of papal authority. It left
no scars because it hurt no one. But this was surely the most
sinister aspect of the curious little anti-drama that we have
been watching. It illustrates the ability of everyone concerned in the case to make themselves comfortable in the
intricacies of the vast machine of papal government.

In an earlier chapter we asked the question: why was it
that the laity acquiesced in the lowly position assigned to
them in the dominant clerical, social and political theories
of the day? A large part of the answer appeared to be that,
whatever their generalities, in their detailed application

these theories were moulded to accommodate secular interests – for instance in the areas of finance and war. We now find that the same explanation can be extended to cover the area where the clerical hierarchical theory was most obviously successful – in the management of purely ecclesiastical affairs. In this area secular interests suffered some very obvious and even spectacular reverses. Kings and laymen lost their direct control of most ecclesiastical appointments; they lost their jurisdiction over ecclesiastical persons and causes; they lost their power to deprive incumbents of ecclesiastical offices; they could not defy the pope for very long. All this was most dramatically displayed in a series of incidents which have caught the imagination of later generations – Henry IV of Germany at Canossa, Henry II of England in his shirt at Canterbury, King John a vassal of the pope, the family of Frederick II destroyed, a papal nominee on the throne of Sicily. But these incidents do not tell the central truth that secular rulers had only to learn the rules of a complicated game in order to dispose of a larger reservoir of ecclesiastical wealth and talent than ever before.

The primitive rulers of Europe before the twelfth century had depended on their almost unrestricted control of ecclesiastical appointments for many advantages. This control had given them reliable agents in peace, troops and treasure in war, a regular replenishment of their income at every vacancy, a reserve of gold and silver in times of need, a variety of places to stay on their journeys. Naturally they viewed with apprehension the loss of these privileges. But by a slow process of adjustment they discovered that they had been unnecessarily alarmed. True, they could no longer simply appoint bishops or exact entrance fees for ecclesiastical office, they could no longer take ecclesiastical property or interfere with ecclesiastical law. But more than ever before they could use ecclesiastical wealth to finance the growing activity of secular government. Clerks in holy orders, though personally subject only to ecclesiastical jurisdiction, were the most effective agents of secular government in the twelfth and thirteenth centuries. They expected ecclesiastical promotion as the reward for their labours, and kings never found any difficulty in providing this. Ecclesiastical office was the main source of treasure from which secular rulers paid their ministers. Everyone from the pope downwards acquiesced in this situation. Naturally therefore the army of royal officials grew by leaps and bounds. Papal dispensations made it possible for the most successful of them to accumulate very large revenues; and at the end they could expect a bishopric.

For all this a royal *fiat* was no longer enough. There were rules to be kept. Where there are rules, there must be experts; and where there are experts, there will be loopholes. The clergy themselves provided the experts who showed the king how to use the ecclesiastical treasure according to the rules of ecclesiastical discipline. These experts, men like Henry of Susa, also expected ecclesiastical rewards from the secular ruler, but so long as the business was managed carefully there was no occasion for bitterness. The dramatic disputes arose either from clumsiness or ignorance or over-confidence or personal hatred. By keeping the rules and not going too far all unpleasantness could be avoided.

The case of the bishopric of Winchester from 1238 to 1244 shows a king not going too far. It also shows how little was lost by losing in the right way, and how little the pope gained by winning according to his own rules. Certainly there was nothing very corrupt in what had happened during these years, but secular motives were everywhere uppermost and everywhere prevailed. We can understand why many contemporaries were beginning to think that the church was a conspiracy between secular and ecclesiastical authorities for the exploitation of ecclesiastical wealth, and that the pope as the head of this conspiracy was in fact anti-Christ. These views were not yet very influential, but they were disturbing. And they were destined to grow.

The lawyer-popes

There is one fact which more than any other sums up this period of papal history: every notable pope from 1159 to

1303 was a lawyer. This fact reflects the papacy's pre-eminent concern with the formulation and enforcement of law. It was here that the papal position was strongest. At a time when the tradition of ancient law and government had been almost completely obliterated in Europe, the popes retained the elements of a legal system on which they could build. Besides this they could claim a legislative authority to which no other ruler of the West could aspire. Every circumstance of twelfth-century society favoured the rapid growth of papal law, and this growth was given a steady impulse by the great succession of lawyer-popes – Alexander III, Innocent III, Gregory IX, Innocent IV, Boniface VIII. The fundamental order of medieval, and to a large extent of modern, society owes a great debt to these popes. They brought to their task clarity of mind, firmness of principle, and a capacious practical wisdom. But they had the weaknesses of the lawyer at the head of affairs. They aspired less and less to provide the leadership which always seemed just beyond their grasp, and increasingly they devoted their energies to keeping the wheels of government turning. In great affairs they were increasingly content if they achieved a formal victory reinforced with resounding generalizations. Increasingly they devoted their energies to the petty business of building up, defending, and ruling the papal state. The measures they took to this end were indistinguishable from those of other secular rulers. Instead of the vast fraternity of obedient kings or knights of St Peter of which earlier popes had dreamt, the thirteenth-century popes contracted their vision to the work of keeping a client king in southern Italy and ruling central Italy with the help of their own relatives. Each successive pope was driven by the uncertainties of political allegiance to form a group of nephews, cousins, and kinsmen faithful to his interests and dependent on his favour, and the political map of Italy became a palimpsest of these uninspiring combinations. More than any theoretical criticism, the necessity for these measures mocked the words of Jeremiah which Boniface VIII quoted in his last great statement of the papal position, 'See, I have this day set thee over the nations and over the kingdoms, to root out, and to pull down, and to destroy, and to throw down; to build and to plant.'[39]

III. THE INFLATIONARY SPIRAL,
c.1300–c.1520

In 1309 Clement V moved to Avignon. In most ways it was a very good thing. It removed the papacy from the fierce tensions of Italian politics and installed it in a low-pressure political area. Geographically the new seat of government was much more convenient: for the inhabitants of four fifths of western Christendom it cut the time spent on a visit to the papal court by five weeks. It is true that Avignon did not stimulate great thoughts, and ardent spirits longed to be back in Rome. But great thoughts had done the papacy little good in recent years, and if the work of the papacy was to lie mainly in the daily routine of judicial business – and from this there was now no escape – then Avignon was a much better centre than Rome. It had the atmosphere of an up-to-date governmental head-quarters.

The mere fact that the popes could operate for seventy years without any physical contact with Rome is a remarkable symptom of the distance travelled in the two centuries before the move. Papal power dissociated from Rome would have been unthinkable at any time before the middle of the thirteenth century; in the fourteenth century it could be accepted, perhaps with regret, but certainly without difficulty. The papal court was now mainly a place where business was done. No one could contemplate its disappearance, and nothing could greatly alter its character. Such as it was it had to be accepted, and the more convenient its place of operation the better.

39. *Extravagantes Communes*, I, viii, 1 (Friedberg, *Corpus Iuris Canonici*, ii, 1246). The words come from the Bull *Unam Sanctam* which Boniface composed and wrote (so it was reported) with his own hand: see H. Finke, *Aus den Tagen Bonifaz VIII*, 1902, p. 147n.

All forms of government had grown rapidly in the last two centuries, and in many areas of government a degree of complexity had been achieved that had a suffocating effect on the efficient conduct of business. Various causes contributed to this result. In the first place, the ease with which an army of officials could be maintained virtually free of charge on ecclesiastical endowments had encouraged the expansion of government beyond the limits of effective action. This was a factor in the growth of papal, no less than of secular, government. Arising from this, the tendency for judicial business to become increasingly complicated created a need for more officials, who in turn created more work. The papal government suffered from all these symptoms of over-elaboration. Business continued to grow in bulk, but the growing business did not carry with it a corresponding increase of papal influence in European affairs.

If we turn back to the quiet months of 1244 we can see that there were already signs that the papal system of government was beginning to produce its own anti-bodies which limited the area of effective development. Conspicuous among them was the secular ruler operating for his own ends within the papal system. In the friendliest possible way Henry III of England had been able to profit by the delays in papal justice to an extent that William Rufus might have envied in the days when papal justice was in its infancy. But whereas Rufus had ecclesiastical opinion everywhere against him, Henry III operated in a favourable climate of opinion with the skilled help of a famous canonist. This mode of operation presented a much more insidious danger to the papal position than the rough violence of Rufus: against respectability there can be no sanctions.

Another sinister feature of the documents of 1244 were the indications that excommunication had been overplayed and was losing its effectiveness. The pope's letter forbidding further excommunication and interdicts in the diocese of Toulouse for a period of five years was an acknowledgement of an essential defeat, for without this sanction the whole papal position would be radically weakened. The Italian towns could have provided many more indications of the same waning influence of the pope's most powerful weapon. The danger signals were here very clear. Most of the great Italian cities suffered papal excommunication at some time or other in the thirteenth century, sometimes for periods of several years. They dealt with the situation in a spirit of commercial calculation, as they might have dealt with a shortage of food or raw materials. It was a considerable nuisance, but it was not a terrible disaster. The ultimate papal weapon had ceased to be a sanction on a different level from any other.

Again, within a few years of 1244 we find the beginnings of a sustained clerical opposition to papal actions. Everyone would now agree that, on the famous occasion in 1253 when Bishop Robert Grosseteste refused to admit a nephew of the pope to a canonry in his cathedral at the pope's command, he was acting on a lofty doctrine of papal authority.[40] But his action was nevertheless a sign that papal power was no longer an adequate protection for ecclesiastical rights. Papal power had grown largely because it satisfied the needs and aspirations of the great mass of the ecclesiastical hierarchy. If it ever ceased to do this, or if it ever appeared that some other power – for instance the king's – could better satisfy these needs and aspirations, then the days of papal power would be numbered. This was still far in the future, but the doubt was already there.

These new factors set limits to the future growth of papal power, but they did not immediately affect the growth of business. If we go on just a hundred years from 1244 and make a similar survey of surviving papal records during the first six months of 1344 we find a remarkable growth in three forms of activity: the issue of indulgences; papal arbitration in international affairs; and the elaboration of the system of papal appointments to ecclesiastical benefices. An examination of these three fields of activity will tell us

40. The best study of Grosseteste's position is W. A. Pantin, 'Grosseteste's relations with the Papacy and the Crown', in *Robert Grosseteste, Scholar and Bishop*, ed. D. A. Callus, 1955, 178–215.

something about the adjustments taking place in the relationship between the papacy and European society in the last centuries of the Middle Ages.

Indulgences

The granting of papal indulgences on a large scale goes back to 1095, when Urban II announced that participation in the Crusade would be reckoned a substitute for all other penances – or, in popular language, would ensure the immediate entry into Heaven of a Crusader who died in a state of repentance and confession.[41] For a long time after 1095 these plenary indulgences, which the pope alone could grant, were reserved for very special occasions. They were given mainly as a reward for taking part in a Crusade on terms laid down by the pope; similar grants for any other meritorious act were very rare indeed. Nevertheless they were from the beginning a peculiarly personal expression of the papal plenitude of power, and there were no limits to the use the popes might make of their privilege.

One of the earliest examples of the exercise of this power provides a touching illustration of the pope's personal involvement. John of Salisbury has described the scene. One day in 1150 Pope Eugenius III was sitting in his court hearing a divorce case, in which the count of Molise sought a divorce from his wife on grounds of consanguinity. After a time the pope could bear it no longer. He burst into tears, rose from his throne, and threw himself at the feet of the count with such violence that his mitre rolled in the dust. When the bishops and cardinals had set him on his feet and retrieved his mitre, he begged the count to take back his wife, adding these words:

To make you more ready and willing to do this, I, the successor of Peter and vicar of Christ, to whom the keys of the kingdom have

41. For an account of the origins and development of the system, see N. Paulus, *Geschichte des Ablasses im Mittelalter*, 3 vols., 1922–3, and H. Delehaye, 'Les lettres d'indulgence collectives', *Analecta Bollandiana*, 1926–8, xliv, 342–79, xlv, 97–123, 323–44; xlvi, 149–57, 287–343.

been delivered, will give your wife an inestimable dowry: provided
that you are faithful to her, she will bring you immunity (from
punishment) for all the sins you have so far committed, and I
shall be responsible for them on the Day of Judgement.[42]

Although the later pronouncements of medieval popes
on the subject of indulgences are seldom as attractive as
this, we see here the deeply felt personal responsibility
which is never far from the best of them. The later history
of indulgences, disastrous though in the end it became, is
simply a development of what we see on a small scale in
this incident: the power and desire of the popes to extend
more and more widely the immunity which Eugenius III
begged the count of Molise to receive.

The stages by which this wide immunity was offered to
Christendom need only be sketched in the briefest outline.
By the end of the twelfth century we find Innocent III
extending the plenary indulgence of Crusaders to those
who helped with money or advice as well as those who
fought; and to the full immunity from punishment he added
a promise of increased rewards in heaven for good works.[43]
In the middle of the thirteenth century Innocent IV took
the further step of granting plenary indulgences in special
circumstances without any condition of service at all. At
first these grants were very infrequent. Like Eugenius III's
grant to the count of Molise a hundred years earlier, they
were spontaneous acts of the pope, moved by the merits of
religious men and women like St Clare or the Franciscan
chronicler Salimbene; but by the end of the thirteenth
century they were being granted to secular rulers for
political reasons.

Soon, by a further extension of the papal clemency,
individuals began to be able to buy the privilege of receiving a plenary indulgence from their confessors at the moment
of death. By 1344 this free use of the papal power had grown
to massive proportions. In the first six months of this year
Clement VI granted this privilege to no less than two

42. *Historia Pontificalis*, ed. R. L. Poole, 1927, p. 84.
43. Paulus, op. cit., i, 207: for the full text see *P.L.* 214, 828–32.

hundred people in England alone.[44] Necessarily they were all people of some substance, able to pay the fees for such an indulgence, but the price was not high – less than ten shillings sterling in the scale of charges at the papal court. Even when we have made allowance for many additional incidental expenses, the plenary indulgence at the hour of death was within the reach of people at many levels of society. In 1344 knights, parish priests, and townsfolk shared the privilege with the Queen of England and other members of the royal family. They were all assured that in the last resort it would suffice for a layman to pronounce the words, 'May the Lord absolve you from your guilt and punishment according to the privilege which you say you have received from the supreme pontiff', for the indulgence to have its full effect. It was a saying of Clement VI, the pope of 1344, that 'a pontiff should make his subjects happy'.[45] He could scarcely have done more to put this basic maxim of government into effect.

Individual indulgences necessarily cost money, but Clement wished further to extend to those with no money but only stout legs the final gift within the papal power. He had the example of Boniface VIII before his eyes. In 1300 Boniface had granted a plenary indulgence to all repentant and confessed sinners who in the course of this year, and every hundredth year in the future, visited the churches of the Holy Apostles in Rome. In 1343 Clement VI reduced the interval to fifty years, on the authority of the text of Leviticus 'ye shall hallow the fiftieth year and proclaim liberty throughout all the land unto all the inhabitants thereof'. He accompanied this decision with a full statement of the papal theory of indulgences:

One drop of Christ's blood would have sufficed for the redemption of the whole human race. Out of the abundant superfluity of Christ's sacrifice there has come a treasure which is not to be

44. *C.P.R.* iii, pp. 4–8, 95–181: the compilers of this calendar did not arrange the entries in chronological order, and the letters of Jan.–June 1344 will be found confused with earlier and later material.

45. G. Mollat, *The Popes at Avignon* (English translation), 1963, 9th ed., p. 38.

hidden in a napkin or buried in a field, but to be used. This treasure has been committed by God to his vicars on earth, to St Peter and his successors, to be used for the full or partial remission of the temporal punishments of the sins of the faithful who have repented and confessed.[46]

In 1389 Urban VI, on the reasonable ground that most men do not live for fifty years, reduced the period between Jubilees to thirty-three years; and in 1470 Paul II, after further reflection on the fragile state of human life, reduced the interval to twenty-five.[47] Thus in the course of an ordinary life anyone capable of reaching Rome could obtain a full remission of his purgatorial pains.

Meanwhile, however, further developments were going on which made the journey scarcely necessary. From the later years of the fourteenth century onwards the extension of similar plenary privileges to local churches on special occasions had become very common. Moreover the privilege of obtaining a full remission from a confessor at the hour of death, which we have noticed as a flourishing recent innovation in 1344, became vastly extended in the course of the next hundred and fifty years. The propensity to carry every innovation to its limits and to elaborate every conceivable detail was fully satisfied in these developments. There were remissions at the hour of death; remissions for a single danger of death; remissions for a multiplicity of dangers of death; remissions obtainable from the papal chancery; remissions obtainable from those commissioned by the pope for this purpose; remissions for pilgrims to Rome or other churches; remissions without any condition whatever, except the universal one of repentance and confession. Once the bottomless treasure had been opened up there could be no restraining its distribution. By the

46. *Extravagantes Communes*, v, ix, 2 (Friedberg, *Corpus Iuris Canonici*, ii, 1304–6).

47. For a fourteenth-century account of the development of the Jubilee and the doctrine behind it, see Ranulph Higden, *Polychronicon*, ed. J. R. Lumby, *R.S.* ix, 206–10, giving the text of Urban VI's Bull. For Paul II's Bull, see C. Cocquelines, *Bullarium Pont. Romanorum*, 1743, iii, part 3, p. 128.

end of the fifteenth century the ramifications of the system
are beyond any useful computation. Many influences
combined to produce a general profusion: the desire of
rival popes to extend their influence and improve their
finances; the claims of local churches, rulers, and towns to
a share in the treasure; the universal demands of all mankind for an assured salvation. There is no need to pursue
the story further. It is more important to attempt to
understand the situation in which the popes found themselves and the reason for their predicament than to trace
all the expedients they employed to satisfy the instinctive
drive for expansion.

In these pages we are concerned to study the system of
indulgences mainly in its governmental aspects, but before
we draw any conclusions about its significance from this
point of view, it is well to return to the point from which we
began and recall the deep personal and emotional springs
of the whole development. We have seen how Eugenius III
in 1150 took an important step under the influence of a
strong emotion, and it would be quite unrealistic to suppose
that a similar emotional impulse was absent in the fifteenth
century. The scattered records of pilgrimages organized to
obtain the papal indulgence read like accounts of movements
of flagellants and *illuminati*; and the popes themselves can
scarcely have been unmoved by their environment.

A small incident in the year 1476 may serve to illustrate
the emotional background to the developments we are
discussing. In this year, Sixtus IV, with some cardinals,
was paying a visit to the Franciscan nuns at Foligno. The
nuns' confessor asked him for an indulgence, and he gave
them a plenary indulgence for the approaching Feast of
the Virgin Mary. Then, feeling moved to give something
more, he added, 'Besides this, you may have a full immunity
from *poena et culpa* every time you confess your sins.'
'What?' shouted the cardinals, '*Every* time?' 'Yes,' said
the pope laying his hand on his heart, 'I give you everything I have.' Then the cardinals went down on their knees
crying 'Us too!', and the pope said 'All right; you too.'[48]

48. Paulus, op. cit., ii, 305.

If this scene had not been recorded by a bystander we should never have known that behind the extraordinary papal privilege for the sisters of Foligno, which was finally drawn up in 1482, there lay no searching for precedents and no subtleties of calculation, but just an old man putting his hand on his heart and giving what he could.

Incidents like this have a beauty of their own, but from the point of view of papal government what we have is a clear case of inflation. Of course it is inflation of a peculiar kind, for the treasure which provided the backing, so to speak, for the spiritual currency was limitless. Nevertheless the consequences of the unrestricted issue of these documents were similar to those which face other issues of paper money: the abundance of the notes brought about a decline in the value attached to them. The symptoms of this decline can be seen at a quite early stage in the inflationary process, long before there was any doubt about the genuineness of the treasure at the disposal of the pope. We can see it in the decline in the numbers of those who took advantage of the Jubilee after 1300. It seems possible that as many as two million people made the journey to Rome in the year of the first Jubilee. It is a major event in the literature of that period.[49] At the next Jubilee in 1350 contemporary chroniclers scarcely mention it, and the crowds were clearly much smaller. The recent plague had no doubt given men other things to think about, and those who sought salvation most urgently sought relief in more violent measures than a journey to Rome. And for people of a quieter disposition there were individual plenary indulgences which could now be obtained on fairly easy terms. Instead of attracting these people to Rome, the Jubilee provided an occasion for the issue of many private privileges to princes and their families and to religious bodies. If we may continue to use the monetary analogy, the issue of this easily obtainable currency naturally drove

49. For contemporary accounts of the crowds of pilgrims, see T. S. R. Boase, *Boniface VIII*, 233–6. For the impression made on Dante and Villani, see Paget Toynbee, *Dictionary of Proper Names and Notable Matters in the Works of Dante*, 2nd ed., 1968, 325–6.

the heavier coin out of circulation, and caused a demand for still easier money. In the fifteenth century the Roman Jubilee had to compete with numerous local Jubilees offering the same privileges. Some of these occasions seem to have been greeted with enthusiasm, but in a surprising number of towns local chroniclers continued their record of municipal strife without stopping to mention the great religious opportunity in their midst. Great efforts were made to give publicity to the papal grants, and these campaigns were often successful; but like all advertising campaigns they sometimes aroused stubborn resistance and recalcitrance.

Every relaxation brought the expectation of further relaxations and depreciated the value of what had already been offered. Forgers of papal bulls stepped in to fill the gap between expectation and reality, and still further hastened the process of devaluation. By the end of the fifteenth century it would not have taken a very far-sighted prophet, or a profound student of economics, to see that the day would soon come when the questions would be asked: what, after all, was the backing for the papal currency of indulgences, and what would happen when it was finally presented for payment? It is easier for us to see this drift than it was for the popes struggling with daily intractable problems, from which the lighter side of papal grandeur provided the only momentary relief.

The history of papal indulgences between 1095 and 1500 is an epitome of the history of the papacy during these centuries. Down to the end of the thirteenth century the system had all the marks of success and beneficence: it helped to lighten the load of fear that the old harsh system of penance had thrown over western Christendom, and it brought the assurance that the power committed by God to the church stretched far out into eternity. The theoretical justification of the system was gradually elaborated, and like so many other elaborations it pointed to a final papal plenitude of power. Thus the papal activity was associated with hope, confidence, and control. But after 1300 there began a process of over-elaboration and confusion, not indeed caused by any special moral or intellectual failure on the part of the popes, but by the relentless pressure on every side to drive the system to its limit. In the process, the hope of the earlier period became dim, the confidence was shaken by confusion and finally by doubt, and the popes were left holding threads which exerted no power of control.

A similar process is to be observed in the second field of papal activity that we are to examine.

International politics

'He who denies that the secular sword is in the power of Peter does not understand the words of the Lord. . . .' Boniface VIII in 1302 thus simply summed up the position of the thirteenth-century popes. In virtue of their plenitude of power as Vicars of Christ on earth they possessed supreme political no less than ecclesiastical power. There was indeed a difference in the use of these two powers. The spiritual sword was wielded directly, the secular was wielded through the agency of kings and princes. This indirect control however implied no independent power in the agents who wielded it, no weakening in the controlling power of the pope; it was simply a convenience, an expression of the inferiority of the secular to the spiritual power. Just as the Apostles in order to concentrate on the Word of God had commissioned deacons to serve tables, so the popes commissioned kings. The papal power was in no way diminished by delegation but rather enhanced, for the power of delegation is the ruler's highest privilege.

Nevertheless delegation raised serious practical problems – problems of the choice of agents, of the removal of unsatisfactory agents, of supervising their activities and decisions, of correcting their mistakes, and supporting them against their enemies. No medieval pope understood these problems so well or thought so deeply about them as Innocent III, and his experience must be borne in mind as we turn to the papal predicament in the later Middle Ages.

Innocent III has left a unique record of his thoughts and activities in the highest realm of politics. In the year after he became pope he started to keep a register of letters relating to the business of the empire.[50] It was a critical moment because there was no emperor, and there were three claimants. Now, if ever, was the time for the pope to exercise his power of choosing his senior secular agent. The volume which the pope started in 1199 is therefore not just a product of regular official routine; it is the record of a concentrated effort to solve the pope's most pressing secular problem. It was intended as a guide for his successors, and perhaps as the first of a long series of volumes recording the papal mastery of the secular world.

Yet it had no successors. At first sight this is odd because Innocent's volume on imperial business ends on a note of triumph with the first stage of the work of papal control successfully accomplished. The pope had the emperor whom he wanted – the man whom he had all along supported against all the odds. One of the last documents in the volume records the emperor's complete submission to the pope and his renunciation of every practice contrary to the papal will. This was the long-sought utopia of papal theory. Innocent greeted its arrival with a fervent cry:

> By the grace of God, a true peace and firm concord now exist between Church and Empire. . . . The state of the world, which is falling into ruins, will be restored by our diligence and care. . . . If we two stand together 'the crooked shall be made straight and the rough places smooth', for the pontifical authority and the royal power (both of them supremely invested in Us) fully suffice for this purpose if each helps the other.[51]

Innocent was not an enthusiast. His firm and well-ordered mind never submitted to the wild expectations which deceived many of his contemporaries; but at this point in his career he touched the hem of an apocalyptic vision.

It is on this note that the record of his supreme political

50. There is an excellent edition by F. Kempf, *Registrum Innocentii III Papae super Negotio Romani Imperii* (*Miscellanea Historiae Pontificiae*, xii, 1947).

51. ibid., pp. 385–7 (*Ep.* 179 of 16 January 1209).

engagement ends. There is ample evidence that his successors studied this record, but (ending as it now does in 1209)
it is very misleading. Within a few months, the pope's
emperor, Otto IV, had betrayed his trust. Within two
years, the pope had been obliged to nominate Frederick II,
the candidate whom he had least desired. The way was
opened to that long course of destruction which swept away
the Hohenstaufen family, the empire, and the whole
prospect of effective temporal authority exercised by the
papacy, into a common political limbo.

The failure of Innocent III was hidden from contemporaries and it has often been hidden from later observers
by the appearance of success at so many points. It is also
hidden by the skill of papal letter-writers in covering every
disaster in a cloud of biblical imagery and confident
generalization. The papal rhetoric is much better than the
imperial rhetoric: it conveys a wonderful impression of
command. But it is important to understand the extent of
the failure and the reasons for it, for here lie the seeds of the
collapse of the whole medieval theory of papal authority.

The theory of supreme political authority committed to
the pope by Christ was an integral part of the papal
plenitude of power, at least in the eyes of the thirteenth-
century popes. If this went, everything else was shaken.
But supreme political power could not be exercised by the
pope in person: for this he must have deputies, and the
most important of these deputies was the emperor. The
emperor was not only the most important of the pope's
political deputies, he was also theoretically the most amenable to papal control, for his office was not hereditary and
it depended on papal coronation. If the pope could not
control the emperor, it was unlikely that he could control
any other secular ruler. Hence the single-minded ferocity
of the papal efforts to establish control of the empire in the
thirteenth century. There were other narrower territorial
reasons for the struggle with Frederick II, but it was the
conviction that the whole papal position depended on
victory that gives a certain dignity to proceedings which
would otherwise be simply repellent.

It was in the course of this struggle that the fatal discovery was made that victory could only be ensured by entering the political battle in full strength. Success required that every spiritual and temporal weapon should be used to promote alliances, foment wars, and bring the recalcitrant to heel. The popes found that their participation in politics had to be complete to be effective. Indirect power means nothing unless it is backed by a threat of direct secular action. As a secular ruler however, the pope was insignificant unless he could harness his spiritual authority to political ends. This was the papal dilemma. By deploying his whole strength for political ends, he could win; but then he lost the unique position that made his victory possible. He was lost in the common world of political manoeuvre.

All this took place at the highest level of politics. At a lower level the exercise of indirect political power might still have been possible if the popes could have relied on a body of political agents or observers throughout Europe to report, transmit orders, and see that they were obeyed. But this was impossible. Neither the resources nor the environment of thirteenth-century government could accommodate a system of political Residents. Direct papal jurisdiction in secular affairs alone could carry papal power down to the lowest levels of secular society. At the time of the first forward surge of papal jurisdiction in the mid twelfth century it had seemed possible that some system of secular appeals might have been established, similar to the ecclesiastical appeals which had such a triumphant success. Secular rulers feared this might happen, and their fears had some justification. In 1156 a small Scottish landowner in the valley of the Tweed thought it worth his money to get a papal privilege confirming his possessions and giving him the right to appeal to the papal court if he were molested.[52] At about the same time the earl of Surrey, the heir of King Stephen, seems to have offered the pope a large sum

52. W. Holtzmann, *Papsturkunden in England*, 1952, iii, nos. 115, 153, 321. The recipient was Askitill of Ridale. The grant was first made by Adrian IV, and later confirmed by Alexander III on two occasions.

of money for permission to bring into the papal court a
suit against Henry II about his inheritance.[53] If these had
become common practices, the pope would have indeed
been supreme in the secular world. But the process was
stifled by the rapid growth of secular law and the opposition
of secular rulers.

Nevertheless there was one area where there was room
for the extension of papal political influence in a quasi-
judicial form. This was in the field of international diplomacy, and it arose from the conditions of medieval warfare.

Medieval wars were like modern ones in this respect:
they were very difficult to bring to an end. It was an untidy
kind of warfare, capable of dragging on for years without
decisive results, and often engaging fluctuating groups of
participants. The first step towards peace was to bring
about a truce. In the delicate negotiations to this end
there was an urgent need for an international authority,
however weak in executive power, to act in various pacific
capacities, as arbitrator, guarantor, or simply as a go-
between. This need grew as old feudal relationships broke
up and the complexities of war and peace became increasingly difficult to disentangle. The papacy was very well
equipped for this task. The procedure, which generally
began with an appeal to the pope from one side or the other,
fitted easily into the papal conception of government. It
carried a suggestion of lordship without too much emphasis
on legal authority. So it satisfied papal aspirations without
offending secular susceptibilities. Moreover, it called for a
kind of professional competence in which the papal court
excelled. There was a greater body of experts in law and
negotiation at the disposal of the pope than of anybody
else in Europe, and he had dispensations at his command
to lubricate the negotiations and to complete the treaty
of peace.

We can see the whole process clearly in 1345 when
Clement VI sent nuncios to help bring about peace between
the kings of England and France. They came equipped

53. *Letters of John of Salisbury*, ed. W. J. Millor, H. E. Butler and
C. N. L. Brooke, 1955, i, p. 82.

with a whole armful of lubricating aids: power to confer vacant benefices in the pope's gift, to confer the office of notary on twenty-five clerks, to grant ten dispensations for the marriage of cousins, and a hundred dispensations from the penalties of bastardy; power to converse with and to absolve excommunicates, to commute vows, to grant plenary and lesser indulgences, to impose ecclesiastical censures, to grant safe-conducts, to restrain the speech of obstructive ecclesiastics, and so on and so on.[54] These powers could not indeed bring peace when there was a desire for war, but they could ease the way if even only one side desired peace. They provided the elbow-room which an arbitrator needs.

It was perhaps the English kings who first realized the value of drawing the pope into the regular business of diplomacy. They had a special reason for this. For a century and a half after King John's submission to Innocent III in 1213, the kingdom was a papal fief. Both John and his son Henry III took full advantage of this position. They could rely on the pope's support against their internal enemies and for a favourable hearing in foreign affairs. So their diplomatic correspondence has many examples of appeals to the pope for his help in their foreign affairs. The climax came in 1298 when Boniface VIII was asked to arbitrate between the kings of France and England in the disputes which had kept them at war for the last four years. Boniface was eager to act; the two kings submitted themselves to the pope's judgement; proctors were appointed; all the necessary legal deeds and authorizations were enrolled. In June 1298 the pope delivered his judgement in a series of long and complicated bulls. For a moment we seem to see the pope standing at the height of his temporal sovereignty, judging the quarrels of subordinate kings. But then at the last minute (probably on the insistence of the king of France) he was obliged to make a surprising admission. He had been acting (he said) simply 'as a private person, as Lord Benedict Gaetani, as an arbitrator and friendly umpire in restoring peace and

54. *C.P.R.*, iii, 195–8.

concord between the kings' – not as the Vicar of Christ with a unique responsibility for bringing peace on earth.[55]

It was a great anti-climax. No pope attached more importance to his secular sovereignty than Boniface VIII. Yet in the last resort he preferred to act as plain Lord Benedict Gaetani, rather than not to act at all. It is hard to think that earlier popes would have allowed themselves to be separated from their office in this way. It was left to the supreme definer of papal temporal supremacy to initiate a papal diplomatic rôle that could be developed without reference to temporal supremacy.

The development was wholly beneficent. The pope abandoned a shouting match in which voices got louder as the scope for action grew smaller, and he concentrated on mild but possible ameliorations in a general disorder. During the thirteenth century the plenitude of power in secular affairs had fluctuated wildly between achieving nothing and leaving nothing but ruins. By contrast the 'private person' of 1298 helped to promote civilized intercourse in the most barbarous war of the Middle Ages. It was not nearly as much as the thirteenth-century popes had hoped for; but practically it was much more than either Innocent III or Innocent IV had achieved.

There were several occasions in the next two centuries when popes, in order to act as arbitrators, had to declare that they acted 'not by reason of our authority, but by reason of the power given to us by the two parties' or (as an English chronicler in 1344 put it) 'not as pope nor as judge but as a private man and a common friend'.[56] Declarations of this kind, however, were not often required because there was no need for them. The existence of an acceptable mediator was too useful for rulers to raise unnecessary difficulties. It was generally understood that, when the pope appointed legates to bring about a truce between warring princes, their powers were limited by the contracting parties themselves. Despite the grandiose

55. T. Rymer, *Foedera*, ed. of 1816, I, ii, 894, 896.

56. Adam of Murimuth, *Continuatio chronicorum*, ed. E. M. Thompson, *R.S.*, p. 136, quoted by J. G. Dickinson, *The Peace of Arras*, 1955, p. 79n.

phrases of their commission of appointment, the legates could do no more than ease the way towards peace and add their ecclesiastical censures to reinforce the terms agreed on by the contending parties.

Before we end this survey of the process whereby the popes of the later Middle Ages tacitly abandoned their claim to political supremacy and found a sphere of real usefulness as arbitrators it may be well to mention two points.

In the first place, the popes could act as disinterested mediators in the wars between England and France largely because they had no territorial interests at stake. In Italy the situation was very different. Here the pope's position as a ruler among other rulers gave him a personal interest in the wars of the late fifteenth and early sixteenth centuries. Hence, when the Hundred Years' War ended and Italy once more became, as it had been in the thirteenth century, the military and diplomatic centre of Europe, papal mediation increasingly gave way to active military intervention. But by this time the pope no longer attempted seriously to call to his aid his pretensions as universal temporal lord. He was content to be a prince among Italian princes.

And yet the old fires still burned. Most vividly they burned in the person of Pope Julius II, who in the midst of the vast complications of Italian wars still kept alive the papal claim to pull down and raise up princes throughout Christendom. He called in the universal power of the pope to support his Italian policies, and at his death he left behind him the draft of a bull depriving Louis XII of France of his kingdom as 'the enemy of the Holy Roman Church and destroyer of the fold of the universal church', and conferring both the kingdom and title of Most Christian King on Henry VIII of England in return for his help in the pope's wars.[57] The bull was never published, but it stands as a monument to the persistence of the grand designs of the thirteenth century long after they had lost any chance of being made effective.

57. See D. S. Chambers, *Cardinal Bainbridge in the Court of Rome 1509–1514*, 1965, 38–9.

The struggle for benefices

Finally we come to the long and complicated struggle for the control of ecclesiastical appointments. It is a struggle which fills a large part of the medieval scene, and it gradually spreads from top to bottom of the ecclesiastical hierarchy to embrace not only papal and episcopal elections but also appointments to lesser benefices in cathedral churches and parishes. It is a story of the rise and fall of the papal attempt to control the whole medieval ecclesiastical system, and at one time or another every interest and power in Europe is drawn into its unfolding plot.

But though we must speak largely of a struggle between contending forces, there is a principle behind the struggle which to some extent raises it above the contest of brute force. The principle – an essential one in the ruling of the Christian church from the beginning – is that the ministers of the church at every level are the representatives of the communities for which they speak and act. As a corollary to this basic principle there has been a lasting presumption that the will of the community should somehow be made effective in the choice of its ministers. To give effect to this more or less instinctive urge for self-expression in the community at large has proved a very difficult undertaking; yet the task has never been altogether abandoned, though the history of these attempts is superficially a long record of failure.

The early medieval centuries are not strong in legislation for giving practical effect to large general principles, but the sparse texts about ecclesiastical elections commonly distinguish three elements of consent – of clergy, people, and bishops – which must be present to make an appointment valid. We find no full discussion of these elements, or the part they play, or their mode of operation; and it is a remarkable illustration of the reliance on tradition and habit in the early Middle Ages that no attempt was made to lay down rules of procedure even for papal elections before 1059 – and then only in a very tentative and ambiguous way. The ambition of the early period stretched no further than the repetition of phrases, such as those of Pope Celestine I:

> No bishop is to be imposed on unwilling subjects, but the consent and wishes of clergy and people are to be consulted;

or of Pope Leo:

> On no account is anyone to be a bishop who has not been chosen by the clergy, desired by the people, and consecrated by the bishops of the province with the authority of the metropolitan;

or of a sixth-century council at Orleans:

> No one is to be consecrated as a bishop unless the clergy and people of the diocese have been called together and have given their consent.[58]

These expressions all leave a good deal to the imagination. How they were to be interpreted in practice was left to be determined by the interplay of social forces, until the legislation of the later Middle Ages attempted to arrest those forces at a certain moment in their development. This is the development that we shall consider at three levels of the ecclesiastical hierarchy: the papacy, the episcopate, and the benefices attached to the canonries of cathedral churches.

PAPAL ELECTIONS

The election of a pope was subject to the same general rules as the election of any other bishop. Yet the papal claim to universal authority gave a wider context to the 'consent of clergy and people' which an election required. Until the eleventh century there was only one man in the West who could reasonably claim to represent the clergy and people of western Christendom during a papal election, and this was the emperor. In virtue of the temporal and spiritual powers with which he was invested at his coronation, he could claim to speak with authority for the whole Latin church. There were several occasions in the tenth

58. These passages are all quoted in Ivo of Chartres, *Decretum*, v, 61, 65, 66 (*P.L.* 84, 347–9).

and eleventh centuries when he did so with success. The last of them was in 1046 when the Emperor Henry III presided over the deposition of two rival popes and the appointment of a third.

The emperor seemed at this moment to have an impressive reserve of power at his command, but the reality was quite different. Without the help of a quite unusual combination of circumstances, he was too far removed from the scene of action to be ordinarily effective. He could seldom hear of a vacancy before it had been filled by the men on the spot, and he was never again to be summoned to heal a schism or compose a quarrel. As the universal representative of western Christendom the emperor's rôle ended at the moment of its greatest triumph, leaving the task of electing a pope in the hands of the only effective rivals of the emperor – the clergy and people of Rome, the men on the spot.

In practice the clergy meant the cardinals, and the people meant the local nobility. The nobility have never had a good press. Everyone agrees that the lowest depth of the medieval papacy coincided with – and, many would say, was caused by – the domination of the family of the local counts of Tusculum, which produced three successive popes between 1012 and 1046. Certainly these popes – Benedict VIII, John XIX, and Benedict IX – were not great ecclesiastical rulers and the last may have been a very bad man. But it was not their fault that their sphere of activity was so limited. Nor did the papacy escape from the pressure of local dynastic politics as it grew in universal authority. Quite the opposite.

Throughout the Middle Ages, so long as the papacy was at Rome, the local nobility remained the most important single force in deciding papal elections, and it was never more important than in the thirteenth century when the papacy was at the height of its medieval power. The family policies and dynastic calculations of the thirteenth-century popes are indeed less conspicuous than those of the tenth and eleventh centuries, but only for the reason that the pugnacity of adults is less obvious than that of children:

the blows are subtler, the combination more sophisticated, and much more is going on at any one time. Nepotism, political bribery, and the appropriation of institutional wealth to endow one's family, were not crimes in medieval rulers; they were part of the art of government, no less necessary in popes than in other men. Hence, although there was never again such a single sequence of dynastic popes as those of the early eleventh century, the calculations which brought Innocent III, Gregory IX, and Alexander IV to the papacy from the Conti family, Celestine III and Nicholas III from the Orsini, Honorius III and IV from the Savelli, Boniface VIII from the Caetani, were no less securely grounded in the politics of local power.[59]

Moreover, just as the local magnates of the tenth and eleventh centuries had their foreign rivals in the German nominees of the emperor who incurred their bitter hatred, so the great local magnates of the thirteenth century had their French rivals in Urban IV, Clement IV, Martin IV, and Celestine V. The same tensions recurred, and led to incidents even more violent than those of the eleventh century. We have Celestine V hounded into retirement after creating eight French cardinals in a pontificate of four months; and Boniface VIII, his successor and adversary, is assaulted and insulted to death by a combination of French and local interests. Even the transfer of the papacy to Avignon and the Great Schism itself were a prolongation of the bitter animosities of local Roman families and the pro-French party among the cardinals. It was not in the nature of medieval society that the medieval papacy should be freed from local dynastic rivalries. But this fact only throws into stronger relief the power of the wider social forces that determined its institutional growth.

The great difference between the earlier and later Middle Ages lay not in the existence of dynastic struggles but in the manner in which they operated. In the early Middle Ages popes emerged from the midst of tumults; in the later centuries from conclaves of cardinals who carried

59. For the local connexions and policies of these popes, see Daniel Waley, *The Papal State in the Thirteenth Century*, 1961.

the tumults in their own breasts. The exclusive right of the cardinals to elect a pope was established by a decree of Pope Nicholas II in 1059. No doubt the general purpose of this decree was to purify the papacy by cutting it off from the world – especially from the emperor and the local nobility. It attempted to do this by entrusting the election of future popes mainly to the cardinal-bishops. But both in its general purpose and in most of its details the decree was a failure. The world could not so easily be ejected: the clash of secular interests was simply transferred to the sacred college. Even the emperor could not so easily be excluded: he could always find some supporters among the cardinals. Moreover, the relations between the cardinal-bishops, who were to have the chief voice in elections, and the cardinal-priests and deacons, who were to be consulted, was not clearly determined. If the votes of the priests and deacons were not to be equal to those of the bishops, how were they to be weighed? Did five bishops, seven priests, and one deacon outweigh two bishops, twenty priests, and six deacons? Nobody knew. Hence the hundred and twenty years after 1059 produced most of the anti-popes of the Middle Ages. A single undisputed pope reigned in only forty-five of these years; for the remaining seventy-five years two claimants were always able to find some support from some cardinals to divide the allegiance of the West.

This situation was brought to an end by the Lateran Council of 1179, which pronounced that all cardinals had an equal vote and required a two thirds majority for a valid election.[60] The rule which has guided papal election to the present day was thus established, and (though it has not excluded the world) it has served the church well. It kept the succession of popes free from dispute for close on two hundred years: except for a few months between 1328 and 1330, there was not a single anti-pope between 1179 and 1378. Even the rising tension of the late thirteenth and early fourteenth centuries, which in earlier days would

60. *X*, i, vi, 6. Later changes to the rule laid down in 1179 have been concerned with procedure, until 1945 when the necessary majority was increased to two thirds plus one.

certainly have produced schisms, resulted only in longer periods of indecision at each vacancy. It was only with the growth of national blocks among the cardinals in the fourteenth century that the system of election established in 1179 proved inadequate to the task of holding the western church together. The renewed period of schism from 1378 to 1417 foreshadowed the national divisions of the Reformation. But apart from this break-down, the system of election by the cardinals worked in the Middle Ages, not because it excluded the world, but because the cardinals represented the effective forces of the world sufficiently to ensure an acceptable measure of agreement in their choice of successive popes.

PAPAL CONTROL OF EPISCOPAL ELECTIONS

The control of episcopal elections presented a more intractable problem, partly because the contenders for power were more equally matched, and partly because no system could be devised to meet all circumstances. The theory that bishops were to be chosen by the clergy and people of the diocese meant in practice that from the eighth to the eleventh century they were generally chosen by the lay ruler. There was some obvious justice in this since, like the emperor, kings had a semi-sacerdotal character. They were responsible to God for the religious order of their territories, and they could claim in their own persons to represent both clergy and people.

But, just as in the mid-eleventh century the clergy claimed a formal monopoly in papal elections, so in episcopal elections the same claim was made. It took a long time for this claim to be recognized, but by the middle of the twelfth century the legal position was everywhere established that the canons of a cathedral church had the right to elect their bishop. This result was very largely due to the leadership provided by the papacy. The papal court was open for the investigation of every irregularity, and the popes saw themselves in the rôle of supervisors entrusted with the task of seeing that the rules were observed.

Like every other electoral body, however, cathedral

chapters tended to be divided in an election, and there were few elections to which some exception could not be taken. The records of medieval episcopal elections are strewn with objections that candidates were deficient in age or legitimacy or learning, or that they had no clear majority among the worthier members of the chapter, or that the legal formalities had not been observed. These were matters that could only be settled at the papal court. So the first result of the control of episcopal elections by cathedral chapters was a stream of appeals to Rome.

The pope had no need to exert himself to bring this about. It happened of its own accord. At the same time a theory was developed which prepared the way for more active papal intervention. Formally the theory had its origin in a very ancient document. In the fifth century Pope Leo I had written a letter to the bishop of Thessalonica, who had exceeded his powers in some way or other, pointing out 'that he was not called to plenitude of power, but only to a share of (the pope's) responsibility'.[61] The precise meaning of this phrase in its original context need not detain us. To the twelfth-century lawyers, who wanted to define the relationship between the pope and the bishops, the letter provided the formula they were seeking: to the pope 'plenitude of power'; to the bishops 'a share in his responsibility'. The relationship suggested by these phrases was that of a sovereign ruler and his assistants. It practically meant that a bishop was the local deputy of the pope: like a local officer of a king, his jurisdiction came from his superior.

The phrases *plenitudo potestatis* to describe the pope's position and *vocatus in partem sollicitudinis* to describe the rôle of the bishop slid so unobtrusively into current use that they were established before men asked what exactly

61. *P.L.* 54, 666 (*Ep.* 14), quoted by Gratian, C. 3.q. 6 c.8. By about 1150 the two phrases were in sufficiently common use for St Bernard to be able to write to the pope, 'Juxta canones tuos, alii in partem sollicitudinis, tu in plenitudinem potestatis vocatus es' (*De Consideratione*, ii, 8). For a discussion of some of the wider applications of the phrase 'plena potestas', see Gaines Post, 'Plena potestas and consent in medieval assemblies', *Traditio*, 1943, i, 355–408.

they meant. But, having arrived, they stuck. They expressed the essential doctrine of the medieval papacy. It still remained to discover what in practice they implied.

At first it seemed that these phrases might simply provide an ultimate safeguard for the pope in his task of supervising electoral processes. Even Innocent III, who used these phrases very freely, was reluctant to overrule the rights of local electors. He would spend a lot of time trying to get rival parties in a cathedral chapter to agree on a candidate before he proceeded 'by the royal road' and made a nomination himself. But there were limits to the time a pope could spare for compounding local quarrels. It must have seemed very futile to write to an archbishop or bishop, in whose election the pope had had no voice and of whose conduct he disapproved, reminding him that 'the see of Rome in the plenitude of its power had called him to a share of its responsibilities'. The pressure to give these words a substantial meaning by asserting the pope's direct and universal right to make episcopal appointments was very strong. The surprising thing is, not that the popes in the end asserted this right, but that they resisted so long, and only approached the final step by so many imperceptible movements. It was not until the fourteenth century that a succession of enactments of John XXII and Benedict XII reserved all episcopal appointments to the pope and put the rights of local electors at the disposal of the pope. The words of Benedict XII in 1335 are the clearest possible expression of the position:

> We reserve to our own ordination, disposition and provision all patriarchal, archiepiscopal and episcopal churches, all monasteries, priories, dignities, parsonages, and offices, all canonries, prebends, churches, and other ecclesiastical benefices, with or without the cure of souls, whether secular or regular, of whatever kind, vacant or in future to become vacant, even if they have been or ought to be filled by election or in some other way, . . . [62]

Henceforth the rights of the ordinary episcopal electors were moribund, and the pope stepped in as the universal

---

62. *Extravagantes Communes*, III, ii, 13 (Friedberg, *Corpus Iuris Canonici*, ii, 1266).

representative of them all. This did not however mean that the rights of the secular ruler were also defunct. Quite the contrary: they were revived. Rulers found it easier to deal with a single pope than with a complicated web of local interests represented by a cathedral chapter. The new state of affairs in practice meant that the pope shared the power of appointment with the secular ruler. In this way the papal monarchy prepared the way for the secular sovereign. It is one of the strangest features of this whole development that each stage provided the machinery for its own overthrow. Without the leadership of the papacy, the local electors could never have won control against the power of the secular ruler. The difficulties of local electors in exercising their rights then enlarged the scope of papal supervision and finally led to a complete papal take-over. But the pope could only make his power effective with the consent (and ultimately at the bidding) of the secular ruler. This in turn made it possible for secular rulers (with or without the consent of the papacy) to take over the whole business of episcopal appointments. Here then, as in many other ways, the situation at the end of the Middle Ages tended – though with much greater complication and political awareness – to approximate to the situation at the beginning. The secular ruler became the residuary legatee of ecclesiastical power.

PAPAL CONTROL OF APPOINTMENTS TO MINOR BENEFICES

The process which we have seen at work in appointments to bishoprics is almost exactly paralleled at a lower level in appointments to canonries and other ecclesiastical benefices. The same rival forces were present, the same conflicting claims were made, and over a wide field of appointments a similar result was achieved for similar reasons.[63]

The decree of Benedict XII in 1335, which has just been

63. As an introduction to the very large literature on this subject, see G. Barraclough, *Papal Provisions*, 1935; G. Mollat, *La Collation des bénéfices ecclésiastiques à l'époque des papes d'Avignon*, 1921; B. Guillemain, *La Politique bénéficiale du Pape Benoît XII (1334–1342)*, 1952.

quoted, indifferently drew into the papal net thousands of
small fish together with patriarchs, archbishops, and
bishops: all alike were subject to papal provision. This
massive simplification had not been the original aim of the
papacy, nor had it come about through any special effort
of successive popes. In appointments to lesser as to major
benefices the popes of the twelfth century were mainly
concerned to assert ecclesiastical rights against the laity.
The practice of the early church whereby the appointment
of diocesan clergy had been in the hands of the bishops
had not been forgotten and the popes wished to restore this
situation as far as possible. There was, it is true, a huge
barrier against its total restoration. Over the centuries
lay magnates had built and endowed many churches;
secular legislation had ensured that tithes should be paid
to these churches; and lay patrons had assumed the right
or duty of appointing clergy to churches on their own lands.
This long and complicated process could not be undone.
All that ecclesiastical legislation could do was to strengthen
the hands of the bishops in examining and approving those
candidates who were offered to them for ordination and
institution.

There were, however, never enough vacancies to satisfy
the host of competitors for the more lucrative benefices.
These competitors were of many kinds. Most important of
all were the many learned, acquisitive, and under-endowed
clerks who, in growing numbers from the mid-twelfth
century, had business at the papal court. Very often they
came as the representatives of important people, with
money in their pockets to pay the many expenses of official
business and to gain the goodwill of cardinals and officials.
Their business might take many months, and it was natural
that they should exercise some of their talents and use some
of their opportunities to their own advantage. Such a man
for instance was Master David of London, a clerk of Gilbert
Foliot, bishop of London, who represented his bishop at
the papal court in 1169–70. The purpose of his mission was
to persuade the pope to release Bishop Foliot from the
excommunication he had incurred through his opposition

to Thomas Becket; but he also looked after his own interests. He ingratiated himself so well at the curia that he returned to England with a sheaf of testimonials from the pope and cardinals. The most important of them was a papal letter which read as follows:

> Since it is our duty to provide for learned clerks, and since the bishopric of Lincoln has at present no bishop, we, being called by God not merely to a share of responsibility but to plenitude of power, have by our own authority and that of St Peter made you a canon of the church of Lincoln, and we have granted you the first prebend that falls vacant in this church, by virtue of the power which we wield.[64]

The phrases of this letter deserve careful study. The pope does not claim any general right of overriding a bishop's authority in his own diocese. He acts simply because there is at present no bishop. But then his insistence on his plenitude of power suggests that, if he wished, he could do more than grant a single prospective benefice in a vacant see to a single clerk.

At this stage the pope had scarcely begun to draw on the limitless reserves of his theoretical power. A quarter of a century later Innocent III went further when he began to direct bishops to confer prebends and other benefices on his nominees. Innocent IV went further still when he made the practice no longer exceptional but common. Clement V took a further step when he reserved to himself all appointments in the hands of bishops. John XXII went further and reserved all appointments falling vacant for a wide variety of reasons; Benedict XII greatly extended the scope of the papal reservation. Clement VI carried the whole process into the realm of fantasy when he offered the expectation of a benefice to all poor clerks who came to the papal court in the first months of his pontificate. A hundred thousand are said to have come to partake of this lavish generosity, and twelve volumes of papal letters record only a small

---

64. F. Liverani, *Spicilegium Liberianum*, 1863, p. 547. For Master David's career see Z. N. Brooke in *Essays in History presented to R. L. Poole*, 1927, 227–45.

fraction of the promised gifts. Everywhere the picture of
the fourteenth-century church is of a rising flood of papal
grants and promises of minor benefices to applicants from
every country in Europe. Here for example is a graph showing the number of benefices conferred by successive popes
during the first year of their reign in the diocese of Constance:[65]

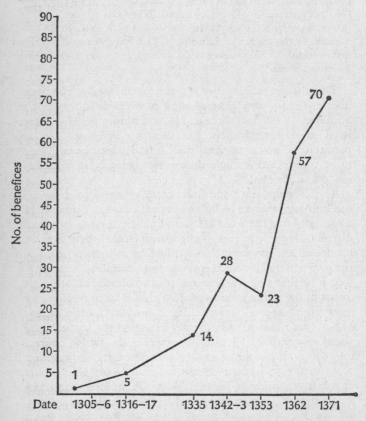

BENEFICES HELD BY PAPAL PROVISION IN
THE DIOCESE OF CONSTANCE, 1305-71

65. The graph is based on the figure given in G. Mollat, *Lettres communes
de Jean XXII, Introduction*, 1921, p. 133.

No doubt the picture would differ for each diocese in Europe, but it is highly likely that the general direction was everywhere the same.

This whole phase of papal activity raises some very difficult problems. In the first place there is the problem of motive. The pope cannot have had any reliable knowledge of the suitability of more than a tiny proportion of the beneficiaries of his grants. Nor could it be thought that the system of papal provisions to minor benefices extended the effectiveness of papal supervision of clerical competence. Indeed the final effect of the limitless increase in the number of clerks with claims to benefices on papal authority was to make more room for the exercise of those local secular influences which it had been a main object of papal policy to resist. The papal profusion recreated the old problem in a new form. If many men had claims which could not all be satisfied, he who had local influence or secular support was most likely to succeed. We have already seen that as early as 1190 the abbot of Bury St Edmunds had a drawer-full of papal nominations for benefices which he proposed to satisfy in strict rotation. The more numerous the claimants, the wider the area of choice. It was inevitable that relatives of the great and those with the support of king or magnates should come first.

Here therefore, as in the field of episcopal appointments, papal plenitude of power in its fullest development reinstated all the influences it had been designed to suppress. With this reinstatement of secular influence the loyalty of the ecclesiastical hierarchy to papal authority declined. Even to make papal mandates effective the clergy was obliged to seek the protection and favour of lay rulers. The growth of papal authority had ironically provided the grounds of its own dissolution.

The popes of the thirteenth and fourteenth centuries could scarcely have foreseen this result, but even if they had it is doubtful if they could have done anything about it. They were the victims of three forces that could only die by being over-extended. The first was the force of the papal plenitude of power, which impelled successive popes to take the steps necessary to translate theory into practice. If they were foiled in one direction, the pressure to advance along an easier route became correspondingly stronger, with the consequence that an over-extended administration tended to turn out increasing quantities of mandates in the areas of least resistance. The second was the force of the papal machine which gained momentum by the exercise of its power. Some of the main beneficiaries of papal power were the officials responsible for driving the machine. They made sure that there would be no turning back. In the circumstances of medieval government no other result could be expected, yet one is often astonished by the largeness of their claims and expectations. The third force was the most fundamental of all, and the one which gave a direction to the other two: this was the tendency to turn all authority into jurisdiction. We have already seen why this happened, but now we see the consequences.

When authority takes the form of jurisdiction it must express itself as an offer of legal processes to all comers within the area of jurisdiction. The *plenitudo potestatis* was a guarantee that this area would be very large, and in principle limitless; the skills of the papal court guaranteed that it would be effectively cultivated. No judge can refuse to admit appropriate litigants to his court, and all who sought papal favours were in a broad sense litigants. They were staking out a claim against all other claimants. The clerk who obtained from the papal court the grant or promise of a benefice was in a position not unlike the layman who obtained from the English king a writ ordering the sheriff to restore land of which he claimed he had been unjustly deprived. He had taken the first step towards getting what he wanted, but he still had a long way to go before he was put in possession; he was only at the beginning of a legal tussle in which he would have to defend his case against adversaries and objections as yet unknown. We may say that the pope gave very little when he distributed claims and expectations of which the greater part could never take effect. He distributed no more than the right to enter the competition from a position of strength. Thereafter, success or failure depended on the resources of friends and money, and the staying-power that the claimant himself could muster. The pope simply laid down the rules of the competition and distributed the tickets; but in making this a main part of papal business in the later Middle Ages, the papal machine profoundly affected the whole history of the papacy.

One last problem remains before we leave the subject of papal intervention in ecclesiastical patronage: how effective was this intervention? This problem can be considered from various angles. We may ask what proportion of papal provisions actually took effect, or (more usefully) what proportion of the benefices in any one diocese at a given time were filled by men who owed their position to papal provision. The first of these questions probably is unanswerable, and the answer even if it could be given would not be very illuminating. We can be sure that only a small proportion took effect, but this does not mean that the papal document was not worth having. Even though all applicants but one must be disappointed, we cannot say that the formality of application is a failure. The proportion of failures is no guide to the efficacy of the system.

It is more useful to inquire what proportion of appointments were filled by those who used the papal system of appointment. This is a question that can be answered to some extent, but even here there are many qualifications to be made. The intricacy of the late medieval system of patronage is such that no single factor can be isolated from the others without distorting the general pattern. In any highly sophisticated society the interaction of mutually supporting elements – however diverse and even contradictory they may be in their origin – is an essential feature of the working of that society. No simple enumeration can properly take account of all the complications. Nevertheless some attempt must be made to indicate the rough outline of an answer to our question.

If we revert to the year 1344, which has already served as a basis for examining the variety of papal business in the third phase of medieval history, and look at the sixty-eight members of the chapter of the cathedral church of Lincoln, the following features appear:[66]

The dean and four of the eight archdeacons held their offices and benefices by papal provision; the sub-dean, precentor, treasurer, and chancellor did not. Of the remaining fifty-five prebends, twenty appear to be held by papal provision, and a further six were claimed by the same title without success. On the other hand an almost exactly equal number of members of the chapter – the chancellor, one archdeacon, and twenty-one prebendaries – held their benefices by royal grant, and a further three claimed prebends by the same title without success. At this comparatively lowly level of ecclesiastical patronage, therefore, the honours were about even between king and pope, and together they disposed of about four fifths of the available benefices. The king, however, was beginning to strengthen his position by legislation, and in comparison with the holders of papal provisions a higher proportion of his nominees succeeded in making good their claims when they were disputed.

The kingdom of England was in various ways exceptional. In 1318 Pope John XXII had remarked that 'the status and, what is more, the liberty of the ecclesiastical dignity is more depressed and trampled on in that country than in all other parts of the world';[67] no doubt the strong position of the king in these appointments was one example of the situation which the pope deplored. In Italy and Spain the proportion of cathedral canons holding by papal provision was probably higher. But everywhere it is likely that the limits of effective papal control had been reached by the middle of the fourteenth century. Certainly at Lincoln a remarkable change had taken place a hundred years later. In 1444 not a single member of the cathedral chapter held

66. This account of the cathedral chapter at Lincoln has been drawn from the revised edition of J. le Neve, *Fasti Ecclesiae Anglicanae 1300–1541*, i, 1962, ed. H. P. F. King, with additional material from U. Berlière, *Suppliques de Clément VI (1342–52)*, 1906, and T. F. Tout, *Chapters in the Administrative History of Medieval England*, 1920–33, vols. iii – v.

67. The text of the letter is quoted in *Histoire littéraire de France* (Académie des inscriptions et belles-lettres), 1914, xxxiv, 402n.

his benefice by papal provision, and – we may add – only two held by royal grant.

It is not easy to explain the change, but it is probably to be connected with changes within the administrative systems of both pope and king. In 1344 a very high proportion of those who held canonries at Lincoln by papal provision were members of the papal curia and their relatives. The archdeacons of Buckingham, Leicester, Northampton, and Oxford were all French or Italian cardinals; so were the prebendaries of Corringham, Cropredy, Leicester St Margaret, Louth, Milton Ecclesia, and Milton Manor, as well as the unsuccessful claimants of Nassington and Thame. Nephews of cardinals held Farndon and Leighton Buzzard; and Nicholas Capucci, a future cardinal, claimed Carlton Paynell. The prebends of Banbury, Biggleswade, Brampton, Caistor, Gretton, and Leighton Ecclesia were all held or claimed by members of French and Italian families linked with the curia. Nearly all these men belonged to the circle of the international papal administrators and curialists. A modest example of this type was Francis Orsini, a papal notary and collateral descendant of a long line of popes and cardinals. He had recently been ejected from the prebend of Farndon by a royal nominee, but he was still treasurer of York, archdeacon of Cambrai, canon of Tournai, Seville, and (in expectation) of Amiens. He was a comparatively small man in a great league, of which the nearest modern equivalent is to be found, not among the clergy, but among the directors of international companies.[68]

Papal provisions created revenues for such men as these, while royal grants made similar provisions for the king's civil service. The list of the prebendaries of Lincoln who held by royal grant in 1344 reads like a roll of the officers of the king's government: at Lafford there was the treasurer of the Exchequer, William de Cusance; at Leighton Manor, the keeper of the Wardrobe, William

68. Although he was a relatively small man, there is a good deal of information about him scattered up and down the Papal Registers and the English *Calendar of Patent Rolls*.

Edington; at Carlton Paynell, the keeper of the Privy Seal, Thomas Hatfield; at Stow Longa, the chief steward of the Chamber, Philip Weston; at Thorngate, the keeper of the Rolls, John Thoresby; at South Scarle, the keeper, and at Farndon, the controller of the Great Wardrobe, Thomas Crosse and William Dalton respectively; at Carlton Paynell, the clerk of the Marshalsea, William Hugate; at Milton Manor, the clerk of the secret seal, Thomas Brembre; and at Thame there was the once great but now disgraced royal servant William Kildesby, who in 1344 was on pilgrimage to Jerusalem hoping for better days.

This, in a single church, was the final result of the plan to extend papal control to the lowest extremities of the ecclesiastical system. It has indeed a certain impressiveness as a feat of organization and as the practical development of a grand theory. But the conspicuous feature which emerges from our survey is the similarity of secular and ecclesiastical development, and the tendency, which is everywhere apparent, for papal activity to stimulate still further the types of secular influence which it was designed in the first place to frustrate.

Our survey of papal activity in the varied fields of indulgences, international politics, and in the control of ecclesiastical appointments, leads to one general conclusion. In the course of the fourteenth century the papal administration reached a level of activity which would have been unimaginable two hundred years earlier. It had everywhere reached the limits of its medieval effectiveness. Except in the one area of indulgences, in which the currency could be debased almost indefinitely because it had no rivals, every further step towards real power stimulated a more than correspondingly great contrary movement, and created complications within the system that nullified the effectiveness of papal action. Consequently there was a growing disproportion between the growth of papal administration and the effectiveness of papal leadership.

The situation foreseen by St Bernard in 1150 was realized two hundred years later. The papacy had become identified with the most complicated, and for its time the best, legal and administrative system in western history. But though it was still superior to all its competitors, it operated on the same level and was subject to the same laws of change as they were.

The atrophy of papal leadership which resulted can be seen at many levels. Not least in the realm of ideas. In the twelfth and thirteenth centuries nearly every new idea had in some way ministered to the growth of papal authority: the Crusade, the elaboration of law and theology, the new religious Orders, the new devotional and scholastic experiments: all of them helped to strengthen, and were themselves supported by, the papacy. But in the fourteenth and fifteenth centuries everything that was most alive in political, ecclesiastical, or theological speculation, in devotional life or religious organization, was in some degree alienated from or indifferent to papal authority. The administrative development of the papacy continued, but it continued without the impetus of intellectual discovery.

This is not to say that the late medieval papacy could have ceased to exist without widespread calamity. The complicated network of papal administration, however choked by petty interests, was still the most stabilizing influence in European society: it could scarcely be touched without bringing on a general convulsion. And at a personal level, the existence of the papacy still gave an assurance of salvation to millions of people who knew nothing about its failures. It was as much part of life as the seasons or the succession of day and night.

5

Bishops and Archbishops

IF we study the medieval episcopate in the documents of
the papal chancery, the impression they convey is of a body
of worldly and undisciplined men being brought to a state
of order and seemliness through the efforts of successive
popes, especially from the mid eleventh century onwards.
We are presented with a picture of bishops being wrenched
free from the secular influences that had controlled their
destinies hitherto and acquiring a new respectability and
usefulness under papal control and direction. In some ways
their office was diminished in the process. The bishops lost
their earlier independent authority in liturgical innovation,
in the canonization of saints, in the supervision of monastic
discipline, and in the definition of law and doctrine. But
they gained in solidity of purpose, in the protection of a
supreme spiritual authority, and in fellowship in an immense common task.

Formally this picture had much to commend it. The
growing papal intervention in diocesan affairs after the time
of Pope Leo IX is indeed the great dividing-line in the
history of medieval episcopacy. Subordination to the papal
office, which had been a wavering, almost an optional,
concept before the eleventh century, was sharply defined
and obligatory after the twelfth. It affected every aspect of
the bishops' activity in the later Middle Ages. In all
matters concerning the appointment, discipline, translation, or deprivation of bishops, the papal word was law;
the local legislation of the bishops re-enacted the general
legislation of the popes; their courts were wide open to
papal directives coming down from above and to appeals
to the pope rising from below. The bishop was a channel of
communication between the pope and the church.

Before we examine the practical results of these changes

at ground-level, there is one general remark to be made. There were many bishops and archbishops in the Latin church of the later Middle Ages – nearly five hundred altogether. They varied greatly in wealth, but many were very wealthy. As a body they took their place among the greatest territorial magnates of Europe. The majority of them were related to the most powerful families in their countries. The episcopal office was generally a reward of high birth, administrative experience, or outstanding service in secular government. It was a reward that a high proportion of men with these qualifications greatly desired. Once appointed it was very difficult, even for the pope, to remove them; and men in secure positions of authority are seldom excessively subservient. Whatever the theoretical claims to their obedience, they were separated from the source of papal authority by long distances and slow communications. In most matters they had to act as they thought best, and this generally meant that they acted in the interests of the institution of which they were briefly the embodiment.

Nearly everywhere bishoprics were the oldest institutions in the neighbourhood. They were generally older than the oldest monasteries and very much older than any secular dynasty or kingdom. They gave their holders not only a palpable social grandeur, but an ancient inheritance of rights and duties guaranteed by venerable documents and watched over by the saints of the church. As the guardians of this inheritance bishops were not easily moved by passing fashions in society or legislation. The weight of a local tradition lay heavily upon them.

Moreover, the office itself was defined in the fundamental documents of the Christian religion, in the Old and New Testaments, and in the earliest history of the church. Although the pope in his plenitude of power called other bishops his assistants, in the essential outline of his office he too was simply a bishop – a universal bishop, but still a bishop like the rest.

All these elements of wealth and birth, local tradition and unchanging authority helped to make the episcopate,

ground though it was between the upper and nether mill-
stones of pope and king, the most varied and complicated
body in the medieval church. No simple scheme can
contain all the varied interests and ideals, the ancient
rights and modern opportunities, that the bishops represented. We can sketch the changing pattern of the episcopal
character, but the bishops themselves, entrenched in their
dioceses, mock every effort to confine them within this
pattern.

Yet the pattern was never wholly ignored, and we may
begin our study of the medieval episcopate with an ideal
that was never questioned. Gregory the Great in his book
on *Pastoral Care* described once and for all the outline of the
true bishop.[1] He was to be above all a teacher and director
of souls. To this end he must be a man of meditation, self-
searching, and humility: 'No art can be taught unless it is
first learned by intense meditation; but the care of souls
is of all arts the greatest; so you may judge the temerity of
those who assume the office without preparation.' The
bishop therefore was to shun external occupations; to
devote himself to preaching, teaching, and admonition; to
perfect his own character so that he could correct others;
'to subdue himself rather than his brethren'; 'to be a
minister, not a master'. In a word, the character of a bishop
was simply that of a Christian writ large.

In the pages that follow there will be few signs that
the cultivation of this character was the main preoccupation of the bishops of the western church. It is as organizers,
administrators, magnates, and politicians that the surviving
documents mainly depict them. It must be supposed that
many, probably most, bishops saw themselves only in these
rôles. But not all; and in unexpected places we find traces
of suppressed or frustrated aspirations which cannot be
assessed in bulk. These aspirations are not to be confused
with the formal language of pious good intentions which
ecclesiastical documents employ with facile ease. They are
to be seen rather in small acts of mercy, in hesitations, and

1. *P.L.* 77, 13–128.

in late repentances. They can have only a small place in our survey, but in the inner history of the medieval church they have a larger place.

I. THE CAROLINGIAN CHURCH ORDER AND ITS BREAK-UP

The formation of a bishop

The impress of Gregory's *Pastoral Care* is to be seen more clearly in the monastic bishops of the eighth century than in the episcopate of any later time. Willibrord and Boniface, in their endless peregrinations, in their unhappiness at the courts of kings, in their unremitting search for aids in their arduous missionary journeys, were Gregorian bishops to an extent that was barely possible for their successors. By their success they made it more difficult for those who came after them to be like them. They made it necessary for bishops to be instruments of government, engaged in ruling the Christian society of Carolingian Europe. As the main assistants of anointed and divinely commissioned rulers, bishops became primarily men of affairs, and they found their model less in Gregory the Great than in the Old Testament. Here they discovered in Samuel the type of Christian bishop: set over the people to judge them, to raise up his voice for the people, to make sacrifices for their sins, to counsel, to go out with their armies, and to anoint their king.

Yet, however necessary these duties might be to ensure the safety of the Christian community, bishops did not throw themselves into secular business without some scruples. St Paul had written that 'no one in God's service involves himself in secular business'. There were some who thought that this referred especially to bishops, and Charlemagne with his usual alertness to practical theological issues put the question to one of his councils.[2] We do not know what was said on this occasion, but later writers gave a clear answer:

2. *M.G.H. Capitularia Regum Francorum*, i, 161.

If anyone who is ignorant of the divine dispensation objects to a bishop ruling the people and facing the dangers of war, and argues that he is responsible only for their souls, the answer is obvious: it is by doing these things that the guardian and teacher of the faithful brings to them the rare gift of peace and saves them from the darkness in which there is no light.[3]

A bishop should indeed undertake secular duties 'not by choice but on account of the people's need'.[4] The divine office, the discipline of monasteries and churches, the adornment of his cathedral, the promotion of Christian learning, were his proper sphere. Just as it was a bishop's duty to assist the ruler in his secular task, so it was the responsibility of the ruler to direct the bishops towards their proper end. Consequently the first substantial body of legislation in the West about the spiritual duties of a bishop in his diocese is to be found in the laws of the Carolingian and Anglo-Saxon kings.

Much of the earliest legislation of Charlemagne was devoted to the duties of bishops and the enforcement of their authority. It was essential for the well-being of a kingdom where Christianity had shallow roots that pagan practices – 'sacrifices of dead bodies, divinations, auguries, incantations, animal sacrifices which foolish men perform according to pagan rites near churches in the name of the holy martyrs' – should be stamped out.[5] The king required his bishops to be diligent in this work. These practices angered the saints whom they were intended to appease. This was not simply a vague or pious opinion. It was a fact as certain as anything in the world. As Alcuin wrote from Charlemagne's court to the archbishop of Canterbury:

We read in the books of Gildas the wisest of the Britons that the avarice of their princes, the iniquity of their judges, the laxity of their bishops and their idleness in preaching, and the

---

3. *Ruotgeri Vita Brunonis Archiepiscopi Coloniensis*, c. 23 (ed. I. Ott, *M.G.H.* pp. 23–4); cf. Widukind, *Rerum Gestarum Saxonicarum Lib.* i, c. 31 (*M.G.H. Scriptores in Usum Scholarum*, p. 44).
4. Ruotger, op. cit., c. 29.
5. *Capitularia*, i, 45.

lust and wickedness of the people, caused them to lose their kingdom. Beware that the same does not happen in our time.[6]

It is not therefore surprising that the legislation of the early kings is full of injunctions to their bishops. It was a matter of urgent public interest to see that they carried out their duties: they are to stay in their own diocese; they are to know the canon law; they are to judge all men in their diocese; they are to examine the faith and learning of their clergy; they are to see that the people know the Lord's Prayer; they are to regulate the payment of tithes and the building of churches; they are to support the count; they are to perambulate their dioceses. All these basic directions for the government of a diocese belong to the time of Charlemagne and were issued on the authority of the king.[7]

In the course of the ninth century the directions became more detailed and they were supplemented by treatises written for the guidance of the episcopate. One such treatise was written by Hincmar, who was archbishop of Rheims from 845 to 882. The heavy round of duties he describes would have made the bishop a very busy man indeed. He had to look after the property of the church throughout his diocese, to investigate the state of its buildings and equipment, to examine, ordain, and supervise the work of the clergy, to consecrate churches, to order penances and perform the rites of reconciliation, to hold synods and enforce obedience, to baptize, confirm, and offer hospitality, to instruct the laity, and to see that princes obeyed the law of God.[8] This was the bishop who emerged from the Carolingian reconstruction of society: he was a man endlessly exercised in the care of temporal and spiritual things, a chief agent in the royal government of the kingdom. In many ways the practice and theory of the ninth

6. Haddan and Stubbs, *Councils and Ecclesiastical Documents*, iii, 1871, 474–8: this letter, which gives a summary of the teaching of Gregory the Great, is an interesting link between the Gregorian and Carolingian ideal of a bishop.

7. *Capitularia*, i, 74–6, 78, 103, 119, 158, 178, 182, 195.

8. *De Officiis Episcoporum, P.L.* 125, 1087–1094. For the practical application of these precepts, see Hincmar's *Capitula Synodica*, ibid., 773–804.

century stamped a character on the episcopate in the West
which it has never lost.

Bishops grew to their full strength at this time. Rulers
who had difficulty in securing loyalty and obedience from
others needed the support of their bishops. At the same time
the great spiritual and temporal resources of the episcopate,
their clear aims and well-defined laws, gave them a growing sense of their corporate power. It is not surprising that,
as the Carolingian dynasty declined in power, the bishops
began to assert their superiority over the secular ruler. Already in the mid-ninth century Hincmar of Rheims could
write:

> This world is chiefly ruled by the sacred authority of bishops
> and the power of kings. . . . But the episcopal dignity is greater
> than the royal, for bishops consecrate kings, but kings do not
> consecrate bishops.[9]

In these words there are the first rumbles of a great
controversy, of which the practical consequences still lay
far in the future. From the middle of the eighth to the
middle of the eleventh century it could scarcely be doubted
that – with whatever flourishes of spiritual superiority –
bishops could only be strong under strong kings.

This was the Carolingian legacy and it was well summed
up in 895 in one of the last of the great assemblies to be
summoned by a descendant of Charlemagne. In this year,
Arnulf, king of Germany, the great-grandson of Charlemagne, summoned his bishops to a meeting at the royal
palace at Trebur near Mainz. The decrees of this council,
issued in the name of twenty-six archbishops and bishops,
form one of the most elaborate codes of ecclesiastical law
in the whole of this period. They range far and wide over
the field of religious discipline, and draw together the legislation of popes and councils and kings for the use of the
German church. There, at the centre of everything stood
the king, 'the most glorious Arnulf who, inspired by the
merciful goodness of Jesus and the humble devotion of his
prelates, decided that the synod should be held'. Arnulf

9. *P.L.* 125, 1071.

is not generally reckoned by historians to have been an impressive ruler, but in this assembly, as he gave directions to his bishops, he was clothed in all the majesty of his ancestors and he spoke with the authority of a consecrated king:

Pastors of the churches of Christ and lights of the world! Carry out that pastoral charge which is laid upon you. . . . You can rely on me to fight all the enemies of the church of Christ. Surely 'neither death nor life, nor things present, nor things to come, nor any creature can separate us from the love of God' or disjoin our sacred unanimity.[10]

As the bells rang out, and the *Te Deum* and royal *Laudes* were sung, the bishops arranged themselves for their discussion. It must have seemed then that the future of the Christian people was assured by the sacred unanimity of kings and bishops. Even at the end of a century in which so much of the might of the Carolingians had been eroded, this unanimity seemed destined to a long continuance.

The break-up of the Carolingian ideal

We know, of course that the future did not lie in this direction, and we may ask why. The simple answer is that the 'sacred unanimity' broke down because the kings failed to maintain their strength. As they became unable to offer bishops the support they needed, the bishops were forced to look elsewhere.

The long history of the break-down of royal power, calamitous in France as early as the tenth century and conspicuous in Germany and Italy in the eleventh, cannot be told here, but its consequences are important. The main consequences were that kings could not control their local officials, nor prevent them from establishing themselves in positions of hereditary power. Consequently they could not guarantee the peace and possessions of the church. In many places kings ceased to be able to control episcopal appointments, and they lacked the resources to reward faithful

10. *Capitularia*, ii, 213.

service or to endow religious foundations. Worst of all, secular rulers in their hour of need were themselves forced to dip into the treasures of the church and to take land from the church to give to laymen. This was always the resort of kings in trouble. The last Merovingians had been driven to it; the Anglo-Saxon kings in their hour of need were driven to it; but it was especially disastrous in the post-Carolingian period because bishops had been raised so high that they had become aware of their corporate sacerdotal power. It made no difference that the bishops owed their great power to kings who now needed their help. Gratitude to benefactors is not a characteristic of great institutions, especially when the benefactors are dead and their successors appear as plunderers rather than protectors. The bishops therefore began to look elsewhere for support.

The kings themselves were not responsible for this state of affairs. No doubt they would have preferred to be rich and liberal, but circumstances made them grasping because they were poor; and they were weak because they could not reward service. We can trace the stages of decline in one small but essential feature of primitive royalty. Kings could rule only by constantly moving from place to place. It was only in this way that they could show themselves to their friends, overawe their enemies, and extort obedience from the unwilling by their presence.[11] Accommodation was a major problem in their lives. If possible they would stay in their own palaces. When these failed they looked for convenient abbeys and episcopal residences. In their prosperity they were welcome. They left behind them magnificent presents and valuable privileges. In the mid tenth century there could be no more welcome visitor than Otto I at the archbishop's palace at Magdeburg for Palm Sunday, or at the nunnery at Quedlinburg for Easter; and when he wanted to turn the church at Maastricht into a royal residence for the good of the kingdom, no one objected. The reason was simple: he had founded

11. For the itinerary of the German kings from 919 to 1056 and its importance in government, see J. H. Rieckenberg, 'Königsstrasse u. Königsgut', *Archiv für Urkundenforschung*, 1942, xvii, pp. 32–154.

the archbishopric of Magdeburg; he had endowed Quedlinburg and sent his daughter there as a nun; and he had
given a rich compensation for the church at Maastricht.[12]
Besides, his presence was everywhere a guarantee of patronage and peace.

This was one side of the coin. The other was displayed
in contemporary France. Here the kings had lost nearly all
their estates in rewarding their vassals. As they lost them,
they had to depend on their bishops for the primitive needs
of hospitality; and as their business declined, they conducted
an increasing proportion of it in episcopal residences rather
than royal palaces. But they could give nothing in return.[13]
This was the quickest way to lose the loyalty of their
hosts. Royal power in Germany never sank as low as this,
but even here in the early eleventh century there were
ominous signs that the old balance of reciprocal benefits
was changing. We hear of the king staying in episcopal and
monastic residences which his predecessors had never
burdened with their presence, and there is a steep rise in
the proportion of abbeys and bishops' palaces included in
their itineraries. To us these seem small matters, but to
contemporaries they were infallible signs that the king had
lost the power to pay his way. He was obliged to take more
and more, and to give less and less.

He who cannot give cannot rule: this fundamental
axiom of government can be verified very often in the
course of medieval history, and not least in the relations of
kings and churches in the eleventh century. Kings had been
the chief, almost the only, large benefactors of the church
in earlier centuries: now they fell behind the local aristocracy in the scale of benefactions. But just because they
had less to give, they depended more than ever on their

12. The Ottonians seem to have tried to be in Magdeburg for Palm
Sunday and at the royal monastery of Quedlinburg, about forty miles
away, for Easter whenever possible. Otto I's action and compensation
in taking over the church at Maastricht for the needs of the kingdom is
described in *M.G.H. Diplomata*, i, 322.

13. For the most recent account of the difficulties of the tenth-century
French kings see J. F. Lemarignier, *Le Gouvernement royal aux premiers temps
capétiens (987–1108)*, 1965.

right to appoint bishops and to receive in return presents, hospitality, loyalty, and armed support. What had been a mutually satisfying combination of duties and interests became a tyranny: *tu pulsas, ego vapulo tantum*, as classically minded men were fond of saying. Slowly but irrevocably the desire for a change in the relationship grew. By the end of the eleventh century the bishops of large parts of Europe were ready for it.

The popes were in the end the main beneficiaries of the change, but they did not initiate it, nor at first welcome it. On the whole, like other men, the popes acknowledged the power of kings over the local churches as part of the divine order of things. They had no wish to exchange the well-established sharing of Christian duties for the frankly predatory grasp of local magnates. Pope John X gave forcible expression to this point of view in a letter of 921. The archbishop of Cologne had consecrated a bishop of Liège who had been appointed by the local duke, 'despite [the pope wrote] the ancient custom that no one except a king with authority received from God should confer a bishopric on any clerk'. The pope was amazed at the archbishop's presumption 'in acting thus contrary to reason and without a royal command, when he should have remembered that no bishop was to be consecrated in any diocese without an order of the king'. For his part the pope had no wish to deprive the king of his dignity: rather 'he rejoiced that the king should retain his dominion intact', and he ordered that the king should continue like his ancestors to set up bishops in all his dioceses.[14]

It took nearly a hundred and fifty years for the papacy to break away from the doctrine of a benevolent royal power cooperating in the ordaining of bishops. When disillusion came it was a complicated phenomenon, but the point on which it fastened was the fundamental *secularity* of kings. All their claims to 'invest', 'ordain', or 'appoint' bishops came to be seen as examples of that constant threat of the

14. The letter is printed in L. Santifaller, *Zur Geschichte des Ottonisch-salischen Reichskirchensystems* (Sitzungsberichte der Österreich, Akademie der Wissenschaften, vol. 229), 1954, pp. 73–4.

secular world to destroy the church. These are the themes
that run through the letters of Gregory VII: 'emperors,
kings, and other lay persons, whether men or women' (it is
hard now to take the full force of this disdainful mingling of
functions and sexes) have been presuming 'contrary to the
statutes of the holy fathers' to confer bishoprics and abbacies
on ecclesiastical persons. This is to stop: if anyone does this
in future his action is declared void by papal authority and
he himself excommunicated.[15]

These words were written almost exactly a hundred and
fifty years after the letter of John X which has just been
quoted. By this time the system which Pope John had
approved was shaken by internal weaknesses. The papal
denunciations did not create these weaknesses, but they
added another element to them – the element of intellectual
uncertainty – and they suggested an alternative. The
combination was sufficient to upset an already tottering
system.

We may illustrate the process of disintegration by the
careers of two contemporaries of Gregory VII, one in
Germany and the other in England – two men of high
respectability, neither visionaries nor monsters, but able
men trying to do their duty as bishops.

Benno II of Osnabrück.[16] In Germany Benno II, bishop of
Osnabrück from 1068 to 1088, was a bishop of the old school.
His early career had been that of a successful scholar and
teacher in the best German schools of the day. Then, like
many scholars before and since, he turned to administration.
He came to the king's notice during a royal expedition
against the Huns in 1051 when he showed outstanding
skill in organizing supplies for the army in a devastated
countryside. This led to his appointment as dean of Hildesheim and steward of the king's palace at Goslar. In these
positions he was responsible for building the great church

15. *Registrum Gregorii VII*, p. 403.
16. For an excellent contemporary biography see *Vita Bennonis II,*
Episcopi Osnabrugensis, by Norbert Abbot of Iburg, ed. H. Bresslau
(*M.G.H. Scriptores in Usum Scholarum*), 1902.

at Hildesheim, and he supervised the building and upkeep of the royal fortresses in the vitally important duchy of Saxony. He had to look after the raising of cattle and crops, the collection of rents, the storage of food, the planning of buildings, the organization of domestic economy.

The qualities of a high-class schoolmaster turned estates-agent, clerk-of-works, and quartermaster may not seem the ideal recommendations for episcopal office, but they were certainly not contemptible. They were needed equally in ecclesiastical and secular government, and Benno used his gifts with impartial zeal in the service of both.

By 1068 he had certainly earned a bishopric, and when the canons of Osnabrück appeared at Goslar in 1068 with the news that their bishop was dead, the king made a good choice in handing the ring and staff of the bishopric to Benno. Benno justified the choice by continued loyalty and assiduity in the royal service. But now a quite new element came into his life. As a bishop he was for the first time an independent agent responsible for promoting the glory of his see. He fortified his cathedral-town and built roads through the marshes of the diocese. He built a monastery beside his cathedral. The buildings, endowments, furnishings, and discipline of his new foundation became the chief care of his life. A monk of this monastery wrote his biography as a memorial of the debt which those who enjoyed the wealth and dignity of the church owed to him:

He was certainly very exacting about the payment of rents, to such an extent that he often forced his peasantry to pay their dues by violence. But those who know the men of this country, their untrustworthiness and cunning, will easily forgive him and acknowledge that he was obliged to do this by pressing necessity. If we mention such points in his behaviour as may seem blameworthy to some, we do so in no carping spirit, but we set down the truth as we knew it so that our readers may pray more diligently for him.[17]

In all these efforts in his diocese he remained a king's man. It was his duty as a bishop to collaborate with God's anointed in the work of government, and he supported the king in the great Saxon rebellion even to the point of suffering exile from his see. But in the last resort the interests of his see came first. This put him in a difficult position when the king summoned a meeting in the cathedral in Brixen in 1080 for the purpose of depositing the pope, Gregory VII. His biographer describes his perplexity:

When he began to doubt how things would turn out, he looked around for a means of escape. He noticed that there was a small cavity at the back of the altar covered by the altar-cloth. He thought he could just get inside, so he pushed his way in, and covered the hole carefully with the altar-cloth. . . . When his absence was noticed, the king sent messengers to his lodgings, but he couldn't be found. So the proceedings came to an end without him. When Gregory had been deposed and Clement elected in his place, Benno slipped from his hiding-place and took his seat near the altar. Everyone was astonished to see him. He said he had never left the church, and he managed to clear himself before the king of the charge of disloyalty. Thereafter, following the precept of the Apostle 'in so far as in you lies, be at peace with all men', he continued to be on good terms with both king and pope – an unparalleled feat for those days.[18]

At the cost of some indignity Benno had managed to evade a choice which his prudent instincts told him would be disastrous. Henceforth he concentrated his efforts more closely on his diocese and on the monastery he had built. In his last years he seldom left the monastery except to preach in the cathedral on Sundays. When he got a royal charter confirming its possessions, he was careful also to get a papal privilege to the same effect. The old unity of life had been destroyed, but he had been spared the necessity of choosing between the two claimants for his loyalty.

The hiding place at Brixen became a symbol of his deliverance. As an act of gratitude he made a replica of his hiding place in the altar of his new monastery at Osnabrück. It was a fitting memorial to the perplexity of a bishop, but it was not always so easy to avoid a choice, as a contemporary of Benno in England discovered.

18. ibid., pp. 23-4.

William of St Calais, bishop of Durham.[19] Like Benno, William
of St Calais, bishop of Durham from 1080 to 1096, was a
king's man. He too had earned his bishopric as a clerk in the
royal service. We know nothing of his early life, but the
king must have thought well of his ability when he put him in
charge of one of the most difficult and dangerous places in
his kingdom. His predecessor had been murdered and the
whole countryside was in a state of wild confusion. Like
Benno, William of St Calais settled down to introduce
order into his diocese, and like him he concentrated his
efforts on building up and endowing a monastic community
in his cathedral town. For him too there came a moment
when the royal interests clashed with those of his church.
He had retained a powerful place in royal government,
but in the great rebellion of 1088 he failed to give the king
the support he demanded. The dispute seems to have
turned on the amount of military service the king could
expect from the lands of the bishopric. It was a point on
which the king was naturally extremely sensitive. The
bishop had failed him, and in revenge the king seized the
lands of his bishopric and summoned him to judgement
before his court. This was a much more serious situation
than any that had faced Benno. William of St Calais had
to use every weapon he possessed to extricate himself. His
most effective weapon was a book of canon law known as
the Pseudo-Isidorean Collection which was in his library
at Durham. He drew from this collection texts to prove
that he ought to submit only to the judgement of his
fellow-bishops – or possibly the king and bishops – but
certainly not the barons and laymen of the king's court.
He failed to convince the court, and in the end he was
driven to appeal to the pope 'to whose judgement all major
ecclesiastical cases and the trial of bishops have been reserved
by the ancient authority of the apostles and their successors'.[20]

19. The main sources for his life are in Symeon of Durham, *Opera
Omnia*, R.S., i, 119–39, 170–95. H. S. Offler has disputed the authenticity of parts of the evidence which I accept: see *E.H.R.*, 1951, lxvi,
321–41, and R. W. Southern, *St Anselm and his Biographer*, 1963, 147–50.
20. Symeon of Durham, i, 184.

This was a step that had not been taken in England since the days of St Wilfrid. But unlike Wilfrid, William of St Calais was not in any sense a papalist; he was simply a royalist bishop in a difficulty. This made it all the more significant that he should see the papacy as his only hope in time of trouble. He had no ideological preference for papal government, but it served his turn. The king let him go and confiscated his bishopric. There is no reason to think that the bishop pursued his appeal as far as the papal court. He waited in Normandy for the king's anger to cool, and after three years of exile he was back at the king's right hand. The king was glad to have him back. He heaped privileges on the see of his old minister. He did more than restore the lands he had seized: he improved the terms on which they were held and he extended the area of the diocese into Cumberland and southern Scotland. In return he got five more years of faithful service and staunch support against the more dangerous, because more convinced, papalism of Archbishop Anselm. So far as William of St Calais was concerned, all was well. He was able to start building his cathedral and he left a blessed memory among the monks of Durham. He had done his duty by his diocese by flourishing the new weapon of papal power, without pressing it so far as to hurt the king.

The careers of Benno and William of St Calais illustrate a number of aspects of the episcopal office in the break-up of the Carolingian church order.

In the first place they illustrate the onset of doubt about the sufficiency of the king to protect episcopal interests. Whether this doubt arose from the ineffectiveness or illegitimacy of the king's patronage of the church, the result was the same: it made bishops look further afield for support, and they could look only to Rome. There was nowhere else to look. When we find considerable numbers of bishops in the late eleventh century confessing that they paid money to a lay ruler for their sees, resigning their office into the hands of the pope, and receiving it back as a papal gift, their motives were no doubt very various. But behind everything there was a doubt about the efficacy of royal protection. Hence the forward movement of the Roman curia was met by a reciprocal movement from outside: without the latter, the former would have been quite ineffectual.

Indeed, looking a little deeper, the two movements were one and the same. Both of them were the result of efforts to preserve and consolidate for episcopal sees rights and privileges that were thought to be part of the unchangeable constitution of the world. The personality of a bishop was wrapped up in his see. The preservation of its rights was his most sacred duty. 'I would not dare to appear before the judgement-seat of God with the rights of my see diminished,' St Anselm said. Other men no doubt had other motives – pride, duty, gain, or the hope of a good name in history. But over all of them there brooded the ever-watchful vigilance of the saints who would brook no diminution of their rights on earth. A bishop who, even by unworthy means, had preserved the rights of the saints might hope by their intercession to be forgiven.

This motive was operative at every level of the ecclesiastical hierarchy, and it gives respectability to the uninhibited pursuit of rights and privileges, which bishops sought with at least as much ferocity as other men. The eager pursuit of the most flimsy and far-fetched claims was the most powerful force in the institutional development of the medieval church, combining as it did the most ordinary of human motives with the nobility of an ideal vision. Every office holder, and especially the holders of the more ancient offices, had a sacred duty to defend the rights, privileges, and possessions of his office and to drive them to the furthest limit. One ought not indeed to seek too much, or by unjust means; but in a world of uncertainties it was well to stake out an ample claim.

The bishops of the late eleventh and twelfth centuries, who in an age of reconstruction struggled to make good their exuberant claims, had the passionate support of their cathedral chapters; and those who satisfied their chapters were often rewarded with laudatory biographies. On the

whole these contemporary praises do not make a good
impression on a modern reader. The privileges, possessions,
and buildings so vigorously enlarged seem now only remotely
connected with an eternal order, while the serious duties
imposed on Carolingian bishops were largely forgotten. We
hear little of bishops examining their clergy, perambulating
their dioceses, or holding synods, and much of their duties
as magnates. These secular duties moreover were no longer
closely linked with the care of the Christian community;
they were duties owed to kings, and to kings who had lost
their sacred character.

The bishops of this period of transition had the weaknesses of the Carolingian bishops without their strength.
The great weakness of the Carolingian episcopate lay in its
alienation from the people; its strength lay in its grand
conception of episcopal government. The alienation remained; the grandeur diminished. When a late-eleventh-
century bishop visited the churches of his diocese, his
biographer could describe this eccentricity as an unusual
exhibition of pious curiosity. And the biographer of one of
the best bishops of the twelfth century could count it among
his eminent virtues that he insisted on dismounting from his
horse to confirm the children 'however great his hurry or
fatigue, however rough the road, or bleak the weather'.[21]
Virtue takes many forms, but it is hard to evoke the situation in which it was a notable virtue in a bishop to refuse
to lay hands on the children from his saddle, while his
cavalcade kicked around and his officers distributed blows
among the screaming throng.

Yet contemporary opinion deserves to be heard. It at
least indicates what was thought to be possible at the time.
At the worst, these busy and persistent men, however great
their limitations, maintained the episcopal office and even
enhanced its standing in society, at a time when they were
exposed to the full force of social and political change.

So far as bishops and archbishops were concerned the
most important result of this period of change was the

21. *The Life of St Hugh of Lincoln*, ed. D. L. Douie and H. Farmer, i,
127–8.

emergence of papal government, and we must now ask how they adapted themselves to exposure to this new force.

II. BISHOPS IN THE SERVICE OF THE POPE

At first it might have seemed that the intrusion of papal jurisdiction into the everyday affairs of the diocese would mean the end of episcopal independence. The bishops could do nothing to stop the removal of monasteries, and soon whole religious Orders, from their supervision. The loss of authority was bad enough, but the reason for it was even worse. All the new religious orders sought, and obtained, freedom from episcopal supervision, because it appeared to be a purely restrictive and Oppressive force in the organized religious life. Besides all this, the bishops had to watch litigants of every class ignoring their jurisdiction in favour of that of the pope. They had to read papal letters which insisted that their rôle in the church was to assist the pope in exercising his plenitude of power. To drive home this message they were required with increasing frequency to carry out papal directions and to co-operate with papal judges in their own dioceses. They lost their power of liturgical innovation and their importance as creators and interpreters of ecclesiastical law. In these conditions there could no longer be any idea of episcopal independence.

Of course the process had its compensations. In many parts of Europe papal support was highly efficacious in recovering lost ecclesiastical property, especially tithes. The process of disengaging the bishops from lay investiture, the most obvious formal sign of the authority of the ruler, was carried through without any loss of episcopal property. There was one dangerous moment in the process of disengagement, in 1111, when Pope Paschal II agreed to a formula for ecclesiastical freedom which would have entailed large losses of territorial rights. The agreement was blocked by an opposition in which the bishops of northern Italy and Germany played the leading part. They did not relish the freedom which comes from having little to lose. They wanted the pope to help them defend their ancient rights, not to act as a broker in relinquishing them. In this they succeeded.

Moreover, papal control, if it brought a loss of independence, also brought substantial benefits. Although the growth of papal government took business and patronage away from the bishop, it was itself only a symptom of a general governmental expansion in which the bishops also shared. Administratively and judicially they were much busier at the end of the twelfth century than they had been at the beginning, and they were still busier a hundred years later. Like every other European magnate, the bishops became the masters of an elaborate jurisdictional and administrative machine. The first results of this development are visible in episcopal charters quite early in the twelfth century when bishops and archbishops began to gather staffs of clerks and lawyers for the conduct of complicated judicial business. With the help of these men the episcopal functions quickly regained and soon surpassed the level of activity that had been reached in the ninth and tenth centuries. By the beginning of the thirteenth century the outlines of the fully developed medieval bishop have appeared. Besides being a great landowner and political magnate, he was a judge and legislator, head of the local ecclesiastical hierarchy, and an indispensable agent of both royal and papal government. Like the secular ruler, the bishops had found that when the tide of papal authority had rolled over them they were still left with most of their functions intact, even though these functions had to be exercised in a new and more complicated way, and in careful conformity with the procedures of the papal court.

The papal framework brought a general uniformity into the development of the episcopal office everywhere in Europe, but bishops varied greatly in their social and political standing. The main line of division lay between the bishoprics, mainly in Italy, which retained the ancient civic pattern of the Roman Empire, and on the other hand the much larger bishoprics of most of northern Europe. This division corresponded in part, but not entirely, to a further distinction between bishoprics in areas of great commercial activity and those which were mainly rural. Cutting across both these divisions, there were bishoprics in areas of acute political strife and those in more or less peaceful communities. The way in which the episcopal office was exercised depended on the bishop's place in this pattern of social and political activity. Consequently the only way to understand the wide diversity of the episcopal species, and the variety of episcopal activity within the general framework of ecclesiastical law, is to take a few examples from different parts of Europe.

An archbishop in northern France

We may look first of all at a model archbishop in the most peaceful and best adjusted society of western Europe. Odo Rigaud, archbishop of Rouen from 1247 to 1276, came from a family of minor nobility in the Île de France.[22] He was a university lecturer in Paris in the 1230s, and like several other academic teachers of his generation he became a Franciscan. He was soon one of the most distinguished theologians of the Order. At the time of his election as archbishop, he was warden of the Franciscans at Rouen. In every way his was a copy-book election: here was a scholar and friar without family influence or secular pressure, a leading man in a great religious order, elected on his merits by the free choice of the cathedral chapter, without any external interference from king or pope. This was the pattern of election that reformers had fought for and could seldom achieve.

Odo's career as archbishop was marked by regularity at every stage. He was already a notable man when he was elected, and he stepped into his great position with easy

22. Attention was first drawn to Odo Rigaud and the extraordinarily rich material for his career by L. Delisle, 'Le clergé normand au xiii⁰ siècle', *Bibliothèque de l'école des chartes*, 1846–7, 2nd ser., vol. iii, 479–99. This article, together with Odo's *Registrum Visitationum 1248–1269* (ed. T. Bounin, 1952) on which it was based, still remains the best account of the archbishop's activities.

assurance. He was now the lord of three palaces with extensive estates on both sides of the Channel, a large household, and a wide authority. Once, on his way to Rome, when an open-handed Italian bishop offered to pay his expenses, he declared that half his income was enough to allow him to live in splendour, and he had no need of the other half. Since he was at that time riding with a retinue of eighty horsemen, this was no mere expression of Franciscan humility. He was a grandee.

The journal of his archiepiscopal visitations has survived, and it shows him making the rounds of his diocese and province from year to year. First of all he visited the rural deaneries of his diocese and examined the morals of the parochial clergy. Then he visited those religious communities throughout the whole province which were not exempt from his authority. Like many Franciscans in positions of authority he took a special interest in the administration of the monastic estates, their system of accounts, and their libraries. His recommendations in all these matters show an excellent grasp of the problems of the librarian as well as the estate-agent. Finally, over the years, he carried out visitations of all the dioceses in his province. Each of them was visited three or four times during the twenty years for which his journal has survived.

Naturally this activity was not wholly peaceful. Odo was inclined to be autocratic and to overstep the bounds of his lawful authority. His visitations cost money and, like every other act of medieval government, they had to be paid for by those who were immediately concerned – that is to say by the examinees themselves. In 1251 all the bishops of Normandy appealed to Rome against the cost of the archbishop's visitations, his interference with their jurisdiction, his absolving of persons whom they had excommunicated, and so on. These protests dragged on for several years. They were the inevitable consequence of firm, and sometimes fussy, government. But none of the complaints alter the main impression of peace and regularity.

Above all there was a profound peace in the relations between the archbishop and the king. After Louis IX's return from his first Crusade the king and archbishop were often together, and when the preparations for the second Crusade became intense they were almost inseparable. Odo himself took part in Louis's second crusade; he was with the king when he died, and he brought the king's body back to France. Nothing could illustrate the peaceful and uncontentious relations between secular and ecclesiastical government in France better than this harmonious and affectionate cooperation. Neither man demanded anything that the other could not give. Everything in their relationship reflected the ease of men who knew their duty and were satisfied.

It is not to be expected that the same ease and mutual trust would be found in the relations between the archbishop and the lower ranks of the ecclesiastical hierarchy. Franciscan friars who became bishops were apt to be disciplinarians. Odo Rigaud was no exception, but there were no extravagant scandals or hopeless problems. There was plenty of incontinence, drunkenness, gaming, illicit trading, irregularities of dress and discipline; but these were the common vices of the lower clergy. They were punished by fines, suspension from divine service, and threats of deposition. Yet disciplinarian though he was, there was a note of moderation in all his proceedings. He did not expect too much or drive men to desperation by excessive penalties. Even a priest found guilty of three simultaneous crimes of incontinence, drunkenness, and violence was required to do no more than seal a promise of resignation to become operative if he were again found guilty. This was the level of severity: firm but not unreasonable.

Similarly, the examinations of candidates for holy orders required a standard of latinity that might just suffice for most parochial purposes but no more. The archbishop and his examiners expected candidates to translate a sentence from the Bible, to decline one or two verbs, and to sing some part of the Mass. A moderate performance in these exercises was enough. It was not a difficult test, but it was a serious one, especially in the presence of an examining body which included the archbishop, his archdeacon, and his brothers. There was no levity; just the solemn bleakness of a board of school inspectors.

This is the secular medieval church at its modest best. Disturbed by no serious dissensions, moderate in action, orderly in procedure, every part fitly conjoined to every other; no heretics, no desperate disorders, no impossible standards of behaviour. Church life did not long nor often appear in this peaceful passivity. It is usual to find currents more violent than the gentle ripples which disturbed the placid surface of Odo's administration. The nature of those currents can be seen in the examples which follow.

An archbishop in England

We turn to another Franciscan scholar-archbishop of a slightly later date. John Peckham (to use a convenient corruption of his name), archbishop of Canterbury from 1279 to 1292, was born at Patcham in Sussex about 1230.[23] In many of its features his career was remarkably similar to Odo Rigaud's. He came from a family of some substance but no importance. After studying at Paris and Oxford he joined the Franciscan Order and rose to be the leading Franciscan scholar at Oxford and Provincial of his Order in 1275. Two years later he was appointed lecturer at the papal curia. So it came about that he was at Rome when Pope Nicholas III removed Robert Kilwardby from the archbishopric of Canterbury by making him cardinal-bishop of Porto in 1278. Kilwardby had been a papal nominee at Canterbury, but he was a disappointment. The pope meant now to get someone he could rely on. The monks of Canterbury, supported by the king, tried hard to elect the royal chancellor Robert Burnel, but they tried in vain. The pope, as he was legally entitled to do, took no notice of their petition and he appointed Peckham. Nobody wanted him except the pope; it was a thoroughly legal, but not an auspicious, start.

23. For a full account of his career see D. L. Douie, *Archbishop Peckham*, 1952. There are some additional details in A. B. Emden, *Biographical Register of the University of Oxford to a.d. 1500*, 1957–9, iii, 1445–7.

Peckham descended on England in a flurry of activity. He at once held a provincial synod with the object of promulgating the decrees of the General Council of Lyons of 1274, and he began a long series of visitations to correct the abuses of every diocese in his province. Like Odo Rigaud he has left a very full record of his activity, but unlike Rigaud his activity brought him almost at once into a long series of conflicts with his suffragans and with the royal government, which overshadowed his work as archbishop.

As we have seen, conflicts with suffragan bishops were an inevitable part of the life of an active archbishop, but Peckham's conflicts were conducted in an atmosphere of bitterness and perpetual ill-will, wholly absent from the administration of Odo Rigaud. No doubt this was partly due to a petulant strain in Peckham's character, which comes out clearly in a letter he wrote on 19 November 1282 to Roger Longespée, bishop of Coventry:

> Passing lately through your diocese we saw many things which we thought we had corrected during our visitation – incest, simony, mis-appropriation of churches, children not confirmed. These things need your attention, but you have been absent so long that you seem not to care. We therefore order you, on receipt of this letter, to take up residence in your diocese, so that – even if you are not competent to redress spiritual evils – you may at least minister to the temporal needs of the poor. If you cannot conduct confirmations yourself you must provide some other bishop who knows the language to go round the diocese and do what is necessary. Let us hear from you by the Feast of St Thomas the Apostle [21 Dec.] that you have done this.[24]

An archbishop who writes to a suffragan in these Churchillian terms cannot be popular. Peckham here came up against the easy-going aristocratic churchman who was never absent from the scene for long. Longespée was the kind of man chapters always tended to elect when they had a free hand. He was a nephew of the king, and he had been unanimously elected as long ago as 1256, when Peckham was still a student. The letters of the electors on that

24. *Registrum J. Peckham*, ed. C. T. Martin, *R.S.*, i, 363–4.

occasion have been preserved. They describe Longespée as a man 'whom we firmly believe will be able to reform both the temporal and spiritual state of the diocese'.[25] Whether this was more than the familiar whitewash of ecclesiastical correspondence we cannot tell, but the new bishop soon made it clear that he intended to disturb no one. Peckham was no doubt justified in hitting out at a bishop who had enjoyed his ease so long, but there is no evidence that he hit his target. Longespée lived till 1295, neither disturbing nor disturbed. His funeral, like his election, is very well documented. It too was a grand affair and a harmonious social occasion, disturbed only by some murmuring that the old bishop had lived thirty years too long: from Peckham's point of view this was certainly an under-estimate.

The aristocratic embrace has always been a hindrance to active zeal, but it was not the main obstacle in Peckham's way. The jurisdictional complexities in England were exceptionally difficult. It was impossible to move without coming up against some knotty problem of judicial rights. If a testator died leaving goods in more than one diocese, should his will be proved in the archbishop's court or elsewhere? Could appeals be made to the archbishop from the court of a rural dean or archdeacon over the head of the diocesan bishop? If a man appealed to Rome from a lower court, could he claim the protection of the archbishop during the course of his appeal? If monasteries were exempt from episcopal authority but owned churches which were not exempt were they obliged to attend the archbishop's provincial synod? These and many other similar problems constantly dogged Peckham's footsteps. They caused frequent tensions between the archbishop and his diocesan bishops, and they were an obstacle to effective administration.

The greatest obstacle of all, however, was the long series of petty disputes between the archbishop and the royal

25. The documents of the election, which illustrate the extraordinary complexity of the formal proceedings and the safeguards against irregularity, are given in the Annals of Burton, *Annales Monastici, R.S.*, i, 376–83.

government. We have already noticed a remark of Pope John XXII that no country displayed so many intrusions of secular authority into ecclesiastical affairs as England. Peckham's letters are full of examples of what this meant in practice. The king forbade the archbishop's council to discuss matters touching his Crown, his person, his dignity, or the business of the royal council. The king summoned bishops to appear in his court in cases concerning ecclesiastical patronage. The king forbade the archbishop's court to hear cases alleged to belong to the field of royal jurisdiction. Wherever he turned Peckham found himself confined within a jurisdictional system which limited his freedom in unexpected ways. He would have needed to be either very wise or very lax to keep his sense of direction in this maze. He was neither of these things, so he failed. He could neither acquiesce in, nor see his way through, the tangle; and the issues were too complicated to be solved by heroic measures in the manner of Thomas Becket. Peckham was driven to the safer but even more annoying course of perpetual complaints, which achieved nothing except a general nervous exhaustion.

It may help us to understand his difficulties if we fix our eyes on a single parish church at Chipping Norton near Oxford[26]. The rectory was a valuable living worth about £35 a year, and when Peckham came to England it was held by a royal clerk in plurality. This was one of the things the pope had spoken to Peckham about when he gave him the archbishopric. He instructed the new archbishop to see that illegal pluralism (that is to say pluralism not authorized by the pope) was stamped out. On his arrival in England Peckham obediently set about legislating against this. Consequently, when he came to Chipping

---

26. A simple list of the sources from which the history of this small incident has been compiled will illustrate the complexity of church-state relations at this time: *Registrum J. Peckham*, ed. C. T. Martin, *R.S.*, i-iii, 158–9, 202, 1015; *Select Cases in the Court of King's Bench*, ed. G. O. Sayles (Seldon Soc.), 1938, ii, 166; *Rotuli Parliamentorum*, i, 96–7; *Calendar of Patent Rolls, 1281–92*, 112; *1291–1301*, 46, 120–1; *Register of Richard Gravesend* (Lincoln Rec. Soc. 20), 1925, 231; *Rolls and Register of Bishop Oliver Sutton* (Lincoln Rec. Soc. 39), 1948, iii.

Norton on the first visitation and found the church held by a royal clerk Nicholas Woodford in illegal plurality, he had no hesitation in declaring it void and giving it to one of his own clerks, Richard of Gloucester.

But at this point a difficulty arose. It appeared that in fact Nicholas Woodford had already resigned at the time of the visitation, and the patron of the benefice, the abbot of Gloucester, had given it to another royal clerk, William of Cherington. When he heard this, Peckham climbed down. He promised to find something else for William of Cherington on condition that his own clerk kept the church of Chipping Norton. The compromise was accepted, but it was a lame result for the archbishop's too hasty zeal; and it appears even lamer when we note the sequel.

Peckham's clerk held the church of Chipping Norton for the next eleven years, and he grew rich in his benefice. A list of his possessions made in 1293 shows that he owned plate and jewels, horses and cattle, and that he was a money-lender in a small way, holding bonds from various debtors worth well over £50. Altogether he valued his personal possessions at over £300 – a princely sum for a parson's chattels at this date. But one day the good time came to an end.

In 1282 Peckham had promised to compensate William of Cherington for the loss of Chipping Norton church. It seems he had not done so. But Cherington had meanwhile become a great man in the royal service. In 1293 he was appointed a baron of the royal exchequer at Dublin, and he may have been on his way to take up his new duties when he arrived as a royal judge in the neighbourhood of Chipping Norton to try a case of deer-stealing. The sight of the benefice he had hoped to enjoy upset his judicial calm, and he stepped aside from his official labours to beat up his old rival. He broke into the rectory, seized the contents, read out what purported to be a papal judgement in his favour, and took possession.

Peckham's nominee fled to Canterbury, where he found a Parliament in session. He appealed to the king. The parties were summoned, and William of Cherington blandly denied everything. He had (he said) simply gone as lawful rector to his own house; there had been no violence, no insults, no forcible ejection. The case was adjourned for further evidence, and when the court met Peckham's nominee failed to appear. He never reappeared, and he fades from the scene burdened with a fine of forty shillings for failing to pursue his case in the royal court. The royal court then reversed all that Peckham in his reforming zeal had accomplished – it cannot be said to have been much – eleven years earlier.

The documents in this small case are quite numerous. They speak of the legislation of General Councils and local synods; they describe at length the actions of the archbishop and the grounds on which he had acted; they refer to papal and episcopal records. The case touched the jurisdictions of pope, archbishop, bishops, and king. The means of justice were infinite; but the justice done was negligible. The firm phrases and rules of law simply concealed a primitive struggle for a valuable property between men who knew how to pull the strings for their own advantage. Two royal clerks and one archbishop's clerk had been fighting for an income, nothing more. The high-minded creators and guardians of the system of ecclesiastical government had no defence against this elemental urge. Peckham's general aims and administration were very similar to those of his fellow Franciscan Odo Rigaud in France. In England the political environment was less sympathetic, and for a conscientious and rigid ecclesiastical administrator the frustrations were correspondingly greater. But in both countries, though more roughly in one than the other, ecclesiastical and secular government operated in a web of compromises from which there could be no release.

A bishop in Germany

Our next example takes us into a quite different situation.[27] Liège was the most westerly diocese in medieval Germany.

27. For the career of Henry of Gueldre and the situation in the diocese of Liège in his time, see E. de Moreau, *Histoire de l'Église en Belgique*, 1945, iii, 148–75.

It belonged to the province of Cologne, and its bishop was himself a count of the empire. To the north and east his country bordered on Brabant, Gueldre, and Limburg – the first a Duchy, the two others counties of Germany; but on the south his neighbour was France, and on the west it was Flanders. Hence the bishopric formed a link between two political systems, the French and the imperial, and between two complex alliances, the papal and the anti-papal. In the eleventh century Liège had been a great imperial bishopric and the most important school in northern Europe; but those days were long past. It was now, in the middle of the thirteenth century, a place where the rival political interests of pope and emperor met.

It was with this situation in mind, and with a view to detaching the German episcopate from the emperor's side, that in 1246 Innocent IV forbade cathedral chapters in this area to elect any bishops without the consent of the Holy See. Politics thus played their part in extending papal control of episcopal elections in this area. The bishopric of Liège became vacant within a month of the receipt of this order, and it lay vacant for a year until the papal legate proposed the name of Henry of Gueldre for election by the chapter. On the surface he was not an obvious choice. He was only nineteen years old, already dissolute and not yet literate; but he was reported to be a faithful adherent of the Roman church.[28] More important, he was a brother of the count of Gueldre, a nephew of the duke of Brabant, and a cousin of the count of Holland. This was the group on which Innocent IV relied to provide the core of an òpposition to the Emperor Frederick II.

One of the new bishop's first acts was to take part in the election of his cousin, the count of Holland, as anti-king of Germany against the Hohenstaufen interest. This is what he had been put in his bishopric to do, and for the next twenty-five years he continued with unfailing fidelity to

28. This was the report of the local chronicler: *M.G.H. Scriptores*, xxv, 129. Most of the details which follow are taken from the *Catalogue des actes d'Henri de Gueldre* (Bibl. de la Faculté de Philosophie et Lettres de l'Université de Liège, v, 1900), ed. A. Delecluse and D. Brouwers.

maintain his political rôle of supporting the anti-Hohen-
staufen party in Germany. He had every kind of papal
indulgence to allow him to do this. Innocent IV allowed him
to remain in minor orders 'in order to engage more freely
in the affairs of the church in Germany'. For years on end
he was allowed to keep benefices in his diocese vacant so
that he could receive their revenues. He was empowered to
make grants of tithes to lay supporters of the papal party.
He was simply a political agent in ecclesiastical dress.

By 1273, however, his political rôle was played out. The
Hohenstaufen family had been destroyed, and it no longer
mattered to the pope who was king in Germany. In these
circumstances, the behaviour of the bishop of Liège came
under papal scrutiny. In January 1273 Gregory X wrote to
him about his relations with abbesses and nuns, and
especially about his after-dinner boast that in twenty-two
months he had had fourteen bastards whom he had provided
with ecclesiastical benefices. He was summoned to the
Council of Lyons and given the choice between resignation
and a canonical trial. He chose the former and spent the
rest of his life in a career of wild brigandage and licence.

Of course there are many moral reflections that might
rightly be made about the career of Henry of Gueldre, and
it certainly throws a lurid light on the extent to which
political considerations dominated papal ecclesiastical
policy in the mid-thirteenth century. But a much greater
interest attaches to the steps which the popes took to
minimize the damage caused by their protégé. When
Innocent IV and his legate procured his election they can
have been under no illusions about his personal unsuit-
ability, but they did everything possible to see that it did
not affect the efficiency of diocesan administration. We
should never guess from the large number of Henry of
Gueldre's surviving official episcopal documents that he
was not a model bishop. The administration of the diocese
went on with great regularity: the bishop granted the usual
indulgences for benefactors of churches and pilgrims to
shrines; he ordered the division of parishes that had become
too large; he regulated the relations of patrons and parish

churches; he instituted vicars; and so on. Or rather all these things were done in the bishop's name. The effective supervision of the diocese was in the hands of papal legates. They intervened freely in diocesan affairs, ordered visitations, appointed visitors to carry out the bishop's duties, directed the bishop to treat his subjects less roughly, and generally tried to keep him in order.

The gap left by Henry of Gueldre's total ignorance of ecclesiastical affairs was especially easy to fill, because for over a century expert clerks had everywhere been gradually taking over more and more of the bishop's administrative and judicial functions. Germany had lagged behind this movement; but by 1250 several dioceses had a full-time deputy for judicial business known as the bishop's official. The final stage in this process of delegation came with the appearance of a still higher official known as the vicar-general.[29] He could relieve the bishop of all his work with the exception of the sacramental acts which required episcopal ordination; and these could be performed by a neighbouring bishop or a papal legate. It is not surprising that one of the innovations of Henry of Gueldre's time in the bishopric of Liège was the appointment of a vicar-general. With this omnicompetent deputy in charge of all routine work, and with legates and neighbouring bishops for consecrations and confirmations, the diocese could run itself.

The appearance of the vicar-general all over Europe in the course of the thirteenth century, marks an important stage in the growth of ecclesiastical officialdom. The work of a bishop had so successfully been reduced to routine that the permanent staff could do very well without a bishop. The machine, under the remote control of the pope and the immediate control of his legate, could do everything. In some ways it did rather better when there was no bishop to intrude his personal likes and dislikes into the work of government. No doubt Henry of Gueldre was quite as bad a bishop as any of those whom Gregory VII had attacked two centuries earlier, but he mattered less

29. See E. Fournier, *L'origine du vicaire général et des autres membres de la curie diocésaine*, 1940.

because the work could go on without him. That was the great difference between a diocese under a bad bishop in the eleventh and thirteenth century: in the thirteenth century it scarcely mattered.

An episcopal family in northern Italy

As a final example we may turn to one of the ancient dioceses of Italy – the diocese of Bologna. Superficially the scene is so different from those we have just examined that we seem to be in another world. Despite their contrasting personalities and differing circumstances, the prelates of Rouen, Canterbury, and Liège had conspicuous features in common: they all had a great political position and large estates, and ruled a mainly rural population. The bishopric of Bologna had none of these things. The greater part of the population of the diocese lived in Bologna, where nearly all the wealth and all the activity of the district were concentrated. In this urban community the bishop held a position of only marginal importance: he had no important body of patronage and little influence on the life of the community. The chronicles of the town are filled with details of the comings and goings of all kinds of people – ambassadors, representatives of the common council, friars, flagellants, heretics, popes, and legates; but of the bishop there are only the scantiest notices.[30] Even the schools, which in northern Europe would have been under episcopal authority, were here fostered and conducted by the community of the town. It was the city government, and not the bishop or the cathedral chapter, which made contracts with masters. It brought them to the city, guaranteed their fees, and exacted an oath that they would be faithful to the interests of the community. The masters were able to drive very good bargains in return for their exclusive services. The municipality cherished the schools, for they brought money and reputation to the city and were an important element in its growth and prosperity. In all this the bishop was of no importance.

30. See *Corpus Chronicorum Bononiensium*, ed. A. Sorbelli (Rerum Italicarum Scriptores, 18), 1910–38, vol. ii.

In the annals of Bologna during its great period of development from 1150 to 1220 there is only one important transaction in which the bishop played a leading part. In 1220 a deputation of the city council, headed by its leading professor of law, met the bishop to discuss his conditions for relaxing a sentence of excommunication laid on the city.[31] This was the bishop's only weapon, but it was a weapon that could not be used every day. Apart from this incident there were minor quarrels about jurisdiction and territorial claims, but they only showed more clearly that the bishop was not a force to be reckoned with in the government of the city. The city treated him very much as a modern corporation might treat a bishop – somewhat gingerly but without undue awe, as a man who could neither help nor harm them much.

The situation of the pope was very different. The interests of the pope and commune were closely linked at two levels. They both had an interest in the success of the schools. The city valued the schools for the wealth and reputation they attracted to the town; the pope valued the schools as an instrument for developing and spreading a knowledge of canon law, which was the main prop of ecclesiastical authority. The schools, therefore, were a bond of union between the city and the popes. The greatest day in the history of this union was 3 September 1234, when Gregory IX commended his new collection of canon law to the masters and scholars of Bologna. This act set the seal of papal approval on the town's reputation as the leading centre for the study of canon law in Europe. It was there for all to see. Nearly every copy of the most important volume ever produced for the government of the church had the name of Bologna upon it. Nothing could more clearly have proclaimed the identity of interest of town and pope.

But the pope had another interest in Bologna of a quite different kind. It is almost impossible to travel the length of Italy without going through Bologna. Coming from the north it is the key to central Italy, to the papal lands, and

31. *Cartularium Studii Bononiensis*, 1907, i, no. 38.

beyond them to the kingdom of Sicily. In the great struggle with the Hohenstaufen it was important for the popes to control as many Italian towns as possible, but the control of Bologna was essential. How could this be established?

At first the bishop had been the obvious instrument of papal control. In the eleventh century the popes had succeeded in wrenching episcopal elections from the control of the German kings and placing them under direct papal supervision. For a century this sufficed, but then a new phase of penetration began. By the early thirteenth century the pope appointed the archdeacon also; very soon he began to intervene in diocesan affairs as if the bishop scarcely existed. We can trace the phases of episcopal eclipse in the history of a single family, which Dante has helped to make notorious.

Among the great men whom Dante placed in the circle of Hell reserved for those who disbelieved in the immortality of the soul there is one great ecclesiastical figure – *il cardinale*. This was Ottaviano degli Ubaldini, a member of a powerful Ghibelline family of Tuscany, whom Gregory IX and Innocent IV managed to attach to the papal cause. The tradition that Ottaviano remained at heart a Ghibelline lingered very long in northern Italy, but effectively Gregory IX had secured his loyal service by making him archdeacon of Bologna when he was still a very young man about 1234. Then in 1240, when the old bishop Enrico Fratta resigned, the pope made Ottaviano custodian of the bishopric. He was still too young to be a bishop, but for four years he ruled the diocese as a papal agent. The cathedral chapter tried more than once to proceed to an election, but the new pope Innocent IV set aside their candidates. In the end he made Ottaviano a cardinal with wider political responsibilities and he gave the bishopric to the vice-chancellor of the papal curia. The pope used the occasion to send the canons of Bologna a lecture on papal power:

It is only reasonable [he wrote] that the pope, who is not the deputy on earth of any man but of God, should call here this man, and there another, to share his responsibility and participate in his plenitude of power, according to the nature of the place and the merits of the persons concerned.[32]

In accordance with this high doctrine, he continued, he had found it expedient to elevate Ottaviano to a position of greater usefulness in the church, and he had provided for the needs of Bologna by nominating as bishop the vice-chancellor of the Roman church. As for the persons suggested by the chapter he brushed them aside, declared their election void, and threatened to treat the chapter as rebels if they failed to accept his nominee. The chapter acquiesced, and a new phase in the history of papal control of northern Italy began.

Ottaviano came as legate equipped with some twenty-five papal bulls that gave him unparalleled powers of command.[33] He was legate throughout the whole of northern Italy. Patriarchs, archbishop, and bishops were ordered to show him humble obedience. He had power to remove permanently from office any prelate he pleased in the area of his command. He could translate prelates to other sees when he deemed it necessary. He could give dispensations for any irregularities in ecclesiastical orders or in elections, including dispensations for simony. He could deprive anyone of their papal privileges, indulgences, liberties or immunities. He could excommunicate anyone of whatever degree or order, exempt or otherwise. He could fill parsonages, canonries, prebends, and other benefices throughout his whole legatine area. He could grant plenary indulgences, as if for a crusade, to anyone who fought against Frederick II. He could promise his supporters that the pope would never desert them, and that he would never make peace with Frederick. For all practical purposes he was entrusted with the full papal plenitude of power throughout his whole area, and this plenitude of power was defined in terms that were brutally precise. In the most literal sense the legate was a commander-in-chief in a major theatre of war; the bishops were simply static commanders of local

32. *Registres d'Innocent IV*, ed. E. Berger, 1884, no. 741 (24 June 1244).
33. A. Potthast, *Regesta Pontificum Romanorum, 1198–1304*, 1874–5, nos. 2998–3024.

garrisons under his orders. In the face of such grandeur as this the episcopal office shrank into the shadows.

The archives accumulated by Ottaviano during his eight years as legate in northern Italy must once have been very bulky, but only small fragments of them for a few months of 1252 have survived.[34] Even these disjointed scraps give a remarkable impression of the extent of his operations and influence. He directed the military affairs of Lombardy – raising troops and money to pay them, holding councils of war, conducting negotiations, planning expeditions. A large part of his surviving correspondence is concerned with the troops he had raised in Bologna for the relief of Parma. In these negotiations the *podestà* and council of the city naturally counted for more than the bishop. The bishop, the archdeacon, and the religious orders were in the position of specialized units in the total force deployed by the legate:

Use all your best efforts [the legate wrote to the bishop] to persuade the *podestà* and his court, as well as the council and community of the city to agree to an extension of the period of service of their troops . . . and if they have made any statutes which bind them on oath not to contract debts, take counsel with the Dominicans and Franciscans about dispensations, being assured that you have our full authority, provided you obtain an extension of the period of service for at least twelve days.[35]

The archdeacon was bidden to help the bishop and keep him up to the mark. A stream of letters poured out of the legate's chancery during these critical days as he strove to manage his team of secular and spiritual allies.

This was not the end of his duties. He had to keep the pope constantly informed about the course of events, and to keep up a correspondence with cardinals and kings and collectors of ecclesiastical revenues. In the midst of everything, he even found time to send his chaplain to England to persuade the monks of Malmesbury to continue an old

34. G. Levi, *Registri dei cardinali Ugolino d'Ostia e Ottaviano degli Ubaldini* (Fonti per la storia d'Italia, 8), 1890.

35. ibid., p. 189: the above passage summarizes the contents of an urgent and complicated letter: the correspondence on the subjects mentioned here fills much of the remaining fragments of the register.

payment to his seneschal's brother, an Italian clerk, who held a benefice in the diocese of Salisbury.[36] It was no small part of his business to keep his officials happy; but he also managed to keep on friendly terms with the great enemy, Frederick II himself. His personal sympathy with the imperial cause was one of the great talking-points of the time, and it was with the emperor that Dante fixed him forever in Hell.

Ottaviano's first legatine mission ended in 1252. By this time Frederick II was dead, and the legate moved south to direct the war against Manfred. In terms of real power he was now one of the greatest men in Europe, and it was only to be expected that members of his family should benefit from his greatness. One of his nephews became archbishop of Pisa, and the other two were successive bishops of Bologna from 1260 to 1298.

It shows the wide ramifications of the legate's influence that the first of his nephews to be bishop of Bologna, Ottaviano II, had started his ecclesiastical career as the absentee rector of a church in Kent. Both he and his brother, Schiatta, who succeeded him as bishop in 1295, owed everything to their uncle's influence, but they had none of his commanding authority. They were little men, who as bishops of Bologna were treated by successive popes as lowly agents of their policies. They were not in the same class as the legates or even the papal chaplains who knew the pope's mind.

This comes out very clearly in some letters which Urban IV wrote to Bishop Ottaviano II about a bequest which had been made to the Roman church by a bishop of Avignon who died in Bologna in 1261. In his first letter (on 5 November 1261) the pope wrote to the bishop requiring him to collect the money from the merchants who held it and to transmit it to the pope. In April 1262 the money had not been paid, and the pope wrote to a neighbouring bishop of Modena directing him to compel the merchants to pay. In January 1263 the money was still 'in profane hands' and

36. ibid., no. xxviii. A similar attempt to get the benefice of Bexley in Kent for his nephew was less successful (T. Rymer, *Foedera*, i, 364–5).

the pope's tone became sharper. He gave strict orders to the bishop of Bologna to search out and remove the money 'notwithstanding anything to the contrary in the will of the late bishop of Avignon or even in papal letters which make no specific reference to the present directive'. Five months later the money was still unpaid, and the pope's patience had run out. The bishop was now required to compel payment in eight days on pain of excommunication.[37] What happened then we do not know. It is the tone and subject-matter of the letters that is significant rather than the outcome.

So far as we can tell, these letters are a fair specimen of the subjects which the pope found it necessary to refer to the bishop of Bologna. The tone of the letters is that in which a sergeant-major addresses recruits. Sometimes the pope wrote directly to the *podestà* and commune of Bologna on matters about which he also sent his directions to the bishop. On these occasions his letters to the commune were full of large compliments about the ancient fidelity and fervent devotion of the city to the Roman church. But in writing to the bishop it was sufficient to threaten him 'on his obedience and on pain of excommunication', or to require him to act 'without making difficulty or delay'; or to direct him to obey the pope's commands, and 'to draw up a public instrument with his seal attached giving an account of what he has done, and send it to the pope'. We see here the bishop as the lowly secular subordinate on whom it was unnecessary to lavish any refinements of courtesy.

It would be quite wrong, however, to suppose that, just because the bishop was an insignificant agent in the great affairs of the church, the routine of diocesan life was neglected during these years. The evidence is very scanty, but there is no reason to think that the bishop neglected the ordinary business of his see. Yet even in these matters it was the authority of the legates that really counted. The only considerable body of ecclesiastical legislation for the diocese in the second half of the thirteenth century was

37. For these letters from the registers of Urban IV, see Potthast, op. cit., nos. 18146, 18276, 18469, 18575.

legatine. For instance, in 1279 the legate Latinus Mala-branca made constitutions for all the bishops of Aemilia and Etruria, including Bologna and Florence.[38] He spoke sharply to the bishops. He was amazed at their prodigality in dispensing the Lord's treasure in indulgences which far exceeded the limits allowed by Innocent III. In this they had deceived the faithful, and they were to keep within the limits laid down by the legate, or lose their power for a month. Further, he declared, many monasteries in his legatine area were in a wretched state; therefore all the bishops were to visit all the monasteries in their dioceses during the next six months. The legate complained about the delays of the bishops in examining persons reserved for their judgement, and he ordered them all to have peniten-tiaries who could pronounce the necessary absolutions. As for the dress of the clergy, and especially of the students in Bologna, the legate had much to complain of: they had no proper trousers; instead of honest cloaks they had ridiculous garments like nothing on earth; their dress was often too short. All this must stop; cloaks must hang from *both* shoulders, under penalty of deprivation of scholastic privileges and exclusion from both civil and ecclesiastical actions. And so on and so on.

Brow-beaten by popes and legates alike, lacking the great estates and baronial positions of the bishops of north-ern Europe, socially and ecclesiastically insignificant, the mere bishops of northern Italy in the thirteenth century cut a poor figure in the church.

We may take our leave of Bologna and the Ubaldini family with the death of Bishop Schiatta, the last of the nephews of *il cardinale*, in 1298. They had been lucky to last so long, for the cardinal himself had died in 1272 and Schiatta got the bishopric in 1295 by an unexpected stroke of good fortune. When Bishop Ottaviano died in this year, the cathedral canons had probably not exercised their rights of election since 1213. They were in danger of losing them altogether, and they feared that the slightest delay would bring down another papal nominee. The day

38. J. D. Mansi, *Conciliorum Amplissima Collectio*, 1780, xxiv, 745–58.

after Ottaviano's death, therefore, they elected his brother and sent news of the election at once to the pope. They were just too late. Boniface VIII had heard of the vacancy, and had reserved the nomination. He had already written forbidding the chapter to proceed to an election. At this point however the strict legalism of the papal curia came into play. The election by the chapter had taken place before the pope's reservation. No doubt the pope could have brushed the chapter aside. But he had a legal scruple. Besides, he liked Schiatta. So he turned to his lawyers and asked their opinion. They told him that the election should stand, but that anything done after the reservation was null and void. The pope accepted this advice, and the last of the relatives of *il cardinale* slipped quietly into the see.[39]

The little scene at the court of Boniface VIII shows a rather engaging side of the relations between the pope and the Italian bishops. In this part of Europe more than anywhere else the government of the church became the government of the pope. But the popes were nearly all Italians and shared a common background with the bishops; and the tensions, which might otherwise have developed from the high-handed interference of the popes in diocesan affairs, were largely avoided. There seemed no incongruity in the pope's involvement in the details of diocesan government. The bishops had little independent influence in their cities; the popes could speak with confidence to the urban communities from which very often they themselves had sprung. The bishops accepted this without complaint, for they and the popes understood each other's needs.

In these examples we see the main features of episcopal government as it had developed by the late thirteenth century. The French example represents the contemporary ideal, or at least it comes as near to the ideal as medieval

39. The complications of this election were thought sufficiently significant to justify the inclusion of the papal decretal which settled the matter in the permanent body of canon law, Sext. i, vi, 45 (see Æ. Friedberg, *Corpus Iuris Canonici*, 1879–81, 969–970n.).

Europe ever came. Here we see a relaxed and wealthy society dominated by a landed aristocracy, of which the archbishop was a natural and important member. This society was not much troubled by civic oligarchies clamouring for their rights. It was even less troubled by the spiritual extravagances and heretical sects which generally accompanied the rise of civic oligarchies. The lay and clerical aristocracies acted together in substantial harmony; there were no serious obstacles to the administration of canon law or to the enforcement of the discipline which the law laid on clergy and laity alike.

Turning to England we find a situation more deeply disturbed by political friction. On the whole, Peckham at Canterbury was able to carry out the same general programme of organization and supervision as Odo Rigaud at Rouen, but the tensions were much greater and the measure of his success correspondingly less. The normal tensions between clergy and laity, between archbishop and bishops, between the ideals of a Franciscan archbishop and the ordinary worldliness of monks, clergy, and bishops, were here greatly exacerbated by the conflicts between royal and ecclesiastical jurisdictions and by the king's need for money.

In our German example, politics intruded into ecclesiastical affairs on a much bigger scale even than in England. Liège was in the full current of a great political conflict which scarcely touched the societies of England and France. Even at this distance from Rome the intensity of the papal determination to remove the Hohenstaufen obstacle from their path is felt in every aspect of episcopal government. At the furthest limit of German territory the single-minded ferocity of the papal political purpose seems peculiarly Italian. It brings the ruthless logic of Machiavelli into the blundering family alliances of a coarse aristocratic society. In the pursuit of their general design Innocent IV and his successors did not hesitate to promote and maintain a man like Henry of Gueldre as a bishop; but they tried to atone for their crime by seeing that his episcopal duties were performed largely by others. It would be very difficult to prove that the work of the diocese suffered from the character of its figurehead.

Henry of Gueldre, monster though he seems to have been, was still in outward appearance and real power an ecclesiastical magnate not so very different from his contemporaries in England and France. But when we turn to Bologna we find bishops whose position is much nearer to that of a modern bishop. Socially and politically they have very little importance except in moments of crisis. They are entirely overshadowed by the local force of the municipal community on the one hand and the all-embracing power of the pope on the other. Most of the active movements of the day, whether religious or secular, lay outside their competence, and they had no entrenched social position to compensate for the limitations of their jurisdiction. The papacy was the only power which could stand up to, and to some extent promote the interests of, the chaotic and thrusting communities of the towns. Therefore the popes through their legates, with the acquiescence of the bishops, took over the effective government of the church without a struggle.

Looking back over the whole field of episcopal government during the two centuries after 1050, the clearest feature is the increasing subordination to papal control. This happened everywhere simply as a result of the growth of canon law, which attracted all important disputes to the papal court. From this one cause there flowed a multitude of consequences. Litigants by-passed the courts of bishops and archbishops on their way to Rome. A growing stream of papal directives flowed out in the opposite direction. Legates became more frequent and more powerful, and in their presence episcopal authority grew dim. The popes appointed bishops, clipped their authority, and intervened in diocesan appointments as a matter of course. But despite the immense pressure of papal intervention, archbishops and bishops emerged with more power than might have been expected. Although they had lost ground in relation to the papacy they had gained in other respects. In most parts of Europe they had kept their temporal estates. Their jurisdiction over clerks, ecclesiastical property, testaments, debts, usury, and all forms of moral and doctrinal offences, had increased – partly as a result of papal legislation, but even more as a result of the expansion of European society. Their administrative activity grew because almost every form of administration grew.

Archbishops and bishops were after all the wealthiest ecclesiastical class in Europe. Many of them were men of high ability who came to their office already experienced in the use of authority. That their previous experience and authority had often been more secular than ecclesiastical was an advantage rather than a drawback. It very seldom made them less determined upholders of episcopal rights. No bishops threw themselves more wholeheartedly into the battle for their rights than those whose earlier duties had led them to oppose these rights. This remained one of the essential features of medieval society to the end.

6

The Religious Orders

THE main centres of religious life in medieval Europe were communities specially endowed and set apart for the full, lifelong, and irrevocable practice of the Christian life at a level of excellence judged to be impossible outside such a community. The members of these bodies were known as *viri religiosi*: they were 'the religious' in contrast to all other men whether secular or clerical. Turn where we will in the later Middle Ages, we find towns and countryside sprinkled with communities of *religiosi* of many different kinds, but all united in one respect: they had all taken life-long vows which set them apart from ordinary members of the church. Within a radius of twenty miles from where I write there were twenty-eight such communities, great and small, not counting hospitals and small communities on the fringe of the religious Orders. There were over eight hundred in the whole of England and Wales. In the single diocese of Cambrai in northern France there were more than eighty religious communities; in Paris and its suburbs twenty-two; in London nineteen.[1]

Communities formed for the perpetual and exclusive practice of religious life have been common in other societies and other religions, but there are some special features in the medieval western development which we may mention at the beginning of this survey.

In the first place the great variety of religious communities is very striking. They differed not only in size and wealth, but even more strikingly in the purposes for which they had been founded and in their way of life, each of

1. For a survey of medieval ecclesiastical statistics with a bibliography, see B. Guillemain, 'Chiffres et statistiques pour l'histoire ecclésiastique du Moyen Âge', *Le Moyen Âge*, lix, 1953, 341–65; for England and Wales, D. Knowles and R. N. Hadcock, *Medieval Religious Houses*, 1953.

which claimed to be, in some important sense, better than any other. By the end of the thirteenth century six or eight major types of community had evolved with about twenty derivative branches, some of them so different from the parent stock that they could claim to be distinctive types. The rules which governed the daily life of these communities, their habits of worship, and their relations with one another have become the subject of a huge literature, so great is their diversity and so important their bearing on every aspect of medieval thought and practice. The rich variety of medieval religious organizations has an importance that goes far beyond the immediate purposes for which they were founded. Quite apart from the interest of their rules in defining changing ideas of worship and Christian living, they reflect the society from which they sprang.

This leads to another observation. The proliferation of organizations for maintaining various forms of religious life was a feature of a quite short period of the Middle Ages. For several centuries, until nearly the end of the eleventh century, the tendency had been to develop an ever greater degree of identity of purpose and organization, and to delight in the unity of an achieved ideal. Then within little more than a hundred years all the main varieties of medieval religious organization came into existence. We shall certainly not be wrong in associating the stability of religious ideals before about 1100 with the relatively static society of the early Middle Ages, and the rapid diversification of religious organization after this date with the expansion and growing complexity of western society. The interaction of social and religious change is nowhere more clearly displayed than in the history of the religious Orders: here more obviously than anywhere else the history of the medieval church is the history of medieval society.

Everywhere in the history of the religious Orders we find that associations which were founded as a protest against the world and all its ways had their destinies shaped for them by the society in which they had their being. There were many forces which shaped them, even against their will: their property, their family connexions, their secular functions, and the opportunity which they offered their members for advancement to the highest places in the social order. The 'worldliness' of medieval religious communities has often been remarked and generally criticized, and it is true that anyone who looks at these communities for a pure expression of the aims of their founders must very often be disappointed. The states of mind and aspirations expressed in the Rules and Foundation deeds of the various Orders were not realized in any large measure. The driving forces in their development were quite different from those of the original founders.

This has often been looked upon as a betrayal, but there is another way of looking on it which perhaps does more justice to their achievements. If we consider the conditions under which the religious Orders operated, the needs which they met, and the extent to which they satisfied some of the strongest impulses of a developing society, a very different judgement must be reached. The place which religious communities were expected to fill in society, the methods of recruitment and endowment, the intentions of benefactors, and the religious outlook of laity and clergy alike, all drew the body of men who lived under a Rule away from the intentions of their original legislator. For better or worse these were the forces that combined to shape the professional religious life of the Middle Ages. They ensured that the communities set apart from the world should become a mirror of the world in which they lived. Above all they stamped on these communities – even the most resistant – two features which are found in every part of medieval life: a strong grasp on the things of this world, and an ardent desire for the rewards of eternity. These two conflicting desires, operating simultaneously in the same people, lie behind many of the most important developments in western history, and they are most fully exemplified in the medieval religious Orders.

I. THE BENEDICTINES

Any account of medieval religious Orders must begin with the Order of St Benedict. Not only is it the first of the great western Orders in time, but it held the field almost alone for several hundred years; and even when in the twelfth century it lost its monopoly and resigned its leadership in religious life, its influence continued to be supreme in the forms of worship used by the church. However out-of-date, and even moribund, the Benedictine ideal became in the later Middle Ages, it continued to provide an authoritative standard of normal religious life, more ancient, more dignified, and more stable than any other.

The greatest days of the Order, when in the West it was universally held to be the highest form of religious life and almost the only safe road to heaven, were over by about 1100. During the previous four hundred years there had indeed been other forms of laudable Christian endeavour: the heroism of the Christian warrior, the laborious responsibility of the ruler, the seclusion and austere inner battle of the hermit, for instance. But slowly the completeness and universality of the Benedictine Rule had established its pre-eminence.

At first it had seemed too tame for ardent spirits. In the heroic age of the Germanic migrations and the period immediately following them men had looked for a sterner confrontation with evil – something to match the stature of a Beowulf. The lonely and superhuman struggles with demons – the hand-to-hand combats, the duckings, beatings, draggings through bog and fen, the terrifying visions and awful threats – described in the life of St Guthlac, who died in 714, excited the admiration of a generation that looked for towering strength and personal prowess in its leaders.[2] For such experiences as these the Rule of St Benedict offered little opportunity, but in the course of the eighth century these experiences began to seem less important. Rulers began to discover the virtues of discipline,

2. See Felix's *Life of St Guthlac*, ed. B. Colgrave, 1956, pp. 101–10.

and to find that even earthly battles were won by organized and disciplined troops rather than by the exertions of individual valour. The Carolingian family, the great new ruling family of Europe, had a genius for bringing order and regularity into every branch of social and religious life – not least into the regular life of religious communities. It was in this task that the strength of the Benedictine Rule became apparent, and the Carolingians were among its earliest and most powerful lay supporters. They encouraged and enforced its observance in the territories under their control, and other rulers followed their example. In the ninth and tenth centuries support for the Rule became everywhere a central feature of secular government. From this time its future was assured.

The Rule

At first sight it might seem that St Benedict's Rule was even less well adapted to the rôle of supporting and extending the area of stable government than it had been to the task of supporting the heroic impulses of an earlier age.[3] It had been drawn up in the middle of the sixth century when the bonds of civil society were everywhere dissolving; and it was not written to restore these bonds, but to point the way to a new order accessible only to those who were willing to leave the world to its own devices.

Yet it has that in it which must appeal to anyone who values order and discipline. It is very short – not more than about 12,000 words; it is also remarkably complete and clear. The main officers of the community and their duties, the details of daily life, the provision to be made for new recruits, for visitors, for sickness, for the disobedient and for their reconciliation, are sufficiently sketched to form a recognizable standard for the conduct of life. The psalms to be recited, the books to be read, the distribution of time

3. The most convenient scholarly edition of the *Rule* is Dom Cuthbert Butler, *S. Benedicti Regula Monasteriorum*, Freiburg, 3rd ed. 1935; for a detailed study, the indexes in the edition by R. Hanslik (*Corpus Scriptorum Ecclesiasticorum Latinorum*, vol. 75, 1960) are especially valuable.

throughout the day, the persons responsible for the various activities of the community, are all in outline described. Yet, despite the great emphasis on detail, there is a remarkable absence of rigidity. The Rule leaves plenty of room for development and for improvisation. It would be hard to tell simply from reading it whether it was intended mainly for a society of scholars or labourers, of noblemen or peasants, for a richly endowed community supporting an army of craftsmen and artists, or for a poor house scratching a living from an infertile soil. All are possible, and all in due course claimed to be expressions of the original ideal.

The main element in this ideal was the practice of obedience. The first words of the Rule announce this theme: it is written so that those who follow it may 'by the labour of obedience' return to God 'whom they have abandoned by the sloth of disobedience'. These words establish the pattern of life: it is to be a life of strenuous activity; and the object of this activity is to teach obedience. The obedience is of various kinds. There is the obedience of heart and body to the precepts of spiritual counsel extracted from the Gospels; there is obedience to the Rule; but immediately and constantly there is obedience to the abbot. He is the vicar of Christ within the community; his word is to be obeyed as the voice of God himself. He both teaches and commands: 'the abbot's command and teaching sprinkle the leaven of the divine justice in the minds of his disciples'.[4]

The Rule leaves no doubt about the quality of the obedience that it required: it is to be obedience 'without delay'. Whatever is being done is to be dropped at once, unfinished as it is, so that the voice of command and the act of obeying occupy the same moment of time. Instant obedience without fear or dawdling or lukewarmness or murmuring or answering back is the Rule of life. The Rule abhors murmuring, which is the first movement of disobedience: 'Above all there is to be no murmuring for any cause whatsoever, by

---

4. *Reg. Ben.*, c. 2.

any word whatsoever, or any gesture.' The phrase is repeated in another part of the Rule: 'Above all, no murmuring.' 'Above all' is a phrase used only three times in the
Rule: these are two of them.[5]

The strong emphasis on obedience might suggest that the
author of the Rule was something of a drill-sergeant, if it
were not associated with some other features which suggest
a quite different picture. In the first place obedience must
be seen in relation to its end. The end is an entire self-
negation, which those living under the Rule are required to
practise as an instrument of the return to God. This self-
abnegation, which is the fruit of obedience, is the source of
all other virtues. The monks are to have nothing of their
own; they are to expect nothing; they are to put up with
everything – poverty, illness, harshness – because these
things lead back to God. Secondly all this harshness in the
Rule is accompanied by an unusual tenderness towards
human weakness: the abbot is privately to console and
encourage those who have incurred the penalty of excommunication through disobedience; 'above all' (this
is the third occurrence of the phrase) he is to take care of the
sick; he is to be responsible for the clothes of the monks and
see that they fit. The most surprising mitigation of all is
the provision that the *Gloria* of the first psalm in the night-
office is to be said slowly, to allow those who had failed to rise
at once at the sound of the bell, and go 'with the utmost
speed' to church, a chance of arriving without ignominy.[6]

This unexpected strain of mildness has a pervasive
influence on the Rule. It helped to make it suitable for
communities in widely differing circumstances. But there is
something more than severity tempered with mildness in
the total character of the Rule: there is a sense of universality. Despite the rigour of the regime, the Rule is written
as if it were designed for all men everywhere. Fundamentally, the author believes it is an easy Rule. It is a 'school of
the Lord's service, in which we hope we have laid down
nothing harsh or burdensome'; it is 'a tiny Rule for begin-

5. ibid., cc. 5, 34, 40.   6. ibid., c. 43.

ners' – it aims at prescribing no more than anyone 'who thinks that nothing is dearer to him than Christ' can do.[7] St Benedict writes as if nothing could be easier.

At the centre of every requirement of the Rule there lies the prescription of a daily round of divine service. For the time at which it was written the regulations for these corporate acts of worship are remarkably careful and unambiguous. The whole system is built on two biblical pillars: 'at midnight I will rise to give thanks unto thee', and 'seven times a day do I praise thee' – hence the long night-office, and the seven day-offices of Matins (or Lauds), Prime, Terce, Sext, Nones, Vespers, and Compline. The main structure and psalmody are clearly laid out to ensure the weekly recitation of the whole Psalter and the annual reading (much less clearly indicated) of the greater part of the Bible. Here, as everywhere, there was room for varied interpretations and developments within a well-defined pattern: it is a pattern that has left its mark more or less clearly stamped on the services of every Christian community of western origin.

The mind of the writer whose Rule has had this pervasive effect on religious life and Christian worship everywhere must excite inquiry at the very threshold of medieval history. What sort of man was he? Naturally there have been many attempts to answer this question, and it is one of the greatest surprises in the history of medieval scholarship that all the answers of the past will have to be modified in the light of a recent discovery. It now appears almost certain that St Benedict took a very large part of his Rule, including some of the most famous passages of spiritual teaching, almost verbatim from the Rule of a slightly earlier writer known as 'the Master'. Nearly all the chapters that describe the kinds of monks, the character of the abbot, the basic principles of the monastic life, the stages of humility, the practice of obedience and silence – together with a great deal about the duties of the monastic officers and many details of daily life – come from this

7. ibid., Prol. cc. 5, 73.

earlier work.[8] It has seemed incredible to many scholars, and it is certainly at first difficult to believe, that these large subtractions should have to be made from the personal contribution of St Benedict to his own Order. Yet it is even more surprising to discover that, despite these subtractions, the mind of St Benedict emerges more clearly than ever from a comparison of his work with its main source.

In the obscurity of sixth-century monastic history, one of the great difficulties has been the lack of a substantial environment and a standard of comparison for the Rule of St Benedict. The discovery of its main source now partially supplies this want, and we can read the mind of Benedict in his silent omissions, alterations, and additions, as well as in the material he was content to take without alteration from the Master. The difference between the two documents is immense. The Rule of the Master is diffuse, individual, and indefinite in its liturgical detail, where Benedict's Rule is concise, universal, and clear. In the Rule of the Master there is much that is too general to be useful in common practice – long elaborations on the joys of Paradise and the nature of monastic life for instance. There was even more that was too particular to be significant – regulations about coughing, spitting, and blowing of the nose in a way likely to give least offence to the attendant angels, for instance.[9] Benedict omitted all this. He kept to the middle way of practical usefulness, making everything as short and clear as possible. His most extensive original passages laid down the exact routine of daily offices. But it is in his short additions that he shows his personality most vividly. All the examples of the mild wisdom of the Rule which have been mentioned above are Benedict's additions to his source. He seems not to have had the searching and imperious spirit of the Master.

8. There is an excellent study of the relations between the Rule of St Benedict and the *Regula Magistri* in D. Knowles, *Great Historical Enterprises*, 1963, 135–96. For the text of the *Regula Magistri* see the edition by A. de Vogüé, 3 vols., 1964–5 (Sources chrétiennes, vol. cv).

9. *Reg. Magistri*, c. 48.

In his extensive borrowings he exemplifies the humility which he urged on his monks, and his briefest additions display the humanity he desired in an abbot. While Benedict's abbot was above all to look after the sick, the Master was more intent on discovering malingerers.[10] 'Never despair of God' says the Master; 'never despair of God's mercy' says Benedict, making a slight but significant change.[11] The Master saw absolute obedience as a virtue to be attained only by a few perfect monks; Benedict thought it was easy for anyone with a serious intention.[12]

A comparison of the two documents leaves an unexpected impression on the reader's mind. Benedict, the most influential guide to the spiritual life in western history, appears as an uncomplicated and self-effacing man who was content to take nearly all his doctrine from the Rule of his precedessor. Yet with a few changes, omissions, and additions he changed the whole character of his source. He added strength where it was weak, tenderness where it was strong, and terseness and simplicity where it was diffuse and confusing. In so doing, he transformed an already remarkable document into one of the central statements of Christian living. He also produced the last great monument to the legislative genius of ancient Rome.

The centuries of greatness

It is now time to turn to the future of the Rule and its influence on the medieval church. Perhaps the quickest way to get to the centre of the subject is to consider a problem to which Benedict devoted three chapters of the Rule: the problem of recruitment.

The Rule envisaged three classes of recruits to a monastery: laymen of mature years, clergy, and the children of

10. Compare the chapters on the care of the sick in *Reg. Ben.*, c. 36 and *Reg. Magistri*, c. 69, and on late-comers in *Reg. Ben.*, c. 43 and *Reg. Magistri*, c. 73.

11. *Reg. Ben.*, c. 4; *Reg. Magistri*, c. 3.

12. *Reg. Magistri*, c. 7, 'haec forma paucis convenit et perfectis'; *Reg. Ben.*, c. 5: 'Haec convenit his qui nihil sibi a Christo carius aliquid existimant.'

noblemen. There seems little doubt that Benedict expected mature laymen to be the normal applicants for admission: it was only with these that he dealt at length, trying to foresee the various situations and difficulties that might arise.[13] Yet in the course of time, and certainly by the tenth century, the recruitment of the children of noblemen offered by their parents to the monastery had become a very common, and probably the most usual, method of entry to Benedictine monasteries. The reasons for this change lie deep in the religious and social situation of the early Middle Ages, and the consequences for the history of the Benedictine Order were very grave.

THE SOCIAL FUNCTION

In the first place it is important to understand that the monasteries did not exist solely or even mainly for the sake of the monks who sought within their walls a personal salvation. This motive could never have filled more than a small proportion of the numerous monasteries of the period, nor could founders and benefactors have been induced to part with a large proportion of their wealth to make provision for the aspirations of the few. In the period of their greatest expansion Benedictine monasteries were founded and filled for political, social, and religious purposes of which we hear nothing in the Rule. These purposes cannot be clearly distinguished from each other, but very broadly founders and benefactors saw in the 'cowled champions' of the monasteries the spiritual equivalent of secular soldiers. The monks fought battles quite as real, and more important, than the battles of the natural world; they fought to cleanse the land from supernatural enemies. To say that they prayed for the well-being of the king and kingdom is to put the matter altogether too feebly. They fought as a disciplined élite, and the safety of the kingdom depended on their efforts:

The abbot is armed with spiritual weapons and supported by a troop of monks anointed with the dew of heavenly graces. They fight together in the strength of Christ with the sword of the spirit

13. *Reg. Ben.*, cc. 58-60.

against the aery wiles of the devils. They defend the king and clergy of the realm from the onslaughts of their invisible enemies.[14]

This was how kings and magnates were taught to look on the work of their monks. In a society which did not clearly distinguish between public and private functions, or between natural and supernatural activities, the value of the monastic warfare penetrated to every corner of the secular world:

Look carefully at the things which are provided for you by trained monks living in monasteries under a Rule: strenuous is the warfare which these castellans of Christ wage against the Devil; innumerable are the benefits of their struggle. Who can recount the vigils, hymns, psalms, prayers, alms, and daily offerings of masses with floods of tears, which the monks perform? These followers of Christ give themselves up wholly to these employments, crucifying themselves that they may please God. . . . And so, noble earl, I earnestly advise you to build such a castle in your country, manned by monks against Satan. Here the cowled champions will resist Behemoth in constant warfare for your soul.[15]

The battle for the safety of the land was closely associated with the battle for the safety of the souls of their benefactors. It was this double objective that induced great men to alienate large portions of their property for monastic uses. They and their followers and families took counsel together to provide monastic establishments in every main centre of political power, because they believed that their temporal and eternal welfare equally depended on the warfare of the monks.

THE PENITENTIAL FUNCTION

Even if belief in these large generalities was weak, there were urgent personal and family reasons for founding monasteries. The penitential system of the early Middle

14. Foundation charter of King Edgar for New Minster, Winchester, 966, in the *Liber Vitae*, ed. W. de Gray Birch, 1892, pp. 232–46. Cf. the careful apportionment of military and liturgical services among monasteries by Louis the Pious in 817 (*M.G.H. Capitularia*, i, 349–51).

15. Ordericus Vitalis, *Hist. Eccl.*, ed. A. Le Prévost, 1838–55, ii, 417–20.

Ages provided a special reason for relying on the disciplined work of monks. For serious sins penances were extremely heavy, and even for sins almost inseparable from any form of secular life the penances were sufficient to make ordinary activity impossible. For instance, the Frankish bishops in 923 imposed three years' penance on everyone who had been present at the battle of Soissons between Charles the Simple and Robert of Lorraine.[16] This penance entailed fasting on bread, salt, and water for three periods of forty days in each year – not an impossible undertaking, but sufficient to put a large part of the nobility of northern France out of action for many months. Similarly the Norman bishops after the battle of Hastings enjoined a penance of one year for each man killed by any member of the victorious army.[17] It would have brought the Norman occupation of England almost to a stand-still, and this was certainly not the intention of the bishops who imposed the penance. They knew, and everyone else knew, that there was no need for anyone to endure privation who could pay for someone else to act in his place. The system of substitution was well understood:

When priests impose a penance of many years on certain sin-ners, they sometimes indicate the sum of money necessary for remission of the annual stint, so that those who dread long fasts may redeem their misdeeds by alms. This money payment is not found in the ancient canons of the Fathers, but it is not therefore to be judged absurd or frivolous.[18]

It was indeed a necessary practice if government and society were to survive. The austere Peter Damian, who wrote these words, had himself acted on this principle when he enjoined

16. N. Paulus, *Gesch. des Ablasses im Mittelalter*, 1922–3, i, 16.

17. The full text is in D. Wilkins, *Concilia Magnae Britanniae et Hiberniae*, 1737, i, 366.

18. *P.L.* 144, 351–2, quoted in N. Paulus, op. cit., i, 14n. Paulus remarks that the practice of allowing alms to be used as a substitute for fasting was new in 747 (Council of Clovesho, c. 26: Haddan and Stubbs, *Councils*, iii, 371–2). From this it would appear that the system we are describing developed in the course of the eighth century.

a penance of a hundred years on the archbishop of Milan for simony:

> I imposed on him a penance of a hundred years, and I indicated a precise sum of money for which each year of penance could be commuted.[19]

A great man could either pay the stipulated sum or engage other men to undertake the penance for him. In the impersonal society of the early Middle Ages one man's penance was as good as another's. It was not a question of individual effort, but of the payment of a supernatural debt.

To die with a penance incomplete or without having made provision for its completion was of all things on earth the most to be dreaded. The popular literature of this age, when the doctrine of Purgatory was still unformed, contained stories to prove that he who left his compensation incomplete was forever doomed.[20] No man could be saved till his debt was paid. Monasteries offered a safer way of paying the penitential debt than any other method of substitution, whether by alms or lay-helpers. Monks could be relied upon to perform their service of substitution for ever: they were bound by vows; they were established in perpetuity; their property was safeguarded by appalling anathemas against the disturbers of their peace. No matter how large the debt, it would in the end be paid, and the soul of the sinner would be free.

The *opus dei* of the monks, therefore, was work of a very practical kind: its wages were eternal life, and this was earned for their founders and benefactors as well as for the monks themselves. A personal vocation was no more necessary for this work than for any other work. The monks existed to perform a necessary task like other men and we do not ask of a good workman that he shall like his work, but only that he shall do it well for a just reward. It was

19. ibid.
20. This is vividly illustrated in a story told by Peter Damian of a monk who undertook to share the penance of a brother monk and died before it was complete. *P.L.* 144, 403 (Ep. vi, 20).

no more offensive to the conscience of the age to offer a child for training as a monk than for training as a king or craftsman. The one function was as necessary as the other.

THE FAMILY FUNCTION

Further, in addition to the need for eternal life, the economy of a great family required a monastic outlet for its members. At no time in the Middle Ages, and least of all in the early centuries, were the resources of society expanding fast enough to provide honourable positions in secular life for all the children of noble families. There were severe, and well-justified, restrictions on the practice of splitting up the family property, and it was a very serious problem to provide secure and acceptable positions for those members of the family for whom no sufficient endowment could be provided. The problem was especially serious for the girls of a family. They were not exposed to the hazards of an active military life, which created gaps and unexpected opportunities for the boys. There were not enough suitable marriages for all of them; and those who married were often widowed at an early age.

A great family had to make provision for all these eventualities, and the monasteries performed an essential service in helping to solve this problem. They provided the children of noble families with a reasonably aristocratic life and with opportunities of great splendour.

The use of monasteries for this purpose naturally imposed on families an obligation to make suitable provision for their upkeep. Parents commonly gave large gifts to the monasteries to which they offered a child: the gift of an estate was not unusual. Such gifts helped to counteract the constant process of attrition to which any property is subject. But the main support for a monastery had come from the benefactions of the founder, his family, and their associates in the act of creation. The moment of foundation was all-important in determining the fortune of a Benedictine monastery: it fixed, probably for ever, the place of the new monastery in the monastic firmament.

The intricate combination of purpose – public and

personal, religious, social, and political – that lay behind a monastic foundation could only be met by a great endowment, and in a Europe only sparsely settled, in which rulers disposed of lordly rights over vast areas of country which they could not effectively exploit, there were opportunities for lavish gifts of land. Land that would later cover nearly half a county could be given to a monastery. It could be given the more readily since it continued to provide so much that a ruler needed – cooperation in government, troops and spiritual aids in war, an honourable livelihood for unendowed members of the family, and the hope of eternal salvation for all.

By a natural process of adaptation the pattern of Benedictine life was developed to fit the mould which these opportunities and demands provided. The Rule provided no obstacle to the massive increase in the numbers of child-oblates. It could easily be adapted to a more elaborate routine of divine offices until they filled the greater part of a monk's waking hours. In the course of time the great endowments and social position, which aristocratic society pressed upon the monasteries, became necessities for the full Benedictine life. A monastery could scarcely perform all its varied duties without a large community of monks – perhaps a hundred would be a reasonable average; and they needed a school for the children, workshops for craftsmen, builders and labourers, a large library, and equipment for musicians, writers, artists, and scholars. The aristocratic background of the monks, the size and splendour of the church, the elaboration of ritual, all called for heavy expenditure and large endowments.

Founders and benefactors naturally wanted their children to have congenial companions and to live in surroundings that did not dishonour their parentage; and the monasteries on their side gloried in the nobility of their members. Noble blood was not something to be hidden under a bushel; it was a guarantee of quality of soul as well as body. The chronicle of the nunnery at Quedlinburg reported that when the widow of King Henry founded the monastery she took great care to see that no low-born women, but only novices of the highest nobility, were admitted 'because those who are well-born can scarcely ever become degenerate.'[21] This may be a myth but it helps to explain how the noble life of the monasteries could be accepted as a spiritual as well as a social ideal.

By about 1050 it must have seemed that the Benedictine Order had established itself for ever as the prime expression of the Christian religion throughout western Europe. Its position in the hearts and minds of men and in the social order seemed unshakeable. It made an appeal to men of every class and all degrees of piety. Each monastery was ideally a replica of heaven on earth:

I saw a Paradise [Peter Damian wrote to Abbot Hugh of Cluny] watered by the four streams of the Gospels, overflowing with spiritual virtues. I saw a garden bringing forth all kinds of delicious roses and lilies, heavy with the sweet fragrance of scents and spices, so that God Almighty might say of it 'See, the smell of my son's raiment is as the smell of a field that the Lord hath blessed' [Gen. XXVII, 27]. And what else can I call the monastery of Cluny but a field of the Lord, where such a great company of monks living in charity stands like a harvest of heavenly corn? The field is hoed with holy counsel and the seeds of heavenly discourse are sown in it. There the harvest of spiritual grain is collected for gathering into heavenly barns.[22]

These words were written after a visit to Cluny in 1063, and when they were written they said only what everyone thought. The long development of the Benedictine life had reached its highest peak in the abbey of Cluny, and it seemed that Christianity could go no further: the whole Gospel was here displayed in institution and in deed.

Change and decay

For a generation after 1063 few people would have thought that there was any exaggeration or possibility of mistake in

21. Quedlinburg Annals (*M.G.H. Scriptores*, iii, 54), quoted by A. Schulte, *Der Adel u. die deutsche Kirche im Mittelalter*, 1910, p. 115n., with many other illustrations of the close connexion between benefactions and provision for noble children.

22. *P.L.* 144, 374 (Ep. vi, 4).

this way of looking at Benedictine religious life: it was an achieved ideal. The purposes for which Benedictine monasteries had been founded in recent times continued to command respect and excite imitation. The growth of the Order continued with ever-increasing momentum: there were almost certainly more new foundations and a higher rate of recruitment in the two generations from 1060 to 1120 than in any previous period of similar length. Yet long before the end of this period there were ominous signs of change: the Benedictine monopoly of organized religious life came to an abrupt end; religious men even within the Order began to waver in their allegiance to the established ideal; the new foundations were in some conspicuous ways weaker than those of the earlier period. We shall have to consider the successful rivals to the old ideal in later sections; for the present we shall speak only of the weaknesses within the Benedictine Order. The weaknesses were of two kinds, social and spiritual, and we shall speak first of the spiritual malaise.

THE SPIRITUAL MALAISE

The elaborate, impersonal routine of the Benedictine life which had been developed since the ninth century was based, as we have seen, on a number of requirements: the requirement of continuous penitential activity for founders and benefactors; the requirement of unending battle against the enemies of the human race; the requirement of collaboration in the work of government and family stability. These needs were still intact in 1050: by 1100 they were disintegrating under the impact of those social and intellectual changes that have been described in an earlier chapter. This disintegration revealed an important gap in the Benedictine life as it had developed through the centuries: the individual had been forgotten in the search for perfection in an external routine. This at least is what monks themselves came increasingly to feel: they wanted a deeper personal religion and they were everywhere hindered by the heap of customary regulations that governed their lives. St Anselm worked hard at Bec and Canterbury to convince his monks by his example and precept that the interior fruits of religion could be enjoyed under the weight of monastic customs, even if they seemed useless:

> If a monk thinks he could achieve better and greater things, with more spiritual fervour than the customs of his present monastery allow, he should consider that he may be mistaken; or at least let him think that he doesn't deserve what he desires. Let him patiently bear the divine judgement, which doesn't deny anything unjustly to any man. By impatience he may exasperate the just judge and lose what he already has, or retain without advantage what he does not love.[23]

Appeals to perseverance in useless customs were very powerful when they were backed by the presence of an Anselm, but they must have seemed unconvincing to monks who lacked any stimulating presence in their midst. Certainly the weight of useless custom was not likely to be patiently borne within the monasteries when in the outside world a succession of vigorous popes were proclaiming the need to cast off long-established customs in the name of Christ, who did not say 'I am Custom' but 'I am Truth'. The confrontation of custom by truth, which supported the claims of papal authority, was also a main source of religious disillusionment within the Benedictine Order.

THE ECONOMIC MALAISE

This disillusionment had also a social and economic basis. The great Benedictine houses of the past had been set among large possessions which could be managed from a single centre. The large responsibilities which these possessions brought were a natural part of the monastic duty. But the feudal baronage, which was responsible for most of the later foundations, could confer neither the responsibilities nor the wealth of earlier benefactors. Instead of wide tracts of country, they could give only clippings from the estates that supported their families and their vassals. In addition they could give tithes and churches, which were necessarily scattered among their

23. Ep. 37 (F. S. Schmitt, *Opera S. Anselmi*, 1938–61, iii, 146; *P.L.* 158, 1097).

own possessions. Monastic properties had now to be fitted into the interstices of secular properties. A good example of the new type of endowment can be seen in the foundation of the priory at S. Mont in Gascony.[24] It was given by its founder the profits of forty-seven churches, one hamlet, seven manors, four small parcels of land, one vineyard, six arable lots, one wood, one stretch of fishing rights, and various small rents and tolls. There were hundreds of foundations like this in the century from 1050 to 1150. Some were larger, many were smaller; the properties of some were many miles apart, others were relatively compact. But the variety of rights and the smallness of the units compared with those of the past were a constant feature of the time.

The ill-effects of this type of endowment were mainly seen in the dispersal of monastic effort. Widely scattered properties called for constant attention to petty details of administration. Worse still, they could best be managed by sending monks out to live on the properties in small communities of two or three. This caused a loosening of the monastic bonds, a relaxing of the monastic routine, and a general tendency to sink into the countryside. These arrangements were very tenacious. The fragmented endowments of the eleventh and twelfth centuries lay on the countryside like a powder which could not easily be brushed off. They were too closely intertwined with secular properties, and too well protected by canon law, to be damaged without upsetting the whole social order. They were not subject to the same kind of erosion that steadily ate away the great properties of the earlier period; hence they could only be destroyed by a great political cataclysm. The foundations of this last phase of Benedictine expansion were consequently very tough; but they lacked the mental and spiritual energy of the past.

THE SYMPTOMS OF DECLINE

After the middle of the twelfth century the symptoms of decline are everywhere apparent – most obviously in the

24. See G. de Valous, *Le Temporel et la situation financière des établissements de l'ordre de Cluny du xii⁴ au xiv⁴ siècle*, 1935, p. 7.

general decline in numbers. Yet we must be cautious in interpreting these symptoms. The problems of a great Benedictine monastery were not unlike those of an army: there was always a tendency for the number of 'effectives' to decline, and for the administrative tail, and the roll of those who were sick or on special duties, to grow. At Christ Church, Canterbury, for instance, which had reached its maximum strength of about one hundred and twenty monks by 1120, the number of active monks was down to sixty-four by 1207, with a further thirteen sick. The great officers of the monastery – the sacrist, cellarer, chamberlain, and treasurer – were fully occupied in the supervision of an army of servants and tradesmen, who easily out-numbered the monks. But this accumulation of 'non-effective' man-power is less a sign of monastic decay than an indication of the growing complexity of life.[25]

The number of Benedictine monks fell everywhere, but with varying severity. In Germany, where the proportion of great old monasteries was high, it was worst; in France, where the old monasteries had received many supplementary endowments in the eleventh century, it was less severe; in England, where the monastic revival came late, the decline was least marked. There is no evidence that numbers declined because of any lack of potential recruits. The cause of decline lay rather in falling revenues combined with an attempt to keep up the state and splendour of former days. Contemporaries noticed the disease, but they failed to detect its cause; they supposed that it was due to some new form of wickedness.

In Germany, for instance, there was a deplorable spectacle. In the great monastery of Fulda there had been two hundred monks in the ninth and tenth centuries: there were only twenty or thirty in the thirteenth and fourteenth. At both St Gallen and Reichenau there had been a hundred monks: they declined to ten or less. The revenues would not support more. Since the abbot had to support the

25. For these figures, see *Epistolae Cantuarienses*, *R.S.*, p. xxxii; D. Knowles, *The Monastic Order in England*, 1940, p. 714; R. W. Southern, *St Anselm and his Biographer*, 1963, pp. 255–60.

dignity of the house, he consumed the greater part of the annual income himself: at St Gallen in 1275 he took nine hundred marks out of a total revenue of one thousand and forty-two; and at Reichenau he took two hundred marks out of two hundred and seventy-nine.[26] The remainder could support only a handful of monks, and they could not maintain a full monastic routine. Probably they did not even try. Pope Benedict XII was roused to indignation.

We have heard [he wrote] that formerly there were sixty or seventy monks at Reichenau. But in the course of time, a long-standing evil custom whereby none are received as monks unless they are of noble birth on both sides of their family has brought it about that there are now scarcely eight or ten members in the monastery. Further, because of the power of their relatives, these monks cannot be restrained from unlawful acts nor can they be compelled to observe the rules of the Order. Hence the divine offices are neglected.[27]

In a sense the pope was right. The social exclusiveness of the monasteries became more apparent as their resources contracted. But it was not the cause of the contraction. Monasteries did not become smaller because they became more aristocratic: they became more exclusive because reduced resources made them small. Doubtless they could have lowered their standards of living and raised their numbers, but this was both socially and mentally an impossible feat for institutions that had become set in their ways. The children of the nobility had always formed a high proportion of the monastic population, and the nobility were not easily thwarted in their endless search for a noble and dignified life for their landless children. Abbots were harassed by the demands of their great neighbours. As early as the mid-thirteenth century the

26. For these figures see U. Berlière, 'Le nombre des moines dans les anciens monastères', *Revue Bénédictine*, 1929, xli, 231–61; 1930, xlii, 31–42; also A. Schulte, *Über freiherrliche Klöster in Baden*, 1896. There are also many interesting details of numerical decline in U. Berlière, 'Le recruitement des moines bénédictins aux xiie et xiiie siècles', *Acad. royale de Belgique, Mémoires*, 2nd ser., ii, 1924, where however the author gives too much weight to aristocratic exclusiveness as a *cause* of decline.

27. Letter of 12 Sept. 1339, quoted by Schulte, op. cit.

abbot of Pontlevoy was so overcome by the contradictory pressures of declining revenue and increasing demands for admission that he took a solemn oath to admit no new recruits until the size of the community had dropped to thirty. This caused such an uproar that the pope had to be called in to dispense him from his oath.[28] Sometimes hard-pressed abbots resorted to a device for spreading the responsibility for admission by allowing each monk the right of introducing a novice in strict rotation. These symptoms of distress all helped to show that, whatever else may have gone wrong with the Benedictine ideal, it retained the stamp of quality which was greatly prized in an aristocratic society.

ATTEMPTED REFORM

Many popes and monastic reformers were aware that something was wrong, but they could neither find the cause nor devise a cure. Innocent III made a notable attempt to give the Benedictine houses a greater sense of corporate responsibility and supervision by requiring the monasteries in each kingdom or province to hold triennial parliaments or 'chapters'.[29] The order was widely ignored, and in England where it was enforced the difficulties of any deep-seated change were soon made clear. In 1277 the English Benedictine chapter made a bold attempt at modernization. New statutes were drawn up which made provision for shortening the divine office, encouraging study, and sending monks to the university. They did some good, but they were not liked. There were protests from all sides. Archbishop Peckham forbade the proposed reforms 'as being against God and in contempt of the approved customs and statutes of our Fathers'. As a Franciscan he may also have feared that his own Order would suffer from reforms which had the avowed intention of attracting 'men of outstanding dignity, education, and religion' back to the Benedictines.

28. *Les Registres d'Alexandre IV*, ed. C. Bourel de la Roncière, 1895 etc., 53, i, no. 1211 (4 Feb. 1256). The abbey was in the diocese of Chartres (Dept. Loir-et-Cher).

29. *Concilium Lateranense IV*, c. 12.

Godfrey Giffard, the secular bishop of Worcester, forbade his monks to observe the new decrees because 'novelties breed discord, and we are determined that the customs and ancient uses of our fathers shall be preserved'. The laity saw the shortening of the divine office as a sign of the laziness and ingratitude of the monks; and the monks themselves doubted the wisdom of a change which might drive away benefactors.[30]

It often happens with ancient institutions that the incrustations of time, however much they may be deplored, come to be valued as the most distinctive feature of the institution. The reformer who seeks to remove the scars of time might just as well, in most people's eyes, go further and destroy the institution altogether. This is what had happened to the Benedictine Order by the end of the thirteenth century. If it was accepted as part of the established order, its historic splendour could give a deep satisfaction to onlookers and participants alike. If it was treated as a problem, it was an insoluble one. In the great days of growth, monasteries had cheerfully accepted burdens of property and social position, which had become an almost full-time occupation. They ruled men, collected rents, maintained buildings, provided hospitality for the great, and kept up a ponderous dignity in all the affairs of life and death. No one looked to them for new ideas or new forms of spiritual life: they looked to them for stability, pageantry, involvement in the aristocratic life of the upper classes, and a visible display of continuous religious and family history. These were scarcely the purposes for which they had been founded; much less were they the purposes for which the Rule had been written; but in the end it had to be this or nothing.

THE VIRTUES OF THE OLD ORDER

The Benedictine pattern of life in the later Middle Ages can be vividly illustrated from a detailed survey of Mont

30. The documents of the attempted reform and the reactions to it are printed in W. A. Pantin, *Chapters of the English Black Monks*, i, pp. 60–121; iii, 274–5 (Camden, 3rd ser., xlv, xlvii, liv, 1931, 1933, 1937).

St Michel in 1338.[31] Here the main community consisted of about forty monks, but another fifty monks were housed in twenty-two priories scattered throughout Normandy, Brittany, and Anjou, and as far afield as Cornwall. There were generally two monks in each of these priories; they looked after the estates on which they lived, consumed the bulk of the produce themselves, and remitted the surplus as a money payment annually to the mother house. Economically it was an efficient system: it made about £7,000 a year available for the forty monks in the great monastery at Mont St Michel, while the fifty monks scattered among the estates supported themselves on a total income of only £2,000. These figures, which I have distilled from a very detailed account, show the financial strength of a community drawing its income from many different sources.

Accounts can tell us very little about the quality of life which they are designed to protect. They can only tell us that scattered monks, who can have been little more than celibate country gentry, were relatively cheap. The monks in the great house, living in splendour and ceremony with much hospitality and administration on their hands, were correspondingly expensive. They spent nearly £1,700 a year on food for the community and its many retainers; £2,200 on wine; £500 on clothing for the monks and their servants; £460 on repairs; £500 on taxes; £300 on law-suits; £120 on fuel; £140 on their vineyards; £200 on food for the poor on Shrove Tuesday; £160 on horses and carriages; £120 on lighting; £8 15s. on the bishop.

Behind this façade it is difficult to go; but it is clear that this great monastery and others like it satisfied multiple needs very different from those of the eighth, ninth, and tenth centuries. They were no longer important as centres

31. The following details are taken from a survey of monastic property made as a result of Benedict XII's attempted reorganization of the Benedictine Order following his Bull *Summa Magistri* (*Magnum Bullarium Romanum*, 1727, 218–37). The account of Mont St. Michel is the fullest that has survived. It is printed by L. Delisle in *Notices et Extraits des MSS de la Bibliothèque Nationale*, xxxii, 359–408.

of order in an untamed countryside; they were no longer essential to the well-being of kingdoms or families, or to their expectations of salvation; but they provided a life of busy social importance and activity for able monks. They had books for the studious, and a permanent background of liturgy and worship for those members of the community who were not too able or too busy with other duties to attend the divine office.

Mont St Michel provides an illustration of the social strength of the great Benedictine monasteries in the later Middle Ages. For an illustration of their personal strength we may turn to the brief monastic biographies which were compiled at Christ Church, Canterbury, by an eager antiquary who was a monk of the house from 1418 to about 1480. In 1418, the year in which he made his own profession, he recorded the death of one William Chart, who had been a monk for nearly fifty years. This is what he says:

William Chart died on Monday 17 October 1418 after mattins in the forty-eighth year of his monastic profession. He was buried in the infirmary chapel by the altar of St Leonard and St Benedict. For many years he had been a man of note in the monastery, having been treasurer, penitentiary, twice cellarer, twice almoner, warden of the college at Oxford while it was being built, coroner, sub-prior for thirteen years, and finally granger. Then, broken down by age and infirmity, he gave up all external cares and took a room in the infirmary of St John where he remained bedridden till the end of his life.[32]

This is a career bathed in the late sunshine of the medieval Benedictine life: a monk sent to the university by his monastery, a Bachelor of Canon Law, Head of his Oxford College, an embryonic Justice of the Peace, an active landlord, bursar, confessor, administrator. The life of the community recorded by our antiquary was one of rich ceremonies, frequent visits of royalty and magnates, close attention to liturgical forms, and a mild comfort spread throughout the whole body. He tells us much of processions and antiphons, of the colours of copes, of the order for

32. *Christ Church, Canterbury: Chronicle of J. Stone*, ed. W. G. Searle (Cambridge Antiquarian Society, xxxiv), 1903, p. 9.

funerals and the reception of the great. At the time when this record was made it was all in its last ripeness, but it has the appearance of eternity. Long after the Benedictine Order had ceased to lead western Europe in its religious life, such men as William Chart continued to make an unobtrusive contribution to the religion and government of the countryside.

The great Benedictine monasteries were the main harbourage of such men in the Middle Ages. Later strangely enough it was in England , where the monasteries were all dissolved, that the type survived most vigorously in the clerical society of the cathedral close and the rural parish. We may pass over five centuries from the death of William Chart in 1418 to the death of Canon William Greenwell in 1918, and find the type still strong. He had been the parson of a parish and a canon of Durham for over fifty years; he had been Principal of a University Hall, librarian of the cathedral, Justice of the Peace, Fellow of the Royal Society; he had edited two important volumes of medieval documents; he had discovered in a secondhand bookshop some precious leaves of a manuscript of the age of Bede; he had invented two highly successful flies for catching trout; he had collected seals, and excavated prehistoric barrows. He died in his ninety-eighth year, and perhaps the type died with him.[33] It could flourish only in a society of stable wealth and aristocratic leisure. Far though it was from the original intention of the Rule, this humane and tolerant tradition represented the most lasting contribution of the Benedictine Order to the world.

II. THE NEW ORDERS

The collapse of the Benedictine monopoly in the late eleventh century coincided with the beginning of the period of rapid expansion in western society. It was an inevitable result of the new diversity of life and opportunity

33. See the account of his life in *Archeologia Aeliana*, 1918, 3rd series, vol. xv.

which this expansion made possible. For the first time for several centuries there was room for many different kinds of organized life in a single area; and this was true of religion, no less than other forms of enterprise. The proof is to be found in the new religious Orders which rose to prominence in the half-century between 1075 and 1125. Among these Orders, the two which had the greatest success emphasized two different sides of the Benedictine tradition. These were the Orders of Augustinian canons and Cistercian monks. In a social sense they occupied the right and the left wings of the Benedictine position, and they succeeded because they developed in opposite directions and fitted into the pattern of an expanding society at two quite different levels.

The Augustinian canons

In one way the Augustinian canons presented a greater challenge to Benedictine monasticism than the Cistercians. The Cistercians after all were themselves Benedictines, though they attacked the existing followers of the Rule as backsliders. But the Augustinians made a formal break with the past. Their patron was neither St Benedict nor any other of the traditional guides to the monastic life. Augustine was the greatest name in western theology, a central figure in the growing controversies of the scholastic age, but he had not previously been accounted a monastic leader. He belonged to an earlier and deeper level of religious inquiry than St Benedict, and to an environment vastly more sophisticated than that of the early Middle Ages. While the Cistercians sought to revive the primitive Rule of St Benedict, which his followers were alleged to have abandoned, the Augustinians sought to revive something that went behind the Rule, behind even the organized church – back to the Bible.

THE ORIGINAL IMPULSE

What they sought was at first not very clear to them, but they found in a letter of St Augustine a frame of life within which they could unite. It was a letter of spiritual advice to some religious women about the daily problems of living together. The advice was sensible but (in comparison with the Rule of St Benedict) extremely general: they were to have all things in common, to pray together at appointed times, to dress without distinction, and to obey a superior.[34] As a 'Rule' its great beauty was that it left so much to the imagination, and it could be developed in various ways by the communities which adopted it. Until about the middle of the eleventh century nobody seems to have thought of it as a 'Rule' at all, but its flexibility soon caused it to be adopted by many groups of clergy and laity on the fringes of organized religious life. It gave a pattern of life to a large variety of vocations.

The proliferation of such informal groups was one of the earliest symptoms of the expansion of western society, and already by the early twelfth century two main tendencies could be seen among these new followers of St Augustine. There was a 'severe' school of thought which insisted on rules of abstinence, silence, manual labour, and psalmody; and there was a 'broad' school which allowed the use of meat, denied the necessity of manual labour, and was content to rest its rule on the requirement that all things should be held in common.[35] The outstanding representative of the 'severe' school was the monastery at Prémontré with its dependent houses; the main representative of the 'broad' school was St Ruf near Avignon with *its* cluster of daughter-houses. But these were only major constellations in a firmament of lesser stars. During the half-century from 1075 to 1125 new communities following the Rule of St Augustine appeared all over western Europe – they are impossible to count with any exactness because their early records are very defective – and they exhibited every kind of mixture of customs. Most of these groups were small and unnoticed

34. Ep. 211 (*P.L.* 33, 958–68).

35. For the various adaptations of St Augustine's letter which formed the basis of the Rule, see D. de Bruyne, *Revue Bénédictine*, 1930, xlii, 316–30; C. Dereine, 'Enquête sur la règle de S. Augustin', *Scriptorium*, 1948, ii, 28–36; and 'Les coutumiers de S. Quentin de Beauvais et de Springiersbach', *Rev. d'hist. eccl.*, 1948, xliii, 411–12.

at first, and their spontaneity, variety, and freedom of movement stand in striking contrast to the stability of the older monasteries.

The dearth of information about their early days is itself a significant fact. Benedictine houses could scarcely begin to exist without a substantial endowment, and their earliest days can commonly be traced in imposing charters and acts of foundation. But the early communities of Augustinian canons came into existence without any formal act of foundation. The purpose for which, and the rule by which, they first lived had often been forgotten even by the men of the next generation. To us they must remain extremely shadowy, but there are occasional shafts of light.

One of the best examples of a pioneering community living under the Rule of St Augustine is to be found in the South of France near Avignon. Here the Augustinian abbey of St Ruf had become very famous by the end of the eleventh century. Its early days are hidden in obscurity, but unlike many early Augustinian houses, it had a foundation charter of a sort. This document records that in 1039 the bishop of Avignon gave a church on the outskirts of the town to four clerks 'so that they could live there in a religious way (*religiose*)'; it then specifies in great detail the tithes, offerings, vineyards, woods, and the little bits of land that went with the church.[36] Unluckily it tells us little about the purpose of the foundation. Was it a rescue operation to repair a derelict church and restore it to parochial use? Had the four clerks any charitable or pastoral aims, or did they simply wish to live together in contemplation and religious exercises? We don't know. It was not till sixty years later that no less a person than Pope Urban II came forward with a general theory of what had happened. Although Urban's words are only a preamble to a charter, they place the Augustinian movement in the context of the universal history of the church.

According to Urban the primitive church had had two

36. U. Chevalier, *Codex Diplomaticus Ordinis S. Rufi Valentiae*, 1891, pp. 1–3.

forms of religious life: monastic and canonical. In the monastic life men abandoned earthly things and gave themselves up to contemplation. In the canonical life, they made use of earthly things, and redeemed with tears and almsgiving the daily sins inseparable from the world. The monks therefore played the part of Mary, the canons that of Martha in the church. The rôle of the canons was the humbler of the two, but not less necessary. Nevertheless, in the course of time, the monastic life had prospered, but (said Urban) the canonical life had almost disappeared until it was revived by the canons of St Ruf. In Urban's view, therefore, the canons had revived a neglected primitive tradition of the church – a tradition in which practical service had a dominant place – and had restored a balance which the overwhelming success of Benedictine monasticism in the preceding centuries had destroyed.[37]

Coming from a pope who was himself a Benedictine monk this is a significant statement. It helps to give a perspective to the Augustinian movement. If Urban is right, the basic contrast between the followers of St Augustine and those of St Benedict lay in the extent to which the new canons sought in some humble way to repair the ruins of the world. The Benedictines had indeed brought order into whole countrysides on a grand scale, but primarily they sought to imitate a supernatural order in the midst of flux. The canons by contrast picked up the broken pieces in an already settled world. They rebuilt ruined churches; they restored religious life in broken-down or half-formed communities; they provided a framework of life for diffused religious impulses; they gathered together large quantities of misappropriated ecclesiastical tithes and applied them to religious purposes, for the relief of the poor, the sick, the infirm, and for the endowment of a modest religious life. In all these ways they gave a new turn to the tradition of organized religion, and the large number of popes, bishops, and teachers in the twelfth century who belonged to the Augustinian Order testifies to their success as practical men.

37. ibid., pp. 8–9.

THE IMPULSE OF BENEFACTORS

Yet if the random efforts of two generations of seekers for a new form of religious life in the eleventh century gradually settled into the channel briefly described by Urban II, a secondary impulse soon made itself felt. This impulse was provided by benefactors who saw in the communities of Augustinian canons a type of foundation within their means, and a religious ideal within their understanding. The social upheavals of the eleventh century had brought into secure positions in the feudal structure many new families, of modest means but with the instincts of great landlords. Like their betters they wanted that symbol of territorial stability – a religious house where they would be honoured as founders and patrons, and buried with decency in the midst of their family.

Here in Oxford there was a good specimen of the species in Robert d'Oilly, who was sheriff of the county in 1129. He was a magnate of moderate means with an income of about £100 a year from his scattered estates around Oxford. His family had been settled in England for two generations, and the time had come to consolidate their position by the foundation of a religious house. Robert d'Oilly could not afford very much, but by relinquishing one of his smallest estates (worth about £4 a year) and adding to it some of his Oxford house-property (about another £1 a year), a few small pieces of agricultural land, and – most important – the six churches on his estates and the tithes of his mills, he managed to scrape together enough to produce an income of about £20 a year – enough to support a small Augustinian community, which he settled on the outskirts of Oxford at Oseney, within easy reach of his castle.[38] The greater part of its income came from churches, which after repeated ecclesiastical censures were no longer acceptable property for a layman. So the total loss to the d'Oilly

38. For the endowment of Oseney Abbey, see *Cartulary of Oseney Abbey*, ed. H. E. Salter, 1929, vol. i (Oxford Historical Society, vol. 89); and for the property of the d'Oilly family in Oxfordshire in 1086, *Domesday Book*, f. 158.

family was much less than the total endowment of their religious house. In a competitive age this was an important consideration.

The result of these efforts was a modest religious foundation. The endowment would scarcely have supported a community following the Rule of St Benedict with the ponderous magnificence that Cluny had helped to make inseparable from the perfect observance of the Rule. But the new 'Rule' of St Augustine provided a basis for a humbler and yet respectable way of life. An income of about £3 a year seems to have been reckoned sufficient for an Augustinian canon, whereas a Benedictine monk would be poorly endowed with less than three times that amount. This was no doubt a powerful consideration for benefactors who wished their modest means to go as far as possible, and the new foundation quickly attracted many small donations from the minor aristocracy and townspeople of Oxford. By 1150 Oseney Abbey had tiny fragments of land and churches in a hundred and twenty places in Oxfordshire and the neighbouring counties. A hundred years later this once small community in the suburbs of a prosperous town was able to carry on a large banking business by taking money on deposit and investing in property. While greater monasteries declined, it continued to benefit from the growing economy. By the time of the Reformation, with an income of £654 and a community of twenty-one canons, it had become a place of great wealth and ease.[39]

The same story was repeated with local variations in scores of places throughout England. In Cambridge there was a sheriff, Picot by name, in a position very similar to that of Robert d'Oilly at Oxford. By helping himself after the Conquest to the estates of the free tenants of the ancient abbey of Ely he had amassed a sizeable property, and during his wife's illness about 1092 he vowed to build a church in honour of St Giles. The endowment consisted entirely of churches and tithes, and the community was at first very small.[40] But here also the unpretentious house attracted many small gifts and benefactions. In 1275 the income of the community was assessed and probably under-estimated at £233, on which thirty canons were supported. The secret of their success was the modesty of their needs, their proximity to a flourishing town, and the services they performed for benefactors who were by no means rich by the standards of ancient feudal greatness. Living under a modest Rule the canons performed modest services for men of moderate means and moderate needs:

The rule of the canons regular is the Rule of St Augustine, who drew his brethren to live together and tempered the rigour of his rule to their infirmity. Like a kind master, he did not drive his disciples with a rod of iron, but invited those who love the beauty of holiness to the door of salvation under a moderate rule.[41]

So spoke one of the canons of Cambridge. Here and else-where they had their reward in a sustained period of growth which reached its peak during the half century after 1150 when the growth of the Benedictine Order had almost ceased. The number of Augustinian canons showed no serious decline until the Black Death, and even after this calamity they showed a remarkable power of recovery. With one exception to be discussed later, the followers of St Augustine lived without great upheavals because they stood outside the great movements of history. They watched their rivals rise and fall; and even when the friars came to capture the affections of the citizens of Cambridge, the canons registered only the mild protest of men deprived of their legitimate fringe benefits.:

The friars [they said] with honeyed words have procured for themselves the burials, legacies, and alms of rich citizens, which before their arrival had benefited our community.[42]

40. For the early history of this foundation, see *Liber Memorandorum Ecclesie de Bernewelle*, ed. J. W. Clark, 1907, pp. 38–46.
41. *The Observances in Use at the Augustinian Priory at Barnwell, Cambridge-shire*, ed. J. W. Clark, 1897, p. 34.
42. *Liber Memorandorum*, p. 70.

This was language that everyone could understand, and no one could greatly blame. So they lived in peace.

THE SOCIAL AMBIENCE

The Augustinian canons indeed, as a whole, lacked every mark of greatness. They were neither very rich, nor very learned, nor very religious, nor very influential: but as a phenomenon they are very important. They filled a very big gap in the biological sequence of medieval religious bodies. Like the ragwort which adheres so tenaciously to the stone walls of Oxford, or the sparrows of the English towns, they were not a handsome species. They needed the proximity of human habitation and they throve on the contact which repelled more delicate organisms. They throve equally in the near-neighbourhood of a town or a castle. For the well-to-do townsfolk they could provide the amenity of burial-places, memorials and masses for the dead, and schools and confessors of superior standing for the living. For the lords of castles they could provide a staff for the chapel and clerks for the needs of administration. They were ubiquitously useful. They could live on comparatively little, yet expand into affluence without disgrace. Consequently there were many who were willing to contribute their crumbs. In return they satisfied many modest requirements. For the moderate landowner they provided a religious house where he was received as lord and patron. For the smaller benefactor they provided a place of burial and masses for his soul. They ran many small schools, many hospitals and places of retirement for the sick and aged, for pregnant women, for the blind, for lepers. In an increasingly busy and practical age they appeared to give more than the Benedictine monks. As Pope Paschal II – following the same line of thought as his predecessor Urban II – wrote to the canons of St Botolph's, Colchester, in 1116:

> The dispensation of the Word of God, the offices of preaching, baptising, and reconciling penitents have always been a function of your order.[43]

43. W. Dugdale, *Monasticon Anglicanum*, 1830, vi, 106–7.

Modesty and service were two qualities which appealed to practical men in this period of rapid growth, and the Augustinian canons promised both:

> Their habit is neither splendid nor abject, so they avoid both pride and the affectation of holiness. They do not need a great variety of gear, and they are content with a moderate expenditure.[44]

Or again:

> The monk renders an account only for his own soul: the canons for the souls of others as well.[45]

If we take an extensive view of the communities living under the Rule of St Augustine, it must be judged the most prolific of all medieval religious Rules. The number of communities in the thirteenth century which acknowledged this Rule as their guide is beyond any certain calculation, but it would run to many thousands. To mention only one variety of community – the least well-known and most ephemeral of all – the Trinitarians. It was reported about 1240 that there were 600 houses of this branch of the Augustinian Order in France, Lombardy, and Spain.[46] These were tiny communities each with three clerks, three laymen, and a superior. Their purpose was to relieve the poor and to redeem prisoners captured by the Muslims. Most of them disappeared when the crusading movement petered out, but their existence illustrates another merit of the flexible Augustinian Rule, which is not often appreciated: small communities could die out when the enthusiasm grew cold; they did not leave the church with the problem of a massive territorial structure enclosing the corpse of a once lively piety.

The ends for which the Rule was devised, and for which

44. These phrases, which sum up a widely expressed view, are taken from an account of the foundation of Lanthony Abbey in W. Dugdale, op. cit. vi, 128–34. Cf. Giraldus Cambrensis, *Opera Omnia, R.S.*, iv, 24, 244; vi, 39.

45. R. Foreville and J. Leclercq, 'Un débat sur le sacerdoce des moines au XIIᵉ siècle', *Studia Anselmiana*, xli, 1957, 117–18.

46. *Chron. Alberici Monachi Trium Fontium, M.G.H. Scriptores*, xxiii, 875.

it was praised by Urban II and Paschal II, were better displayed in the branches than in the main body of the Augustinian Order. The main body consisted of quiet communities scattered everywhere throughout Europe, bringing a widely diffused but wan ray of light into the local religious scene. It was left to the branches to maintain the concern for the infirmities of the world which Urban II had singled out as the great work of the regular canons, and to develop the practice of preaching and reconciliation which Paschal II had recommended to the canons of Colchester. Among these branches the organization founded by St Dominic finally broke out from the limitations of the past, and achieved the universal character and distinction that persistently eluded the great majority of those who followed the Rule of St Augustine. But before we turn to the Dominicans, something must be said about the other great organization which destroyed the monopoly of traditional Benedictinism in the early twelfth century – Cîteaux.

The Cistercians

The Cistercian Order came into existence only a few years later than the Augustinian canons, and the two Orders rose to the height of popularity at exactly the same time. Nevertheless they satisfied very different needs. It is one of the signs of the many-sided growth of European society in the twelfth century that it found room for two such different and prolific growths at the same time.

The ideas behind the two Orders were entirely different; the economic resources which they tapped could scarcely have been more dissimilar; their attitudes to the contemporary world were wholly opposed. The Augustinian canons aimed in various ways at serving the society around them; the Cistercians fled from it. The canons became identified with their environment; the Cistercians dominated their surroundings. While the canons made their way forward by the modesty of their demands and the mildness of their rule, the Cistercians brought a strident and aggressive temper into their dealings with the outside world and took special pleasure in the rigour and singularity of their interior discipline. The canons did best in the neighbourhood of a castle or a town, or preferably both; the Cistercians flourished best on the frontiers of settlement. The canons eschewed elaborate buildings and ornaments because they were generally too poor for ostentation; the Cistercians turned from these things from choice and made simplicity a principle of their existence. The Cistercians thought themselves the only true followers of the Benedictine Rule, and in the name of the Rule set themselves against the traditions and customs of the Benedictine Order; the Augustinian canons found an alternative to the Rule of St Benedict, but they had no quarrel with Benedictine customs and were content to follow them at a distance.

Yet the two new Orders shared one quality which was characteristic of their time: they sought in antiquity the justification for their actions. The canons indeed went further in this respect than the Cistercians. St Augustine brought to their way of life an authority and antiquity greater even than that of St Benedict, and they claimed for the principles of their discipline an even higher authority and a greater antiquity than that of St Augustine. Their way of life (they said) came from the earliest days of the Christian community: it was described in the fourth chapter of the Acts of the Apostles and it had been sanctioned in the second century by Pope Urban I. Technically the Cistercians could not claim as much as this. They wished only to restore the Rule of St Benedict to its original simplicity. But this Rule (they claimed) was nothing other than the pure Gospel of Christ:

Whatever St Benedict ordained was altogether established by the Providence of the Holy Spirit, so that nothing can be imagined that is more profitable, more holy, or more blessed. Indeed the Rule of St Benedict is an exposition of the whole Gospel, not allegorically but in terms of simple experience and visible works.[47]

On this common ground the two Orders met as rival claimants to evangelical truth – the Cistercians claiming

47. *Memorials of Fountains Abbey*, ed. J. R. Walbran (*Surtees Soc.* 42) 1863, i, 15.

'the whole Gospel' as their way, the canons the early apostolic church. The difference between these two primitive ideals may not seem very great but in fact it is quite fundamental, and it became a major distinguishing feature in later medieval thought about the religious life. The 'whole Gospel' meant following Christ in poverty and stark simplicity of life: *pauperes pauperem Christum sequentes*. This was not yet quite the 'imitation of Christ' as it later came to be conceived, but it was a step in this direction. The emphasis of the 'apostolic life' was different. It meant activity within the world, and acceptance of whatever was necessary for this activity of preaching, teaching, converting, healing, and serving. Of course the two strands were never wholly separated. Every new Order and every plan for Christian living contained some elements of both. But every new plan tended to go in one direction or the other: to concentrate *either* on evangelical imitation *or* apostolic usefulness. The Cistercian emphasis was on the imitation of Christ through the Rule of St Benedict, and in this emphasis the Franciscans were their spiritual heirs. The Augustinian emphasis was on the apostolic life, and the Dominicans were their heirs. These later developments will be the subject of the next section of this chapter; meanwhile we have some immediate problems on our hands.

The first problem is this. The Cistercian ideal demands complete self-abnegation, poverty, simplicity, retirement, purity, and refinement of the spiritual life. But the historic rôle of the Order and its reputation among uncommitted contemporary observers suggest aggression, arrogance, military (or at least militant) discipline, outstanding managerial qualities, and cupidity. How is this contrast to be explained?

No doubt to some extent the contrast can be explained by ill-will on the part of the observers and human frailty on the part of the Cistercians themselves. Any group which affects singularity in dress and customs, emphasizes its unique righteousness, and is free with its strictures on others, must expect to be charged with arrogance and the secret sharing of the very faults it denounces; and the charge will often be justified. But in the Cistercian case there is evidently more to it than this. There is a driving force in Cistercian expansion which seems to come neither from the ideal nor from the corruption of the ideal through human frailty. The earliest Cistercian rebels against Benedictine complacency saw themselves as a small élite unlikely to make much headway in the world. Yet almost before the words were out of their mouths, they were overtaken by a measure of success that at first sight seems to contradict all the laws of probability. Unlike the growth of the Augustinian canons which can now be recorded only in the most general outline, the growth of the Cistercian, is capable of a very exact portrayal as can be seen on the following page.

No impartial observer during the first twenty years of Cistercian history, when the number of foundations rose from one to seven, could have predicted a rate of growth which in little over fifty years raised the total number to more than three hundred. Everything seemed to be against any large expansion. In the first place, a Cistercian foundation needed much land, and land was becoming scarce. Then, the most obvious sources of revenue for new religious houses were tithes, rents, services, and the profits of churches and altars. It was to these that the Augustinian canons owed their rise; but the Cistercians rejected them with comprehensive scorn. They would take only the plainest agricultural property, and accept only the fullest possession of it. Then again, they turned their face against those incentives to benefactions – confessions, masses, burials within the monastery – which made the canons so widely acceptable. Their statutes decreed that Cistercian monasteries were to be far removed from the towns, cities, and castles which were the growing points of society where the canons found their niche. The severity of their internal discipline, the discouragement of learning, the plainness of ritual, the absence of relics, were all calculated to discourage visitors and (it might be supposed) gifts of benefactors. The Cistercians seemed to run counter both to the established

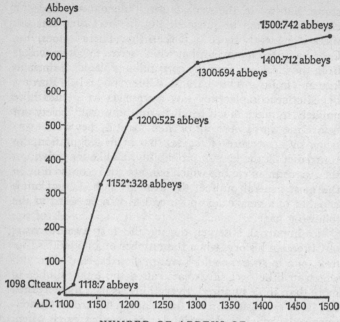

NUMBER OF ABBEYS OF
CISTERCIAN MONKS, 1098–1500

* In this year the Cistercian General Chapter forbade the foundation of new abbeys, but after a short interval the growth began again with one foundation in 1155 and 1156, five in 1158, one in 1159, fourteen in 1162, and so on with an average of about 4.5 a year till the end of the century. There is no doubt that the growth would have been much greater but for this prohibition, which transferred a large part of the potential Cistercian growth to the Premonstratensians, who (though belonging to the order of Augustinian canons) had adopted many of the characteristic features of the Cistercians.

habits of western Christendom and to its most recent intellectual and practical developments.

Nevertheless, all unknowingly, the early Cistercian statutes hit on the way that offered the best hope of economic success. It would have been quite impossible at this date for any new Order to compete with the older monasteries or the Augustinian canons in collecting an endowment of churches, tithes, rents, and services. These sources of endowment were not yet exhausted, but what was left was only a remnant. In rejecting these revenues, the Cistercians thought that they were renouncing the world; in fact they renounced only its shadow. Their principles forced them to go to the edge of the settled lands of Europe; but the most far-sighted economic prudence would have pointed in the same direction. In an expanding society this was where the future lay.

Economically therefore, contrary to all expectation, the Cistercians represented a move in the right direction. In itself however this would not have ensured success if other factors had not been present. These factors were of many different kinds, but they may be roughly classified as the effects of the organization and religious outlook of the Order on the one hand, and the needs and resources of benefactors on the other.

ORGANIZATION

The Cistercian organization was one of the masterpieces of medieval planning. In a world ruled by a complicated network of authorities often at variance with each other, the Cistercian plan presented a single strong chain of authority from top to bottom. There was a single supreme legislative body in the triennial General Chapter of all Cistercian abbots; a simple system of affiliation and visitation which embraced every house in the order; a uniformity of practice; a wide freedom from every local authority whether secular or ecclesiastical. The Cistercians achieved at one stroke the kind of organization that every ruler would wish to have: a system complete in itself, wholly autonomous, equipped with a thorough organization for internal supervision, isolated from external interference, untroubled by those sources of dispute about services and rights which choked the law courts of Europe. The Cistercian system was the first effective international organization in Europe, more effective even than the papal organization because it had narrower aims and a smaller field of operation.

In the economy of each monastery there was the same simple chain of authority that we find in the Order as a whole. By renouncing rents and services, by concentrating on compact estates worked by laymen under monastic discipline, the Cistercians cut through all the complexities of rights and tenures which beset the managers of great estates. Strong though the Order was at the top, it was even stronger at the bottom.

Apart from the simple strength of the organization, the earliest statutes of the Order had two other ingredients necessary for worldly success. The first was a certain military precision and aggressiveness in practical details. The men who were fighting for a new ideal of corporate religious life were not above regulating every detail of daily life – even the activities of their herds of swine:

> Pig-styes can be two or even three leagues from a grange, but pigs, though they can wander by day, must return to the styes at night. Swine-herds and shepherds must get their daily food from their abbey or grange.[48]

The control of the granges was as precisely regulated as the order of divine service:

> No abbot may put granges under the authority of anyone but the cellarer, who has the authority of the abbot.[49]

And the same controlling hand determined how monks and abbots, even the greatest, were to behave in even the smallest details:

> Any monk or *conversus* found in the monastery or granges of Cîteaux during a General Chapter shall be brought before the Chapter and beaten before the assembled abbots; and no one, not even the abbot of Cîteaux, may offer any excuse for him.[50]

Such clauses as these are surely very remarkable in an order which claimed to follow nothing but the pure Rule of St Benedict, and claimed that this Rule was itself nothing

---

48. *Statuta Ordinis Cisterciensis*, ed. J. M. Canivez, 1933, i, 12–32: *statutorum annorum praecedentium prima collectio, 1134*, c. 59.
49. ibid., c. 68.   50. ibid., c. 76.

but the pure Gospel in action. The clauses I have quoted were not later accretions to the Cistercian code: they all belong to the first generation of Cistercians, and they reflect very clearly one aspect of contemporary secular life – its military harshness. The first Cistercians spoke equally confidently with two voices. The first was the voice of the military aristocracy from which they sprang, and this voice is most clearly heard in their legislation. The second voice was the one which they used in the cloister – it was the voice of mutual friendship, of introspection and spiritual sweetness.

Here we have the typically puritan paradox of the Cistercians. They rose to eminence in the midst of the most crudely expansive period in medieval history and were the most articulate prophets of this expansion. 'The exposition of the whole Gospel in visible works' can never have been more deeply dyed in the spirit of the age. It was not an accident that the chief Crusading orders adopted the Cistercian rule, for there was a close affinity in their aims and methods. The Cistercians were essentially a frontier organization engaged in a work of colonization which was partly religious, partly military, and partly agrarian. No one – least of all the Cistercians themselves – knew where one type of colonization ended and the other began. They scarcely needed to know, for they all led to the growth of Christendom. They were the last generation of medieval men to believe that it was good for all men to be monks, or at least to belong in some degree to a monastic organization, if only as lay brethren participating in the work and rewards of monks.

This brings us to another source of strength in the Cistercian organization – the lay-brethren or *conversi*. Earlier monasteries had used lay helpers to relieve monks of the chores of daily life, but it was the Cistercians who first made these lay helpers the basis of their economy and gave them a strict rule of life.

The *conversi* were second-class monks – second class in the sense that they were illiterate and therefore unable to take a full part in the life of the community. Moreover they were required to remain illiterate and forbidden ever to aspire to a full monastic status. Yet they were monks in the sense that they followed a simplified monastic regime: they rose at the sound of a bell to listen to the later part of the monastic night-office; their food and clothing were similar to those of the monks; they were required to keep silent like monks and to pray at the times of the divine office, even though they could not be in church; they had their own chapter-houses where they met on Sundays, and they were required to communicate seven times a year. Like monks they had a year's noviciate and made a binding profession of life-long obedience at the end of this period of probation. This act of profession, in which the *conversus* put his hands between those of the abbot and promised to obey him, was a curious mixture of feudal and monastic ceremonial; it emphasized the binding obligations undertaken by the aspirant, but it did not give him the rights of a member of the community. It was a kind of monastic vassalage.[51]

These celibate monastic vassals were not simply a convenience for religious life. They were an essential part of the whole economic organization of the Order. Their existence made it possible for the Cistercians to organize large areas of undeveloped land, to reject the conveniences of rents and services, and to turn their backs on the world without giving up the ideal of a highly organized religious life. Their numbers varied from house to house, but they normally exceeded the number of monks, sometimes by as many as three or four to one. On them devolved the whole business of the monastic estates. So long as recruits to the lay-brotherhood could be obtained and the system was in full working order, it brought an immense economic strength to the Cistercians: a disciplined labour force which required no wages, had no families to support, and could not withdraw its labour, was the perfect recipe for

51. The best account of the status of the *conversi* is E. Hoffmann, *Das Konverseninstitut des Cisterzienserordens* (Freiburger Historische Studien, i), 1905. The ceremony of admission is described in the 'Usus conversorum', c. 13 (*Les monuments primitifs de la Règle Cistercienne*, ed. P. Guignard, 1878, p. 285).

agrarian efficiency, especially when it was concentrated in well-defined units.

We may ask why such large numbers of labourers should have been willing to serve in such unattractive conditions, and in answering this question it is first of all necessary to observe the chronology of dissatisfaction. To judge by the records of rebellion, it does not appear that the conditions of service caused much violent discontent until about 1190, but thereafter there is an average of about one revolt every two years until the end of the thirteenth century.[52] Thereafter the whole system fell into disuse. The great period of Cistercian expansion therefore coincided with the period in which the system of *conversi* was in full operation and aroused least discontent. It was the time of great movements of colonists into the undeveloped lands of western Europe and along its frontiers, when a sufficient surplus of labour existed to make a very harsh regime acceptable to a large number of people. The Cistercians were the religious beneficiaries of this state of affairs. They possessed the secret of utilizing and organizing this surplus labour, and in addition, virtually for the first time in the history of medieval western Christendom, they offered a full assurance of salvation to illiterate men.

RELIGION AND CAPITALISM

In determining the causes of the success of the Cistercians, we must also reckon with the side-effects of their religious outlook in promoting their worldly success. Their earliest statutes forbade all forms of adornment in buildings, liturgy, chant, manuscripts, food, and dress. This legislation was of course prompted by purely religious considerations, but in a time of economic expansion it had an unexpected consequence. The old Benedictine houses had encouraged expenditure up to the limit of available income. It was the glory of an abbot's or a prior's term of office to have added some costly object to the monastic scene – a new tower, an enlarged chancel, an improved water supply,

52. See J. S. Donnelly, *The Decline of the Cistercian Brotherhood*, 1949, pp. 72–80.

or at least some carpets, paintings, copes, or crucifixes. There was always some work on hand which had been held up by lack of money, and no more worthy object could be imagined than to complete what others had been obliged to abandon. This is the attitude of the great lord in a static society: his first duty to the world is to spend; and his greatest glory is to be able to spend lavishly. Such, in the higher sphere of divine service, had been the duty of the Benedictine monasteries.

The Cistercians put an end to all this. Forbidden to spend on embellishments for their churches and common life, they were often, at least in the twelfth century, faced with the problem of an unexpendable surplus. Almost of necessity they were driven to spend the surplus which they could not devote to present needs and adornments on the improvement and increase of their estates. They did this not from policy, but from the pressure of opportunity. They had no intention of leading the way in agrarian improvement. In 1182 the General Chapter forbade any abbey with a debt of over fifty marks to buy land or extend its buildings except for some urgent necessity.[53] This somewhat half-hearted and ambiguous prohibition was repeated at intervals. But an institution cannot long renounce its opportunities of growth. The improvements were prompted by instinct and continued because they had become a way of life.

This was probably the biggest single factor in giving the Cistercians the reputation for covetousness and greed which was very widespread at the end of the twelfth century. They offended against the unwritten law of aristocratic society that he to whom much is given must spend much, without hoping for any return except the greater glory of his name. These puritans of the monastic life incurred the penalty of puritanism; they became rich because they renounced the glory of riches, and powerful because they invested wisely. They were blamed for being rich and powerful by those who went out for glory and invested badly or not at

53. *Stat. Cist.*, i, 90–91 (1182, c. 9): there is considerable obscurity in the wording of the prohibition, and this obscurity grows deeper when the rule is amplified in 1188 (ibid., i, 109).

all. Such men naturally distrusted the religious motives of monks who rose on other men's losses.

THE BENEFACTORS

All these internal seeds of growth would have been sterile unless they could have found a suitable soil in which to lodge. The Cistercian Order would never have grown to a great place in medieval society if it had depended on the efforts of small groups of dissidents like those who in the early days had gone out from Molesme to found the abbey of Cîteaux or from St Mary's at York to found the abbey of Fountains. These were the pioneers, but great success depended on great benefactors with the right kind of property. The old Benedictine houses were already secure in the settled countryside, and the Augustinian canons were already filling the gaps which the older foundations had left. The Cistercians needed much land, but they did not need it where others were already established. They needed it on the edge of the wild, and they found it wherever the frontiers of cultivation were being pushed back.

On all these frontiers there were landlords with much unsettled or half-settled land on their hands. To these men the Cistercians presented themselves as an organization capable of bringing formidable advantages to their patrons: they provided the religious comforts of great and spacious communities; they were eminently suitable as organizers of large tracts of land of uncertain loyalty; and in the wilder parts of Europe their system of agrarian *conversi* was easily extended to accommodate a military element that could be used for aggression and defence.

It was on the frontiers of Christendom that the Cistercian expansion was most remarkable.[54] In Castile between 1132

54. There are good accounts of Cistercian expansion in the *Dictionnaire d'histoire et de géographie ecclésiastiques* (art. 'Cisterciens', and under individual houses). Some of the statistics in these articles require correction: see F. Vongrey and F. Hervay in *Analecta Cisterciensia*, 1966, xxii, 279–90; 1967, xxiii, 115–52. See also M. Willibrord Tijburg, 'Les Relations de S. Bernard avec l'Espagne', *Collectanea Ord. Cist. Reform.*, 1951, xiii, 273–83; 1953, xv, 174–89. For a chart of affiliations which shows the strength of the formal organization of the Order, see L. Janauschek, *Origines Cistercienses*, 1877.

and 1148 Alfonso VII founded thirteen great Cistercian houses, and his successor Alfonso VIII added six more between 1158 and 1214. In Portugal there were thirteen houses, including Alcobaça, the biggest monastery of the Order, all of royal foundation or with royal benefactions. The same story is repeated in Aragon, Hungary, Poland, Sweden, Austria, Wales, and on the Scottish border. In Bohemia King Ottokar II founded the Cistercian monastery of Goldenkron in honour of the Crown of Thorns which Louis IX had recently brought to France. The area was a wild and empty country on the politically sensitive frontier of Bohemia towards Austria, and the foundation charter of 1264 describes the monastic lands with the grand abandon of a Merovingian or Anglo-Saxon royal founder. Rivers and mountain ranges form the boundary marks, and the whole estate comprises a compact mass of land thirty miles across from east to west and from north to south: it is to be held 'in that full liberty and lordship which we and our predecessors have enjoyed, without any diminution'.[55] It was a great gesture of piety, and perhaps of calculation, for it ensured that the land would be filled with reliable developers of its resources. The development duly followed: the map of the area compiled from the medieval charters of the monastery shows seventy villages where there can have been very few when the monastery first began.

All these foundations for Cistercian monks were frontier monasteries in the most obvious sense; but even within the settled lands of Europe there were still plenty of areas of internal colonization, and it was to these especially that the Cistercians were drawn. Much of France, and more of Germany and England, was still very primitive and ripe (as we say) for development. Wherever there was a pocket of underdeveloped countryside the Cistercians, the great developers of the twelfth century, found their way. Of course in the long-run the great endowments of the Cistercians represented a corresponding loss to their lay bene-

55. The charters, with a map, are printed in M. Pangerl, *Urkundenbuch des ehemaligen Cisterzienserstiftes Goldenkron in Böhmen* (*Fontes rerum Austriacarum*, 2ᵉ Abt., xxxiii, 1872).

factors; but far-sightedness is the rarest of qualities, and the least useful. In the short run the Cistercians brought consolidation and order at relatively little cost to many a chaotic area of Europe.

The great benefactors on the frontiers were often very primitive and had not yet felt the subtle influences of twelfth-century sophistication. Their charters are reminiscent of the Benedictine charters of an earlier age:

I fear [writes a Spanish countess at the beginning of a Cistercian foundation charter] the pains of hell and I desire to come to the joys of paradise, and for the love of God and his glorious Mother, and for the salvation of my soul and those of my parents, I give to God, St Mary, and all the saints my whole inheritance in Retoria.[56]

There is something primitive in this bluntness, as also there is in the need to plant reliable settlers and organizers in empty and undeveloped lands. Just as the kings of the Franks and Anglo-Saxons had used Benedictine monasteries for this purpose in the early Middle Ages, so now the Cistercians were agents of government in the new lands of the twelfth century. Their benefactors could be sure of having foundations of great stability and corporate strength, capable of imposing an effective estate-management and a close supervision on a wide area of country. In some ways the new benefactors got less than the old founders of Benedictine houses. They could expect to have little influence in the choice of abbots, no rights during a vacancy, a limited power of placing relatives in the monastery, and fewer prayers and masses than the founders of the older monasteries had enjoyed. The Cistercian houses belonged less to the family and more to the countryside than the Benedictines. This was the price to be paid for their powers of organization.

These general conditions of growth affected all Cistercian

56. F. Anton, *Monasterios medievales de la Provincia de Valladolid*, 1942, p. 256. This work is largely architectural in content, but the Appendix contains a useful collection of documents which illustrate the primitive impulses of the donors and the very large areas of country available for their gifts.

monasteries, but each individual house reacted to the conditions in its own way. The only astonishing feature is the speed with which each house according to its opportunities followed a similar pattern of development. Even a foundation like that at Fountains, which could claim (if any house could) to have sprung from a pure religious impulse, can be seen within thirty years of its foundation vigorously applying the Cistercian formula for economic growth to its peculiar situation – consolidating its estates by buying intervening plots of land, making use of its accumulated capital to disinherit landowners in financial difficulties, paying for its new acquisitions by a mixture of spiritual benefits and ready money, founding new granges and organizing great areas of land under a single centralized direction. All these operations can be traced in abundant detail throughout the second half of the twelfth century in the excellent records of the monks of Fountains.[57]

Not every foundation succeeded equally well. Some succumbed to the difficulties of poor sites and insufficient endowment. But even in these cases the vigilance of the Cistercian organization could save a tottering house from extinction or bring its agony to a speedy end.[58] There was much less chance of material and disciplinary degradation than in the independent Benedictine foundations which had to battle against misfortune on their own. In failure the Cistercians proved their strength, and when they succeeded in their material struggle, their success was greater than ever before in monastic history. A brief account

57. An interesting example is the grange of Baldersby which belonged to Fountains in the thirteenth century . It comprised three earlier villages of Baldersby, Birkhow, and Easby, and there are over a hundred charters in the Fountains cartulary which record the stages by which the property was built up. See C. T. Clay, *Early Yorkshire Charters*, 1963, xi, 339–51; *Memorials of Fountains Abbey*, ed. J. R. Walbran (Surtees Soc. 42), 1863, i, 90–112. For a similar process at Markingfield, see *E.Y.C.*, xi, 180–86, and for the whole subject R. A. Donkin, 'The Cistercian Grange in England in the xii and xiii centuries', *Studia Monastica*, 1964, vi, 95–144.

58. See the prompt and efficient measures taken by the Cistercian visitors to deal with the failing monastery at Sawley, a house founded 'in terra nebulosa et pluviosa ita quod segetes iam albae ad messem per consuetudinem in culmo computrescunt' (*E.Y.C.*, xi, p. 55).

of the monastery of Les Dunes in Belgium will show how
the Cistercian economic formula could turn a poor community on an inhospitable shore into one of the biggest
agrarian enterprises of the Middle Ages.

A NOTABLE EXAMPLE: LES DUNES

The monastery of Les Dunes developed, as did many other
early Cistercian houses, from a small hermitage in a
desolate place. In the early twelfth century a hermit called
Ligerius settled among the sand-dunes about twenty-five
miles west of Bruges. He presumably eked out some kind of
living for himself from the sea, and in course of time he was
joined by others who recognized him as their leader. They
faced a dreary future among the dunes, and these first
hermits could not have known as we do that the centre of
commercial activity in Flanders was beginning to move
north-eastwards from the port of Wissant to Bruges, soon
to be one of the great cities of medieval Europe. The
sketch-map shows the position of the monastery and the
rough outline of the coast in the twelfth century:

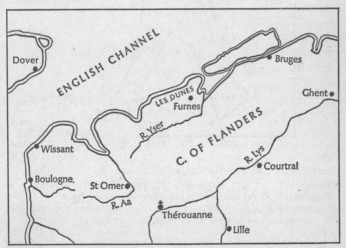

THE ABBEY OF LES DUNES AND ITS NEIGHBOURHOOD
IN THE EARLY TWELFTH CENTURY

The early stages of adopting a religious rule are obscure, but in 1138 the community was affiliated to Clairvaux and received a colony of Cistercian monks under a new abbot. From this date the fortunes of the house were assured. The monastic chronicle has preserved a record of the recruitment of monks and *conversi* from 1148 to the end of the Middle Ages, and – reduced to a yearly average – the figures given in the chronicle may be shown as follows:[59]

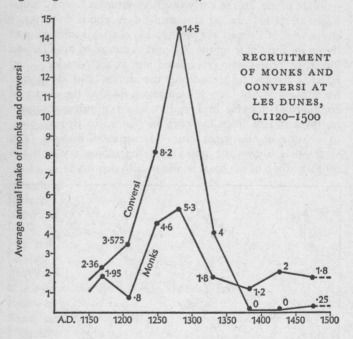

RECRUITMENT OF MONKS AND CONVERSI AT LES DUNES, C.1120–1500

Note: The total figures of recruits are as follows:

Monks: 1138–89, 97; 1189–1230, 32; 1230–58, 134; 1259–99, 211; 1305–54, 89; 1354–1406, 61; 1406–42, 73; 1442–87, 84.

Conversi: 1138–89, 118; 1189–1230, 143; 1230–58, 247; 1259–99, 577; 1305–54, 202; 1354–1406, 0; 1406–42, 0; 1447–87, 17.

59. I have extracted these statistics from A. But, *Chronica Abbatum Monasterii Dunensis* (Soc d'Émulation de Bruges), 1839. Additional details are taken from the *Codex Dunensis*, ed. J. Kervyn de Lettenhove (Coll. de chroniques Belges inédites), 1875, xvi.

The main points which emerge from this graph are the very steady growth both in monks and *conversi* till the end of the thirteenth century. This growth was accompanied by a massive growth in economic activity. By 1190 the monastery had its own fleet of ships and the General Chapter had to legislate against the growing practice of carrying general cargoes in these ships for profit.[60] The importance of the monastery's foreign connexions at this time is shown by the fact that the abbot was the chief agent of the Queen of England in negotiating the ransom and release of King Richard I from captivity in 1193-4.[61] The monastery was already a force to be reckoned with in the world, but the golden age of its prosperity still lay in the future. This was reached under Nicholas of Balliol, abbot from 1226-53. The monastery had then 120 monks, supported by 248 *conversi* who made up a skilled labour force of weavers, fullers, tanners, skinners, shoe-makers, smiths, carpenters, masons, etc.[62] It was a contemporary jest that the sand-dunes on which the monastery was built had become a mound of silver for an abbot who knew how to manage it. Materially it was a good time. A new church was being built, and it was rapidly filled with the memorials and coats-of-arms of the noble benefactors who were buried in the monastery.

Late in the thirteenth century university men first appeared among the monks, bringing with them a new style of academic learning. These men were a symptom of a great change in the order. In 1231 the General Chapter – in a spirit very different from that of the earliest statutes – had recommended that novices should be received who were capable of doing honour to the order by their learning.[63] This had been followed in 1244 by the establishment of a college in Paris, and similar establishments were set up in other universities in the next fifty years. The new eloquence in the pulpit, which was one of the results of this development, was sufficiently notable in the now somnolent piety of Les Dunes to be thought worthy of an entry in the

60. *Statuta Cist.*, i, 130 (1190, c. 63).   61. But, op. cit., pp. 41-2.
62. ibid., p. 46.   63. *Statuta Cist.*, ii, 93-4 (1231, c. 12).

domestic chronicle.[64] At the same time the monastic estates continued to grow. By the end of the century twenty-five monastic grangers supervised the cultivation of 25,000 acres. By any standards Les Dunes was now a very large enterprise indeed.

The good times continued till the death of Abbot William de Hulst in 1317. After this date the monastic chronicler noted that a great change suddenly came over the whole way of life in the monastery. Our graph shows one side of this change: recruitment of both monks and *conversi* began to fall off, and the number of *conversi* was destined to fall to zero before the end of the century. As the number of monks declined, life became more comfortable for those who were left. A taste for comfort is insidious, and yesterday's luxuries become today's necessities in monasteries no less than other places. The history of the use of wine among the monks of Les Dunes is a case in point. At first it was only for invalids; then for special feast-days; afterwards for Sundays also; by 1350 it was taken on Tuesdays and Thursdays as well; quite soon daily; by 1375 the ration had been increased to a pint a day. Then one luxury begets others of the most diverse kinds. Gregory XI, himself a Cistercian, gave the abbot the right to use the insignia of a bishop; and lay benefactors got into the habit of leaving gifts for the monks to enjoy a supplementary dish or some other comfort on their anniversary day. It must have been a most agreeable bachelor society.

There was always a sprinkling of learning, but most of the monks were engaged in the work of country gentlemen, looking after estates which could no longer be tended by an army of *conversi*. The abbots were able men who took care of themselves and their aristocratic community. They retired to Bruges to die under the hands of the best doctors, and the election of their successors was a matter of high social consequence. Yet here at least some spark of the old Cistercian spirit remained. The monks of Les Dunes could not escape the aristocratic embrace, but they could still choose their conqueror. Thus in 1442, when the duke and

64. But, op. cit., p. 62.

duchess of Burgundy both strove to get the nomination for their ex-chancellor and nephew respectively, one of the monks roused the spirit of the community to the extent of procuring the election of his own brother.[65] So a certain love of liberty survived the decay of every other ideal.

THE PERSISTENCE OF CISTERCIAN VIRTUE

The Cistercian Order, as we survey its main lines of development, can be seen to have represented a powerful impulse in three different but related areas of medieval life. In the first place it represented a return to primitive simplicity, in reaction against the elaboration of customary rules which had characterized the early period of the Middle Ages. Secondly it represented a search for system and rational organization in place of the accumulation of variegated customs that had satisfied the imagination and aspirations of the earlier period. And thirdly it represented the ruthless and aggressive side of European activity in its most expansive period. Simplicity, system, and energetic exploitation of resources are three strands in European development which came into prominence in the twelfth century: they were nowhere more effectively combined than in the Cistercian Order. In one way or another these three characteristics long survived, but in the end they fought a losing battle against the forces of custom, localism, and aristocratic display. The Cistercians themselves increasingly felt the pull of these enticements to acquiescence, and by the end of the thirteenth century most Cistercian houses were distinguished exponents of the very qualities which they had come into existence to denounce.

In one sense therefore the Order may be said to have failed, and the moment of incipient failure can be located about the year 1200. Until this date it was still reasonable to look on the Order – whether for praise or blame – as a disturbing influence in the life of the community. Even so violent and apocalyptic a character as Joachim of Fiore could still, in the last years of the twelfth century, look on the Cistercians as the angelic Order destined to purge the

65. ibid., p. 87.

corruptions of the church and prepare the way for the end of the world.[66] And even so practical a pope as Innocent III could still in his early days as pope see the Cistercians as the most effective instruments for the conversion of the heretics of Languedoc.[67] In the fields of apocalyptic vision and missionary activity, as also on their great estates in Spain and elsewhere, the Cistercians were still frontiersmen in 1200. But no one could think of them in this way a generation later. In the Joachimite apocalyptic scheme they had been ousted by the friars. Equally the friars had taken over the missionary activity which Innocent III had entrusted to the Cistercians. Their failure as missionaries demonstrates the failing grip of the Cistercians more clearly than anything else. They failed because, in succeeding as an Order, they had adopted the habits of the established order.

Since they no longer themselves represented a revolt, they made no appeal to others who were in revolt. They no longer travelled light. Indeed, to do them justice, it had never been part of their aim to lessen the weight with which established institutions pressed upon the individual. They saw themselves as rebels in the interests of discipline. They had no quarrel with society, still less with the holy Rule of St Benedict: they only wished to simplify the monastic institution in order to make it stronger and to organize society in order to make it a more effective instrument of Christian aggression. They were from the beginning an aristocratic movement, the product of the society of northern feudal Europe. They had a natural disdain for the lower orders and for all stirrings of those whom St Bernard characterized as 'rustics without learning or fitness for war'.[68] They shifted the emphasis of the monastic Rule from personal obedience to corporate discipline. In every way it was inevitable that the Cistercians should be a reactionary force in the dissolving social order and confused town-life of the later Middle Ages.

66. Joachim nevertheless had reservations about the Cistercians: for his 'double attitude' see Marjorie Reeves, *The Influence of Prophecy in the later Middle Ages*, 1969, pp. 152–8.

67. Ep. vi, 243 (29 Jan. 1204); vii, 76 (31 May 1204): *P.L.* 215, 273, 358.

68. *Sermones in Cantica*, lxv, c. 8 (*P.L.* 183, 1093); lxvi, c. 1 (ibid., 1094).

Yet the impetus of their initial attack, the genius of their founders, and the economic success which was the inevitable result of their spiritual programme, gave the Cistercians a character of their own at least till the fourteenth century. Certainly it was a character different from anything that could have been imagined or approved by the earliest advocates of the Order. It was a character which combined solid virtues and solid learning with solid prosperity.

The copy-book Cistercian of the later Middle Ages was the man who became pope in 1334 as Benedict XII.[69] He was a very serious reformer after the manner of his day. We have already noticed some results of his great inquiry into the wealth of the Benedictine houses throughout Europe – an inquiry which had the typically Cistercian aim of promoting the economic efficiency and orderly administration of monastic houses.[70] He was a Doctor of Theology who had studied at the Cistercian College of St Bernard at Paris. In this he represented the Cistercian conversion to academic learning which had taken place in the late thirteenth century, and he wished to see theological study firmly established in his Order. To this end he drew up a plan which required that every monastery with more than eighteen monks should have one student, and those with more than forty monks two students, at Paris or some other university. Intellectually there can be no doubt that this was a move in the right direction, though it might have seemed odd to anyone who studied the early Cistercian statutes. Odder still from this point of view was the pope's scale of payments for monks in Paris: £105 a year for masters, £50 for bachelors, £30 for lectors, £20 for single students – payments which were perhaps not exorbitant for the aristocrats of the schools but far removed from monastic austerity.[71]

69. See J. B. Mahn, *Le Pape Benoît XII et les Cisterciens* (Bibl. de l'école des hautes études, 295), 1949.

70. See above p. 238, n.31.

71. Mahn, op. cit., p. 57. These payments which Benedict XII laid down in his Bull *Fulgens sicut stella* of 13 July 1335, are considerably more than he allowed the Benedictines in the following year. The sums of money are in pounds *tournois*.

Yet, however far we have drifted from the original Cistercian pattern of life, the virtues of organization, discipline, and a certain austerity of purpose continued to dominate everything that Benedict did or planned. He himself in his younger days as a student and university teacher had enjoyed every kind of dispensation from residing in his monastery, but he had remained scrupulous in his attention to the divine office. Later, his life became a busy round of General Chapters, university disputations, legal actions in the defence of the monastic property; as bishop of Pamiers he was an active and exemplary super-visor of the Inquisition in his diocese.[72] There is always the same impulse towards order and uniformity – broken reflections of the primitive Cistercian spirit. He would have all monks engage in study; but he insisted that they should study only theology, and he maintained the Cistercian prohibition of canon law. He wanted all monks to be as nearly as possible alike, and he wanted them all to be as Cistercian as the circumstances of his day allowed: well-organized, well-endowed, prudent in the management of their possessions, learned, devout. It is easy to smile at his quiet acceptance of the aristocratic amenities of life, but it is difficult to know what else or what better he could have done. There was no longer any fire in the Cistercian heart. That had long ago departed. But a formidable consistency of purpose and rigour of execution remained. Strangely enough a large part of the fire had found its way into a branch of the least inflammable of all medieval religious orders, the Augustinian canons.

III. THE FRIARS

The Orders of Augustinian canons and Cistercian monks were the religious creations which best met the needs and fitted into the social pattern of western Europe in the period from 1050 to 1200. In the same way the Dominican

72. See *Le Registre d'Inquisition de Jacques Fournier (Benoît XII), évêque de Pamiers (1318–25)*, ed. J. Duvernoy, 3 vols., 1965.

and Franciscan friars were the creations which best performed this function in the thirteenth century. In one
sense they were a development of the two earlier creations.
The Dominican friars followed the Rule of St Augustine.
The Franciscans were wholly original in their Rule, but in
their piety they were the heirs of the Cistercian devotion
to the person of Jesus. And in their government both
Orders of friars took the centralized direction and control,
which the Cistercians had pioneered a century earlier, a
long step forward.

Yet, though the line of descent on both sides is clear
enough, in a much more important sense the friars were
something quite new in the religious life of Europe. For
one thing they belonged to an environment which had
scarcely existed a hundred years earlier – the environment
of the great towns and universities. Without the towns the
friars would never have come into existence; without the
universities they would never have become great. We may
begin therefore by saying something about the ways in
which towns and universities of the thirteenth century
created a demand for some new kind of religious organization, and the ways in which the friars first of all met and
then succumbed to the new demand.

The environment

THE TOWNS

The general effect of the growth of towns on the development of the religious consciousness of Europe has already
been touched on, but only in broad outline and only in
connexion with a late phase in this development. We must
now look somewhat earlier and examine more closely the
manifestations of urban religion. The chronicles of the
city of Bologna will provide a starting point. Under the
year 1204 we read:

In this year brother Albert of Mantua came to Bologna and
preached there for six weeks and many were converted.[73]

73. *Corpus Chronicorum Bononiensium*, ed. A. Sorbelli, ii, p. 68.

This simple annal raises many problems. We don't know anything about Albert of Mantua, nor what he preached, nor to whom, nor what they were converted to. Nevertheless the event is of some interest. We have an unknown man, calling himself 'Brother', though he is, so far as we know, a member of no religious order. He is an itinerant preacher, who apparently on his own authority conducts a mission in an episcopal city, makes a substantial number of converts, and goes on his way to another town. There is no suggestion of heresy, nor of unusual hysteria or disorder – simply of preaching and conversions. Now until this time, and for hundreds of years previously, within the Christian community the word 'conversion' simply meant conversion from secular occupations to life in a religious Order. But this is clearly not intended here: the conversion is evidently some kind of interior conversion from a 'formal' to an 'effective' religion.

This peaceful mission is further amplified by the only other notice we have of Brother Albert's activity. In the year 1207,

on 6 May Brother Albert of Mantua went to Faenza and there made peace in ninety-five cases of homicide; then he made peace in Bertinora; then in Siena; and then in Castel Nuovo; then in Forlimpopoli; and finally in Imola he made peace in twenty-eight cases of homicide.[74]

Here then was a man carrying on a private missionary activity of conversion and peace in a turbulent society. It was an activity outside the framework of the organized church. Indeed the organized church of the Middle Ages had so far scarcely considered the problems of urban society. Despite all the natural disasters and disruptions which afflicted the countryside, it was possible to treat the rural community as a stable and inert mass amenable to organization and control. But what was to be made of the towns – anarchic, engaged in pursuits doubtfully permissible in canon law, embracing extremes of wealth and destitution, subject to over-employment and unemployment, quite

74. ibid., p. 69.

different from anything known in the rural community? To such a society the ecclesiastical organization had not yet, and perhaps never has, adapted itself.

Above all it had not adapted itself to one element in the urban mentality, which is not illustrated in the activity of Brother Albert but cannot be overlooked – the element of hysteria. Hysterical outbursts are to be found at all periods and in every environment, but they are far more common in towns than anywhere else. When we read the following annal for 1260 in the chronicle of Bologna, we are certainly in the presence of a hysterical outburst, and the cause can be identified:

> In this year, the whole of Italy was plagued with many flagel-lants and the country was defiled with many vices and sins. First the people of Perugia went barefooted through their town beating themselves; then the Romans, and after them people all over Italy young and old, nobles and common people, went two by two beating their backs with leather thongs, beseeching God's mercy with many tears. And not only men but also women did likewise all night long. This was done throughout all the fortified places and towns of Italy, so much so that it was thought to be irreligious if anyone did not beat himself in this way. This began in October and lasted for the whole month. . . . And on 10 October the men of Imola came to Bologna beating themselves and crying 'Have mercy, oh God, and send peace'; and on 19 October the men of Bologna did likewise and went to Modena. Then the Romans set free all the prisoners for the love of God; the family of the Castelani were freed from prison and they fled from Rome in fear of death.[75]

This outburst was certainly caused by the expectation of the imminent end of the world, which had been foretold by Joachim of Fiore, just as the even more spectacular outbursts in northern Europe in 1349 are to be associated with the Great Plague. The hysteria to which these events bear witness was never far beneath the surface of urban life, but it did not ordinarily take the form of mass terror. More often it is to be seen simply in violent gestures of renunciation and self-immolation either in individuals or

75. ibid., pp. 156–7.

groups. The Italian chronicler Salimbene describes such a group of seventy-two men calling themselves the Apostles, whom he had seen in 1284 between Modena and Reggio going along the road to Parma to meet their leader. A few days later he saw twelve young women making the same journey for the same purpose. At their meeting they set up a rhythmical chant 'Pater, pater, pater', then they cast off their clothes and stood around naked until their leader clothed them again and sent them on their way to the four corners of the earth, to Rome, Compostella, Monte Gargano, and across the seas.[76]

This association of Apostles did not last long, but their brief history shows how easy it was to get a movement started in a population which always had time on its hands, poverty in its midst, and alms to spare for people who had broken out of the drab cycle of surfeit, destitution, and communal violence, into the freedom of poverty and eternity. Of course decent people did not at all approve of the goings-on of the Apostles, least of all (by this time) the friars, who felt that their territory was being invaded by men who went further along their private road than they did; but the grounds on which they were to be condemned were not at all clear.

The perplexity of ecclesiastical authority in the face of a movement like that of the Apostles is instructive for the background of the early friars. They were not heretics, and it was hard to say that they endangered anything but public decency. For long they were tolerated and even encouraged. Even after their indecencies had been condemned in 1274, their leader lived in Parma, sometimes in prison, at other times in the bishop's palace sharing the bishop's table; and then in the end he was burnt as a heretic in 1300. By this time a harsher religious climate prevailed. But the earlier ups and downs of the leader and his movement reflect the initial difficulty of knowing how to treat

76. *Chronica Fratris Salimbene de Adam Ordinis Minorum*, ed. O. Holder-Egger, *M.G.H. Scriptores*, xxxii, pp. 264–5, 563–4. Salimbene's long and hostile account of the Apostles, pp. 245–77, shows how close (and therefore dangerous) they were to the friars 'who taught all men to beg'.

spontaneous outbursts of religious emotion in the urban population of Italy. The final act of violence which brought the Apostle movement to an end reflects the hardening of attitudes during the last years of the thirteenth century. It was the freedom of the earlier years of the century which made possible the rise of the friars.

THE UNIVERSITIES

Besides the freedom of the towns, the freedom of the universities provided the other prerequisite for the development of the friars. By the beginning of the thirteenth century the universities of Paris and Bologna were the leading intellectual centres in Europe. They were the places where nearly all the new ideas in theology and law were to be found, and they also provided a sound training in the liberal arts. Oxford was just beginning to get an international reputation in the fields that Paris had made her own in the previous century; and in the course of the century several new universities would be founded, especially in Italy, but also in France and England. But apart from these places that could technically be called 'universities', there were many other schools with a high reputation in one or other field of study. These places of learning, which provided organized teaching and a recognized test of performance in all the known areas of learning, had decisively taken the place of monasteries as centres of intellectual effort and attainment by the beginning of the thirteenth century. The training they offered was in great demand, and towns and rulers were prepared to bid high for the loyalty of academic masters. The agreements between the city of Bologna and the masters of the schools are like treaties between two equal and independent parties; they amply illustrate the high value which a hard-headed mercantile community attached to the services of distinguished masters in their midst. Kings were equally solicitous, as the following letter of Henry III of England to the masters and scholars of Paris testifies:

We humbly sympathize with your sufferings under the iniquitous laws of Paris and we wish to restore you to your rightful liberty. We therefore write to you to invite you to come to our realm of England and to stay here for the purposes of study. We will assign to your use whatever cities, boroughs, or towns you select for this purpose and gladly assure you of liberty and tranquillity, which will be both pleasing to God and fully adequate to your needs.[77]

The reasons for this obsequious solicitation of learned men by secular powers was the same in all cases. Scholars were necessary for the conduct of business; their presence brought repute to a town or kingdom; they provided a storehouse of technical advice, and ensured a succession of future servants of government. Yet with all this eagerness to found and encourage universities, and despite the growing numbers of students and the growing elaboration of programmes of study, scholars and teachers suffered from many uncertainties. They could not live on encouragement alone. The students had to look to their friends to support them while they studied; the masters in their turn had to rely on their students for their livelihood; and over both masters and students there hung the perennial problem of a career. A university was a place for young men. All students had to lecture to obtain a degree, but few could support themselves by teaching when their period of obligatory lecturing had run out. Nearly all of them relied on obtaining a benefice. This meant finding a patron, and a patron generally required a clerk to qualify for preferment by making himself useful as an advocate or administrator. The moment when a man is pushed out of the university into the world is never very pleasant, and the medieval student (even if he had managed to stay the course) often found himself in an embarrassing position:

I am unable to leave Bologna because of a mountain of debt that weighs me down and destroys my substance. So far as I can reckon, ninety pounds would scarcely suffice to clear the principal that I have borrowed, not counting the interest of two and a half years. No month passes without my having to raise another twenty-one shillings for my debts. I had hoped for a better income from my

77. *Calendar of Patent Rolls, Henry III, 1225–1252*, p. 257.

rents, and this expectation has led me to spend more and stay longer in Bologna than I could afford. That is always the way things happen.[78]

This is the kind of letter that occurs so frequently in medieval letter collections that it is often looked on as a kind of joke or idle exercise; but it can have been no joke at the time. The new universities of the Middle Ages very quickly built up a stable corporate organization, but the stability did not extend to individual scholars. For them, the future was full of uncertainty.

There is a permanent propensity for universities to attract more able men than they can provide with employment. This is especially true in times of intense activity and discovery, and it was certainly true in the thirteenth century. Only a very able or well-endowed master could live on the fees or gifts of his pupils; the remainder had to push out into the world to seek preferment at the hands of men whom they could serve. It was into this scene of intellectual activity and social insecurity that the friars came.

Aims and origins

The origins of the friars are wrapped up in the hidden struggles and resolutions of the two great founders, Dominic and Francis, which we cannot here even attempt to probe. But though the interior stages of growth must forever remain mysterious, the general circumstances and direction of the two movements which they initiated are fairly clear.

The origin of the Dominican organization goes back to a chance encounter in Montpellier in 1206 between a Spanish bishop returning from Rome and three Cistercian abbots whom Innocent III had charged with the task of combatting heresy in Languedoc. The Cistercian mission was having no success, and a member of the bishop's household, an Augustinian canon called Dominic, saw the reason: the three abbots were moving around with

78. F. Liverani, *Spicilegium Liberianum*, 1863, i. p. 627. This is one of a series of letters written from Bologna by a Master David of London who studied there in the 1170s.

the heavy pomp of ecclesiastical dignitaries. These trappings cut no ice with people disposed to regard the whole establishment as an affront to the true religion, whatever that might be. To succeed (so Dominic saw) they must adopt a simpler, more 'apostolic', life. This was not a new discovery. The *vita apostolica*, as we have seen, had been the inspiration of the Augustinian movement a century earlier. Its significance for evangelical work, however, had been largely submerged in the later development of the Augustinian canons, and Dominic's first great service was that he brought it to the surface again. The idea took immediate possession of him, and for the next fifteen years, till his death in 1221, he worked to give it an institutional existence. For ten years he had only a meagre success, but by 1217 the shape of things to come was beginning to emerge. In this year Dominic and his small band of preachers held a meeting at Toulouse from which they dispersed in all directions: four went to Spain, seven to Paris, four stayed in Toulouse, and Dominic himself went to Rome. They had no resources, little learning, almost no books; but something of the world-wide scale of later operations was already envisaged in the wide scattering of the little band. Also, the high proportion sent to Paris shows an immediate appreciation of the rôle which the universities were to play in the recruitment and development of the new Order.

These then were the foundations of the Dominican Order: it aimed at combating heresy through preaching reinforced by a primitive simplicity of apostolic life. As its main tool in this work it used academic discipline supported by a universal organization. After 1217 the special emphasis on the conversion of Languedoc was abandoned, and the centre of gravity in the Order shifted to Paris and Bologna, the main scholastic centres of Europe. With the first general chapter at Bologna in 1220 the movement began its triumphant career as a new universal Order in the Church.

But before we follow the later stages of the movement, we must turn to the quite different circumstances of the

Franciscan development. It would be quite useless in a few words to attempt to trace the personal development of St Francis from the affluent son of a cloth merchant of Assisi to the man of twenty-eight who in 1210 went with eleven ragged followers to Rome to lay a new way of life before the pope. Four years earlier he had given up everything, and this was the result. His aims were much less clear than those of Dominic. So far as the Rule of 1210 can now be reconstituted, it seems to have consisted mainly of a call to total renunciation – selling everything, giving everything to the poor, giving up every form of worldly glory, wealth, aid, comfort, organization, everything, 'to live according to the form of the holy Gospel'.[79] In his total renunciation Francis was following a pattern of conversion that can be found in all ages; but the sharpness and extremity of his impulse was in some way prompted by the violence, glitter, and instability of the emerging municipal oligarchies of Italy. All earlier religious movements had been guided by a strong sense of order and tradition. Of this there is little trace in the words of Francis that have been preserved. His idea was to cut through all the accretions of monastic development, whether Benedictine, Cistercian, or Augustinian, and to live literally the life of Christ. He called for a total surrender, symbolized in following precisely the Gospel precept to sell everything and give to the poor.

It may at first sight seem absurd to say that the Franciscan conception of poverty was something new, for the ideal of poverty had been part of every earlier religious movement. But poverty was not the special mark of these movements. The poverty of a rural society is so deeply rooted in the nature of things that it could never in itself seem a very important part of renunciation. The Rule of St Benedict had laid its main emphasis on *obedience*, not on *poverty*. *Paupertas* is a word it uses only once, and here the reference is to an unusual state of affairs: 'If the exigencies or poverty of the place make it necessary for the monks

79. J. R. H. Moorman, *Sources for the Life of St Francis of Assisi*, 1940, pp. 51–2; cf. *Testamentum S. Francisci* in *Opuscula S. Patris Francisci*, 1904, p. 79.

themselves to gather the harvest, they are not to groan. . .'.[80]
This kind of poverty was not part of the Benedictine Rule.
The essential poverty of a Benedictine monk lay in the
denial of self-will. The literally *poor* were those outside the
monastery whom it was the duty of the monks to feed.

For St Francis it was quite different. He and his followers
were to be the most abject, the most wholly deprived, of the
poor. He saw poverty and wealth as perhaps only a man
brought up in the rapid accumulation and sudden destitution of an urban community could see them. He did not
have the comfortable sense that all wealth is natural,
whether it consists in the command of labour or the fruits of
the earth, and that no man is so poor as to be wholly
destitute of wealth. He could see only that wealth is profit,
which men create for themselves; it is something corrupt.
Hence poverty shone as an ideal of purity and romance,
and it occupied the first place in his attempt 'to follow the
life and poverty of Jesus Christ'.[81]

For St Francis therefore poverty, which was merely a
channel of communication for Dominic, was the end towards which his greatest effort was directed. It was the
essential element in the imitation of Christ, which was all
he wanted. He seems to have had very little idea of leadership or organization, but in showing how the destitution of
the towns could be accepted with joy and made service-
able for salvation, he touched some deep emotional
springs in an urban society. Faster than Dominic's well-
planned campaign, the unregulated movement which
Francis brought into existence became an organization
covering the whole of Christendom. When the two leaders
met in Rome in 1218, Dominic was still the leader of only a
handful of preachers, while Francis was the reluctant
head of an organization with branches in nearly every
country in western Europe.

It will be seen at once that the two organizations which
came into existence as a result of the work of Dominic and
Francis were in principle very different. The Dominicans
were an off-shoot of the Augustinian canons, and this

80. *Reg. Ben.*, c. 48.   81. *Opuscula S. Patris Francisci*, 1904, p. 76.

connexion went much deeper than a simple constitutional adherence to the same Rule. Practical evangelical work and the ideal of the *vita apostolica* had been the main impulses of the earliest followers of the Augustinian rule. Although many communities of canons had quietly abandoned, or never experienced, these impulses, yet in others the work of maintaining schools, running hospitals, redeeming captives, and preaching had never ceased to be part of their Augustinian way of life. Dominic simply gave a new impetus and concentration to this activity by pointing to preaching as the central task. Everything else – organization, studies, rules about poverty and liturgy – was subordinated to this one purpose.

By contrast the Franciscans are much more difficult to place in the historical development of religious organizations. They do not belong to any of the types of organization that have so far been described, but to the succession of ephemeral urban movements, like the 'Apostles' mentioned above, which appeared spasmodically throughout Europe from the mid eleventh century onwards. All these movements had in various ways protested against the wealth and formalism of the ecclesiastical hierarchy, and against the whole tendency for religion to become engulfed in secular values and the pursuit of secular ends. They all stirred some sympathy among serious men, but most of them in the end (including an important section of the Franciscans themselves) were condemned and persecuted. Where the Franciscans differed from all other movements of the same type was in their immense success, their universal appeal, their permanence and – despite multiple condemnations of individuals, groups, and ideas within the Franciscan order – their ability to settle down within the framework of an ecclesiastical organization. This last feature, which they owed largely to their imitation of the Dominican organization, prevented them from going the way of the other sporadic urban movements.

The extent to which the two Orders borrowed from each other does not here concern us in any detailed way. We are concerned only with the forces which determined the way in which the two organizations developed. Among these forces the importance of rivalry must not be overlooked. The members of both organizations very quickly developed a passionate desire to develop their own Order to the extreme limit of its possibilities. In this they were simply following the most deeply rooted instinct of the Middle Ages – the instinct for corporate survival. This instinct was not yet associated with the secular state, but it was intensely active in every kind of religious organization, and it inevitably led to vigorous competition between organizations trading (so to speak) in the same market.

This situation accounts for many features in the history of the two Orders which would otherwise be difficult to understand. For one thing it accounts for the extent to which they borrowed from each other those elements which had the highest value for survival. Thus (to the dismay of St Francis himself) the Franciscans borrowed large parts of the Dominican organization and followed the Dominicans into the universities. The Dominicans on the other hand borrowed the Franciscan attitude to poverty which gave them much of their urban strength. In a large sense the Dominicans provided the intellect and the Franciscans the instincts which led to universal success. Without their rivals the Dominicans would perhaps have remained a relatively small order dedicated to a single task of combatting heresy; without the Dominican example the Franciscans might not have survived at all. Standing together against the rest of the world, while bitterly contesting every inch of the ground occupied by the other, they grew with astonishing speed.

Growth and achievement

GROWTH

The growth of the two Orders presents some striking points of difference within an overall similarity. Almost from the beginning they both took the whole world for their parish in a way that would have seemed wholly visionary if it had not so quickly been justified by the event.

By 1217 the Franciscans had already divided the known world into provinces which show very well the areas of the greatest initial impetus: there were six provinces in Italy, two in France, and one each in Germany, Spain, and the Middle East. By 1230, Germany had been divided into two provinces, France and Spain into three each, and the provinces of England and Austria had been added to the list. Within a few years therefore the basic territorial organization which satisfied all medieval requirements had been created.[82]

The Dominicans proceeded with greater deliberation. In their first provincial plan of 1221 there were only five provinces (Lombardy, Rome with southern Italy, Provence, Spain, France) to which Hungary, Germany, England, Poland, Denmark, Greece, and the Holy Land were added by about 1230. By this date therefore, along somewhat different lines which reflected the greater Dominican emphasis on border lands, the two Orders were deployed for their world-wide tasks.[83]

Numerically the Dominicans with their more clearly defined objectives were never as successful as the Franciscans. By the early fourteenth century the total number of Dominican houses was about six hundred as against about fourteen hundred Franciscan houses. Any estimate of the number of friars in these houses is extremely uncertain, but an average figure of twenty in each house would probably not be far wrong. This would indicate a total of about 28,000 Franciscans compared with 12,000 Dominicans at the peak of the medieval development of the two Orders.[84]

In themselves these numbers do not mean very much, and it is very difficult to make any comparisons with the

82. J. Moorman, *History of the Franciscan Order*, 1968, 46–62, 62–74.

83. There is a useful summary of these developments in A. Walz, *Compendium Historiae Ordinis Praedicatorum*, 2nd ed., 1948.

84. Estimates of numbers in the two Orders differ very widely. For the Franciscans, see Moorman, op. cit., 155–76, 351; and for the Dominicans, besides Walz, see F. Mandonnet, *Saint Dominique*, 1937, i, 187–8, and (for England) Hinnebusch, *The Early English Friars Preachers*, 1951, pp. 271–8. The earliest official list of Franciscan houses in 1331 is printed in Eubel, *Provinciale Vetustissimum*, 1892.

development of earlier Orders. The records of the friars, so abundant for their intellectual activity, are much more fragmentary in all that concerns their material circumstances than the records of all earlier Orders. Nevertheless a comparison between the growth of the Cistercians in the twelfth century and the friars in the thirteenth provides some significant contrasts. In number the houses of the Dominicans reached a total roughly comparable with that of the Cistercians, while the Franciscans' total was very much greater; but all the houses of friars put together represented a capital investment that was only a fraction of that absorbed by the Cistercians. The period of growth of the friars, which scarcely extended over more than eighty years, was much shorter than the two centuries of Cistercian growth. But the most striking difference between the friars and the Cistercians was in distribution. Whereas France accounted for one third of all Cistercian houses, it held only about one sixth of the Dominican and probably a still smaller proportion of the Franciscan houses. Conversely Italy, which had just over a tenth of all Cistercian houses, accounted for a fifth of all Dominican and an unknown but certainly very high proportion of all Franciscan houses. This broad geographical shift is a symptom of an important difference between the friars and earlier religious Orders. The friars were basically a Mediterranean and urban movement; the Cistercians were agrarian, French, and feudal.

LIVELIHOOD

Wherever there was a town there were friars; and without a town there were no friars. This was a necessary consequence of their way of life. A single beggar can survive in the countryside, but an organized community of beggars cannot. In order to survive, such a community, however small, needs a fairly large population of people who are not themselves on the verge of want. The friars therefore made at once for the towns. They would not have looked on themselves as men who were tapping a hitherto under-exploited source of urban revenue; but this is in effect what they did. The Augustinian canons had in some respects anticipated them. As we have already seen, there were complaints from the canons that the friars competed with them in the pursuit of 'burials, legacies, and alms of rich citizens'. But the area of economic competition was marginal. The Augustinian canons were an endowed Order, who supplemented their basic income from casual sources. The friars found their main livelihood in acts of transitory charity. The two organizations operated within two quite different contexts and at different economic levels.

It is interesting to compare the attitude of the friars to town life with that of the Augustinian canons, who were the most urban of all the earlier Orders. We saw that many houses of canons began in the suburbs of towns, in ruined or ill-served churches. These churches were conveniently placed to serve the needs of an urban middle-class, too poor to found abbeys themselves, but rich enough to desire a stake in a regular religious community. The canons therefore very often had an urban background, but they were not an urban phenomenon: they came to the towns by accident, because they found there unoccupied land, decayed churches, and unappropriated tithes. The friars by contrast came to the towns, not for the churches or tithes, but because it was in the towns that they could find the people for whom they had a message, from whom they drew their earliest recruits, and on whom they depended for their means of life. By preference they came not to the suburbs but to central sites, however awkward they might be. Very often when their numbers grew they had to move away from the centre, perhaps even outside the city wall. But they stayed as near to the centre as they could, and they sometimes got permission to destroy part of the city wall so that they could still remain inside the city.[85] Their whole way of life depended on their association with the town, and this determined the direction of their later development.

85. There are valuable notes on Dominican sites in England in Hinnebusch, op. cit., and on the sites of all Orders of friars in numerous volumes of the *V.C.H.*

In cities a body of men may hope to live on almsgiving, but even in a city it is not possible to live utterly without possessions. This raises a problem for anyone who wishes to be one of the poor. No one, and certainly no community, can for long be utterly poor. This is the paradox of poverty as an ideal: it is so easy to be poor by chance, so difficult by policy. The older monastic orders had solved the problem by adopting as their ideal individual poverty in the midst of corporate possessions. But it is evident that, in the face of real poverty, monastic poverty of this kind is only wealth under another name. On any ordinary interpretation of the phrase, long before the thirteenth century, the claim made by monks and canons to be *pauperes Christum pauperem sequentes*, 'the poor following Christ in poverty', had ceased to have any respectable meaning.

It was a main part of the mission of St Francis and his followers to give a new meaning to this well-worn phrase. But their experience showed that the path they wished to follow could only be followed instinctively: as soon as it was thought about and pursued in an organized way it raised problems of insuperable difficulty. Western Christendom had hitherto been shielded from these problems by the monastic formula to which I have referred, but they had long been familiar in the religious life of India where total poverty was a more comprehensible ideal. Here is a Buddhist description of the progress of property which catches exactly the dilemma of the early Franciscans:

The disciples began by making robes torn into a rough shape with their hands: so the Leader allowed them to use a knife.

They sewed the pieces with bits of bamboo: so the Leader allowed them to use a needle.

The needles became blunt: so the Leader allowed them a needle-case.

The knife and needles got lost: so the Leader allowed them a bag to carry them in.

The bag became a nuisance, so the Leader allowed them a shoulder-strap.[86]

86. The *Kullavagga*, V, 11 (*Vinaya Texts*, transl. T. W. R. Davids and H. Oldenberg, in *The Sacred Books of the East*, 1885, vol. xx, p. 90).

Where should this process stop? To the Franciscan this was a major problem which almost tore the order to pieces in the first century of its existence. To the Dominicans, whose ideal was not so much the imitation of Christ's poverty as the following of the *vita apostolica*, the problem was less severe. In the end the mutual interaction of the two orders led to a compromise, which in effect allowed the friars (or custodians acting on their behalf) to possess whatever buildings and equipment were necessary for their work, but not to own income-producing property.

The effect of this property limitation was much diminished by the acceptance of fixed annual alms which were indistinguishable from a regular rent. Despite this, the difference between the friars and the earlier religious Orders on the question of property remained very great. The friars never became great property-owners. Most of their income came from small gifts in money or kind, from legacies, and from fees for burials and masses for the dead. Even when door-to-door begging had become a formality or a memory, the public accessibility of the friars and their dependence on an urban environment was still obvious in the sources from which they drew their income.

The friars were forbidden by their rules to hold more land than they needed to occupy for the immediate purposes of life. This meant that they had no need for the cartularies, estate records, and surveys, from which we derive our information about the benefactions that supported the earlier religious foundations. The gifts on which the friars lived are known to us mainly from the numberless wills which have survived from the later medieval centuries. It has been reckoned that in the last half of the fourteenth century one third of the wills of the citizens of Oxford contain bequests to the Franciscans; and though the Franciscans were the most popular, a high proportion of these wills contained bequests to other friars as well. The gifts were very small in comparison with the endowments of monastic foundations, but they were very numerous and they came from a wider area of society than any previous religious benefactions of which a record survives. The wide range of donors and donations is well illustrated in the records of the Oxford Franciscans. At the top of their list of benefactors stands the king who paid them £33 6s. 8d. every year from 1289 until the Dissolution in 1538; at the bottom of the list are the people of St Ebbe's church, in whose parish the Franciscan house stood, who paid sixpence a year. Between these two extremes there are earls and archbishops, monks and nuns, clergy and laity, merchants and knights, wives and widows, all paying a few pounds or pence, annually or in a single payment. The evidence is fragmentary and it only becomes full when the first vigour of the friars had declined, but such as it is it leaves a sufficient impression of the wide area of the friars' appeal.[87]

Wills and last testaments only begin to be available in large quantities from the late thirteenth century onwards. From this date they are one of the best sources of evidence for popular religious sentiment. They show very clearly that the dying were no longer overpowered by the fear of hell as they had once been. Instead they trembled at the prospect of prolonged purgatorial pains, and they sought to shorten and mitigate these pains by widely scattered acts of charity. The surviving wills show that, in making their dispositions, even the wealthiest members of society had little land to spare; but even the humblest of those who rose to the dignity of making a will had much miscellaneous personal property and a few pounds in cash to distribute for pious purposes. The friars were ideal recipients: they could make use of small gifts, and they could confer small but precious benefits to ease the way to heaven. They took their natural, and almost necessary, place in the distribution lists of final acts of charity. The will of one Richard Brampton, an Oxford butcher of modest means who died in 1362, provides a picture of the minimum offerings that the soul's health of a tradesman required.[88] He left:

87. For the details in this paragraph see A. G. Little, *The Greyfriars in Oxford* (Oxford Hist. Soc., 21), 1892.

88. *Oxford Deeds of Balliol College*, ed. H. E. Salter (Oxford Hist. Soc., 64), 1913, pp. 198–9.

two shillings for the repair of the porch at All Saints' church where he hoped to be buried;

six shillings and eightpence for the payment of any tithes or offerings which he had neglected or forgotten to pay;

one shilling to the parish priest, and sixpence for his clerk;

ten shillings for distribution to the poor on the day of his funeral;

ten shillings for distribution among the mendicant friars of Oxford;

three pounds, six shillings and eightpence for a chaplain to say a daily mass for his soul for a year;

and his house property in Oxford to the Augustinian canons of Oseney Abbey after his wife's death.

That is a basic late-medieval mixture. As we rise in the social scale the sums become larger, the number of masses for the soul increases, the area of munificence is enlarged to include the repair of bridges, the support of anchorites and anchoresses, the relief of prisoners and lepers, the provision of lights for many altars; but the basic ingredients are nearly always present. In the spectrum of diffused charity in an urban community the friars represented a broad central band. In some degree they satisfied every common religious need: they were poor and needed relief; they were a place of burial for the great and of memorial for the less great; they would sing masses for the dead and pronounce an absolution over the dying. They made the road to heaven easier for everyone.

Naturally, like all institutions, the friars quickly developed the vices appropriate to their way of life. Just as Cistercian puritanism led directly to landlordly aggressiveness, so the poverty and institutional begging of the friars led to a search for legacies and fees, and easily suggested a lenient treatment for penitents who were also benefactors. We scarcely need evidence to prove that practices which sprang so naturally from the nature and circumstances of the life of the friars were very common, but at the worst these vices were not those of aristocratic ease. They required exertion, and there was never any danger that friaries would become closed corporations of the well-born living in comfort. Even in the relaxed atmosphere of the late Middle Ages they retained this mark of their urban origins, that they were more notorious for sharpness than for sloth.

RECRUITMENT

It is not difficult to understand the flow of gifts and alms which made possible the rapid growth of the Orders of mendicant friars in the thirteenth century and ensured their support till the end of the Middle Ages. The problem of recruitment, however, is more difficult, and the difficulty underlines the difference between the friars and the earlier monastic Orders. A high percentage of recruits to the monastic Orders came from the same class of society as their great benefactors, the landed aristocracy and gentry. But those who gave most to the friars had least desire to see their children adopt the mendicant life. It was a nightmare for well-to-do families that their children might become friars, and more especially Franciscans. No doubt this abhorrence sometimes had the effect of investing the poverty of the friars with the appeal of high romance; and disgust with social respectability was probably as strong a motive for disobliging the expectations of parents in the thirteenth as in the twentieth century.

Yet, repellent or romantic though the life of organized mendicancy might appear to the prosperous, to the very poor it was a haven of security and respectability. It seems likely that the Franciscans, whose conditions of entry with regard to literacy were easier than those of the Dominicans, gathered into their ranks many who already lived on alms. In the chaotic social conditions of a growing city the transition from secular to religious begging offered many attractions, and this may help to account for the unmeasured multiplication of Franciscan houses throughout the towns of Italy in the thirteenth century. Indeed, not many years ago in Naples it was still possible to visualize the close affinity between the friars and the many gradations of those employed in soliciting alms. This was the environ-

ment of the early friars, and probably one of their early
sources of recruitment lay in those who were already
mendicants by necessity.

Like everyone else, however, the friars believed in the
virtues of gentle birth, and there were two classes of men
over whose conversion they especially rejoiced: the well-
born and the learned. Their enemies told many stories of
the efforts of the friars to secure the enlistment of such
men, and not all these stories were untrue. As early as
March 1244 Innocent IV wrote a letter to the archdcacon
of Turin which must suffice to illustrate a whole class of
complaints about the friars which grew in volume
as time went on. The pope related how the schoolmaster
of Asti had appeared before him with the following
story:

While studying in Vercelli the schoolmaster's servants had been
bribed to dope his drink. Whereupon certain friars induced him
to join their Order by pronouncing (he was incapable of further
speech) the simple word 'Yes'. They then seized his goods, tore
off his clothes, and invested him with the religious habit. They
were about to tonsure him when he came to his senses, seized the
scissors, and chased his attackers from the house. The friars,
fearing a scandal, gave him back his goods; but the schoolmaster
appealed to the pope for release from his enforced vow.[89]

It is never possible to check the truth of this kind of
story, but it seems highly likely that the story related by
Innocent IV was substantially accurate. Yet it would be
absurd to suppose that the friars rose by tricks of this kind
to the academic excellence which gives them their great
place in medieval history. They had something to offer
academic scholars and teachers that no other organization
could give. They offered freedom from the scramble for
ecclesiastical preferment, an opportunity for prolonged
theological study and teaching, and an incentive for
scholastic effort that appealed to the noblest minds.

The scramble of scholars for ecclesiastical preferment has

89. *Registres d'Innocent IV*, no. 529.

already been touched on. Nearly every university student needed first of all a family or patron to support him while he studied, and then a benefice (or better still several benefices) to support him when his studies were finished. Normally he would be a Master of Arts by the time he was twenty-five, and he would then have to make his career in the practical world of secular or ecclesiastical administration before he could return to the university to study for a higher degree in theology or law. By the time he was a Doctor of Theology he would probably be about forty, and he would be ready for promotion to the higher offices of church and state. Of course there were exceptional masters who taught all their lives in the university without the support of a religious foundation, but they were a rarity: most men had to combine an academic career with a struggle up the ladder of promotion.

The friars opened a way of escape. University teachers who joined the friars abandoned the struggle for benefices and could dedicate themselves to academic work. Some of the earliest recruits were regent masters who had not yet become involved in making a career; others had already gone quite far; in either case the friars saved them for the universities and made it possible for them to turn their backs on the world. The careers of three Englishmen at the universities of Paris and Oxford in the early thirteenth century will illustrate the situation.

Robert Bacon. Robert Bacon had become an M.A. in Paris by about 1215. He then returned to England and started a modest career with half the rectory of Lower Heyford in Oxfordshire as his benefice. He owed this preferment to the abbey of Eynsham, and it seems likely that he obtained it because his family were tenants of the abbey. Materially his prospects were not brilliant; but he was within reach of Oxford, and here he came to study theology. While he was doing this he joined the Dominicans, probably in 1227. Now he could resign his benefice. He had no need to struggle any longer with the world. He had an assured academic position, and he continued to teach theology in Oxford with universal applause till he died in 1248.[90]

Richard Rufus. Richard Rufus, a Cornishman studying in Paris in the 1220s, took a similar road. He was an M.A. who had started to study theology when he joined the Franciscans in Paris, in about 1230. Thereafter his academic career was assured, and it was a notable one, entirely devoted to the study and teaching of theology in Paris and Oxford. Opinions about him among contemporary Franciscans differed. Thomas of Eccleston calls him an excellent lecturer; Roger Bacon more sourly says that his fame was greatest with the ignorant multitude. But criticisms such as these are the buffets that academic persons must expect. At least he was saved from the squalid race for promotion in the world. He had the satisfaction of working with famous men and he left writings widely scattered throughout the Franciscan libraries of Europe.[91]

Alexander of Hales. Alexander of Hales was an older man, probably from Hales-Owen in Shropshire, who had advanced quite far in his career before he became a Franciscan. He had studied and taught in Paris in both the arts and theology faculties during the first quarter of the thirteenth century. With canonries at both London and Lichfield and the archdeaconry of Coventry, he had advanced solidly but not brilliantly along the road of ecclesiastical preferment. Then in about 1236 he threw it all up and became a Franciscan. He was then in his mid-fifties; he had a distinguished reputation as a theologian and a social position in the ecclesiastical hierarchy. So he gave up a great deal when he became a friar. But he did not give up his academic career. On the contrary, he was now anchored more securely than ever in the university. His conversion had great importance for the Franciscans in Paris because it gave them their first university teacher of

90. For his career see A. B. Emden, *Biographical Register of the University of Oxford to A.D. 1500*, 1957–9, i, 87.
91. ibid., iii, 1604–5.

theology. This was a distinction that the Dominicans had long enjoyed, and the Franciscans had long desired it in vain: their joy was so great that it has helped to keep Alexander's academic reputation bright among Franciscans down to the present day.[92]

ACADEMIC ACHIEVEMENT

The motives of these men in joining the friars are of course hidden from us. But there is one theme common to all of them: the friars needed them, as no one else did, not as administrators but simply as teachers and students of theology, and of theology in its most advanced form. It was here that they found their niche. For fifty years before the friars came, theological study had made little advance. There had been few new ideas, and few innovations in method. Now the time had come for a rapid advance in absorbing the whole body of Aristotelian sciences and metaphysics into theology. Theologians who saw this prospect ahead of them wanted to expand the subject, to experiment in new forms of discussion and in new systems of instruction. It was difficult to find room for these things in the current curriculum of the universities and in the midst of a secular struggle for existence. The friars offered both an opportunity and a relief from anxiety: a relief from anxiety, because they made it possible for the first time for a scholar to live in a community in the full stream of university life and pursue his work without thinking of his career; and an opportunity, because the friars desperately needed theologians to train their young men as preachers, missionaries, and disputants.

The Dominicans were from the earliest days an Order organized for theological study. Already by 1223 there were a hundred and twenty members of the Order in Paris; and by 1234 nine out of fifteen doctors of divinity in the university were probably Dominicans. The General Chapter of 1228 had laid down that every community in the Order should have a friar in charge of theological studies, organiz-

92. For Alexander's career and importance in the Order see J. Moorman, *The Franciscan Order*, 1968, pp. 100, 131–2, 240–2.

ing disputations and directing the reading of the students in the house; it provided that no member of the Order should preach in public until he had studied theology for at least three years; and it envisaged that there would be three students in Paris from each of the twelve provinces of the Order. No doubt all legislation is to some extent utopian, but the rapid organization of Dominican studies to provide what was virtually a separate university system parallel with the system of secular universities is one of the most astonishing creations of the Middle Ages. In some ways the Dominicans created a stronger organization for advanced studies than any other ever created in western Europe. There has never again been such an organization, directed by a single legislative authority, drawing together an international body of students studying for a clearly defined purpose.

The scholastic legislation of the Franciscans followed that of the Dominicans at a considerable distance. Like every other aspect of Franciscan organization it gives the impression of being on the verge of chaos, but it was not necessarily less effective on that account. There seems to be no direct injunction that every house should have a theological lecturer; but in England alone the Franciscan chronicler boasted that by 1251 there were thirty lecturers holding formal theological disputations, and three or four who lectured without formal disputations. Since this almost exactly coincides with the number of Franciscan houses in the English province, it seems clear that the Franciscan ideal was by this date very close to that of the Dominicans.[93]

All that we know of thirteenth-century Franciscan legislation supports this view. In 1260 the Franciscan General Chapter laid down that two friars from each province in the Order could go to Paris free of charge. These men had clearly already studied two or three years in their own

93. Thomas of Eccleston, *Tractatus de Adventu Fratrum Minorum in Angliam*, ed. A. G. Little, 1951, p. 50; and A. G. Little, 'The Educational Organization of the Mendicant Friars in England', *Transactions of the Royal Historical Society*, 1895, viii, 49–70.

province. There was certainly no lack of scholarly opportunity. At Oxford in the early fourteenth century there
were ninety Dominicans and eighty-four Franciscans.[94] The
two Orders were running neck-and-neck, and together
they must have accounted for well over a tenth of the
academic population. More important, they had invaded
and rejuvenated the study of theology, and profoundly
affected every other branch of scholastic activity.

The friars were able to do this not only because they
provided larger opportunities for prolonged study than
any other organization, but also because they gave a new
purpose to academic effort. They put the excitement back
into scholarship that had been lacking since the mid-twelfth
century. Until the friars came the universities had served
mainly as a training ground for administrators. They
produced the men who developed the legal systems, the law
courts, and the organization of government. This was a
necessary, but increasingly unsatisfying, aim. By contrast
the friars in their studies aimed at the conversion of the
world. They wanted to convert heretics, to confute the
Saracens, to win over the Greeks, to form preachers and
confessors, and to instruct those people in western Europe
who had largely been left out of the calculations of earlier
religious innovators. Theological study was the foundation
for this widely diversified activity: in becoming intellectually
more refined and difficult, it also became practically more
significant. It is hard to imagine an intellectual situation
more completely satisfying or more stimulating to academic
effort – and it could scarcely have existed without the
friars. It is not therefore surprising that all the greatest
names in medieval theology from 1250 to 1350 are the

94. This was the number in 1317; sixty years later, in 1377, the
Dominicans had fallen to 70 and the Franciscans had risen to 103. There
were also 45 Carmelites and 43 Austin Friars in 1317, and 57 Carmelites
and 49 Austin Friars in 1377 (A. G. Little, *Franciscan Papers, Lists and
Documents*, p. 65). The total number of members of Oxford University
in the fourteenth century is very uncertain: the most reliable estimate
(for 1315) is 1500; a hundred years later it was probably about 1000
(H. Rashdall, *Universities of Europe in the Middle Ages*, ed. F. M. Powicke
and A. B. Emden, 1936, iii, pp. 95, 328, 332–3).

names of friars: Albertus Magnus, Thomas Aquinas, Eckhart, among the Dominicans; Bonaventura, Duns Scotus, William of Ockham, among the Franciscans. These are names of permanent importance, standing above time or place. It is a measure of the wide scope of the friars' activities and of the passions which they released that this short list includes the greatest constructor as well as the greatest destroyer in the history of medieval thought. Where all previous religious organizations had failed, the friars succeeded: they satisfied the intellectual demands of the most intellectual century of the Middle Ages.

7

Fringe Orders and Anti-Orders

I. THE GENERAL ENVIRONMENT

WE have now reached the stage when every form of
organized religious life that could be successfully developed
within the social and religious framework of medieval
society – every possible form, that is to say, with regard to
purpose, organization, material support, and relationship
to the world at large – had been explored. The Benedictines, the Cistercians, the Augustinian canons, and the
Orders of friars between them had filled all the main areas
open for development. They met all the main spiritual,
social, and intellectual needs that could be met by organized
religious bodies, and they exhausted all the main sources of
support. There was only one further step to be taken,
and that was in the direction of greater freedom from social
and hierarchical pressures and a greater diversity of
individual effort. Here as in some other fields the last two
centuries of the Middle Ages, partly as a result of their
greater complexity and confusion, saw a return to the more
primitive conditions of life of the early Middle Ages. The
drive towards increasingly well-defined and universal
forms of organization and effort was suddenly relaxed, and
Europe began, from one point of view, to fall apart, and
from another to experience a new richness and variety of
emotional life.

This was a situation highly unfavourable to the production of new organizations like those of the Cistercians or the
Friars, who had been driven to form powerful organizations
to achieve their ends. Instead, we find a return to small,
humble, shadowy organizations for large and indefinite
ends. The solitary religious figure, never indeed wholly
submerged in the organizational zeal of the intervening

centuries, once more emerged as a force in society. He (or, still more significantly, she) no longer appeared in the form of a St Guthlac fighting a lonely battle to purify the land from evil spirits, but in the form of a St Catherine of Siena, a Julian of Norwich, or a Gerhard Groote of Deventer: contemplatives and mystics, critics and reformers who stood somewhat apart from the organized religious society around them. The spiritual warrior was out; the critic and contemplative came in. Warfare, which had provided the spiritual imagery of an earlier age, ceased to be attractive except to profiteers who concealed their true motives behind a parade of chivalry. Even the attempt to recreate the image of the Christian warrior for the purpose of the Crusade fell on deaf ears. In the place of the warrior, the new hope of Christendom lay in the individual prophet.

It often happens that the first breath of change is felt within the organization which stands most strongly for an established ideal. So here. It was in the Dominican Order, the most powerfully unified and orderly of all religious organizations, that in the early years of the fourteenth century the German friar Eckhart spoke words which could be interpreted in a very disruptive sense:

If anyone imagines he will get more by inner thoughts and sweet yearnings and a special grace of God than he could get beside the fire or with his flocks or in the stable, he is doing no more than trying to take God and wrap His head in a cloak and shove Him under the bench. For whoever seeks God in some special Way, will gain the Way and lose God who is hidden in the Way. But whoever seeks God without any special Way, finds Him as He really is; and such a man lives with the Son, and He is life itself.[1]

There are several ways of looking on these words. They may be considered against the background of widespread rebellion against the hierarchical church which can be traced from the twelfth century onwards. Or they may be considered in their future significance as a preview of the quiet evangelical purity of domestic life which is the most lasting contribution of Protestant puritanism to the Chris-

1. Meister Eckhart, *Die Deutschen Werke*, ed. J. Quint, 1938–? (work still in progress), i (*Predigt* 5b), p. 450.

tian life. Or they may be considered as an expression of the growing individualism of medieval religion, and as a criticism of the many attempts to press religious life into an organized system of observance for a professional élite. In all these ways Eckhart's words reflected some of the most important tendencies in later medieval experience, but for our present purpose the last is the most important.

All the great and fruitful movements in Europe between 1050 and 1300 were part of a search for order and organization, and they had all failed in varying degrees to attain their objective. Of course great things had been accomplished and the modern observer is rightly more impressed by the achievement than the failure. But to contemporaries, who saw more clearly than we do the gap between expectation and reality, who felt as we do not the confusion and bitterness of disappointed hopes, and who knew that if a man sets out on a journey nothing is achieved unless he arrives, the failure was very bitter. It was among the friars that the sense of disillusionment was greatest, because they had been the centre of the greatest hopes and the source of the most successful efforts during the thirteenth century. The Franciscan disillusionment found expression in a new wave of apocalyptic hope and rebellion against the complacency of the established order. The Dominican disillusionment was more restrained and found its main expression in some courageous attempts by disciples of Thomas Aquinas to recast and extend the content of his work. Among the works of these disciples, the sermons of Eckhart represent an effort to free religious life from the pressure of institutions, and to give it a centre not in an institution – not even an institution so free from common worldly ties as the Orders of friars – but in the individual.

Eckhart's teaching is beset with difficulties of interpretation, but it seems clear that, in his German sermons which he preached in the Dominican church to the people of Cologne, he gave a new emphasis to the religious value of secular life. He spoke of a union with God that was open to all men, and especially to those who were free from the temptations of the professionally religious. The chief of these temptations was to possess property – not the worldly property which the friars had shunned, but property in prayers, fastings, watchings, and all such outward practices and mortifications. It would be quite wrong to imagine (as many of Eckhart's contemporaries did) that he was a rebel against the outward forms and institutions of the church. If his teaching seemed to depreciate these things, it was partly because they had been overvalued in the past, and partly because he was taking one stage further the search for the liberating poverty that the friars had institutionally failed to find.

The core of Eckhart's message was that this poverty had to be found in the soul itself. It could not be found in the act of giving up this or that form of property, because this act like every other act was a contrivance of the human will, which imposed a barrier between the soul and God. What Eckhart talked about in his sermons was an interior conversion in the soul which would manifest itself in the appropriate way determined by God alone. When men experienced this conversion, all vows, disciplines, religious exercises, and outward forms retreated into the background.

Did then these vows, disciplines, and outward forms have any continuing value at all? This was a question to which Eckhart gave no clear answer. It was a question that kept reappearing throughout the later Middle Ages in many different contexts, and it threatened to break down all the hardly won systems and organization of the earlier period. Even when it did not go as far as this, the search for a single ultimate reality in the individual soul – whether it stemmed from Eckhart or from some other source – had a profound influence on the religion of the last two medieval centuries.

It is important, however, to exaggerate neither the extent of this influence nor the uniqueness of Eckhart's testimony to the religious values of secular life. On the one hand, the starkly individualist position, which Eckhart's words taken out of their context often suggest, had only a limited appeal before the end of the Middle Ages. The vast majority of people remained firmly attached to the religious aids offered by the institutional church. To put it bluntly Europe had sunk too much intellectual, emotional, and material capital in these aids to resign them lightly. Masses and prayers for the dead, indulgences, good works and pious donations for the remission of purgatorial pains, have never been so widely and even wildly popular as they were in the fourteenth and fifteenth centuries.

Yet the eager acceptance of the benefits offered by these practices was never the whole of the popular religion of the Middle Ages. The laity never wholly acquiesced in their position as outsiders, receiving benefits in return for payments and services; they were neither so obedient nor so inert as they were encouraged to be. Eckhart's words only echoed, more sharply than most people would have found acceptable, a permanent and widespread desire to invest ordinary secular life with some of the values of a religious Order. This desire was expressed in various ways, but most coherently in attempts to create a lay fringe around established religious Orders and institutions. Round each of the Orders discussed above associations grew up clinging to the parent body like organisms which drew their life from the parent but developed (as such growths are apt to do) a life of their own.

In these fringe bodies are to be found some of the most original and attractive, and at times also violent and destructive, forces of the later Middle Ages. But before we turn to consider the development of organized religious life on the fringe of the religious Orders, something must be said about two elements in medieval society which we have too long neglected: the behaviour of crowds and the influence of women. They provide a key to the understanding of many features in late medieval religious behaviour which aroused the suspicion of both secular and ecclesiastical authorities.

The behaviour of crowds

From one point of view all the religious movements of the later Middle Ages were an attempt to harness, guide, and express some eléments in popular religion which drew their strength, not from the organized teaching and worship of the church, but from pressures in ordinary life which were beyond all control. The chief sources of mass religious movements were disease and despair, and the two generally went together. It is scarcely necessary to insist on the importance of these two basic facts of human life, except to draw attention to the frightful impact which they made, not only on individuals in the common accidents of life, but more especially on whole communities struck down by natural and social disasters which they could neither understand nor control. These disasters reached their peak in the Great Plague of 1348–9, but they were endemic throughout the medieval centuries. Warfare too made its contribution to despair. At all times the lives and property of non-combatants were at the mercy of armies without any regular sources of supply and with rules of war that took account only of military expediency.[2] Here as elsewhere Europe was saved from complete misery by a limited technology, but armies employed their limited means of destruction with utter ruthlessness. Yet, however great the terrors of war to ordinary people, undoubtedly famine and disease were the main sources of despair. Painful disease, incurable by any human agency, stimulated crowds of sufferers to hysterical outbursts prompted and alleviated by the hope of divine intervention. There are many accounts of these movements of popular despair, but two must suffice.

In 1145 the church of St-Pierre-sur-Dives in Normandy was brought to completion after many years' work and the expectation of miracles brought great crowds of people, who surrounded the altars with frantic appeals to the Mother of Mercy:

If their cure was delayed and they did not immediately obtain what they desired, they stripped off their clothes and lay on the ground naked from the loins upwards, forgetting all shame, men,

2. See M. H. Keen, *The Laws of War in the Late Middle Ages*, 1965, pp. 19, 121, 140, 190–91, 243. In all centuries of the Middle Ages the barbarous treatment of civilians was normal.

women, and children together; and thus stretched on the ground, they crawled not on hands and knees but clawed with their whole bodies to the high altar and then to the other altars crying a new supplication, 'Mother of Mercy', until they extorted a reply to their petitions.[3]

Again, here in Oxford a few years later, there were similar scenes. In 1180 the body of St Frideswide was translated to a new tomb and a rumour of miracles began to spread through the town. In a short time the church was besieged with people suffering from every kind of disease. Most of them were people of humble origin coming in from the towns or surrounding countryside; a number came from as far afield as Exeter, Bury St Edmunds, Southampton, and Shropshire; a few had been disappointed suppliants at other and greater shrines like that of St Thomas at Canterbury. They were sufferers from dropsy, paralysis, blindness, madness, skin-diseases, aches, pains, and wounds of head, stomach, and limbs. The church was filled day and night with sufferers and their relatives; they crowded round the tomb, slept beside it, touched it, scraped up the dust. The canons recorded about a hundred miracles, and then quite suddenly the excitement died down and nothing more was heard of the healing powers of St Frideswide.[4]

These are commonplace scenes, and of course they are not confined to the Middle Ages nor to Christendom. But it is important to remember how frequent they were in medieval Europe, how easily popular expectations were stirred, and what an essential part these expectations played in making life tolerable for large masses of people whose only hope lay in a sign from heaven.

In general these manifestations of popular religious need were too widely diffused to become an organized movement. Yet there was always the possibility that some specially disturbing event would intensify the prevailing mood of worldly despair and supernatural hope until a spontaneous polarization of energy took place. This possibility was most

3. See the letter from the abbot of St Pierre to the monks at Tutbury, ed. L. Delisle, *Bibliothèque de l'école des chartes*, 1860, xxi, 113–39.

4. *Acta Sanctorum, Octobris*, viii, 568–89.

strikingly realized in the plague months of 1348 and 1349, and we can get a very clear picture of what happened at this time under the strain of an overwhelming disaster from the observations of the abbot of St Martin of Tournai in Belgium.[5]

He recorded that on 15 August 1349 a band of some two hundred men from Bruges appeared in the town about supper-time and stayed for twenty-four hours. During the following week they were followed by similar bands – four hundred from Ghent; three hundred from Sluis; four hundred from Dordrecht; a hundred and eighty from Liège. With this last band there came a Dominican who preached a sermon in which he set out the purpose of the movement. He called his companions the Red Knights of Christ and spoke of the blood which they shed freely in frequent flagellations: it was, he said, the most noble effusion of blood since that of Christ himself, and it united them with the blood of Christ. They would all, he added, be saved; they had no need of a papal indulgence; they had no need to honour the saints, for they bore on their own bodies and souls the stigmata of Christ.

At this point the popular excitement in the town exploded. During the next few days a contingent of flagellants was organized under the leadership of four local men, and on 7 September five hundred and sixty-five men with the prior of the Augustinian friars, a canon, and two secular priests set out in the direction of Liège. They did not return till 10 October. Meanwhile the flood continued to pour through Tournai: in the four weeks from 12 September the abbot reckoned that twenty-three bands comprising some 3,500 people from the neighbouring towns had come through. It was beyond all possibility of control.

The abbot who recorded these events was a puzzled man. On the one hand ecclesiastical opinion was against these itinerating crowds: they swarmed into the cathedral and other churches, performing their peculiar rites and dis-

5. See the documents collected by P. Frédéricq, *Corpus Documentorum Inquisitionis Hereticae Pravitatis Neerlandicae*, 1889, i, 190–201; 1896, ii, 100–139.

turbing the orderly recital of the divine office; they kept
their hats on even at the moment of the elevation of the
Host; they behaved in an altogether unseemly way. Yet
the clergy could do nothing for fear of the multitude, who
were strongly in favour of the movement. Everyone felt
the need to do something in the face of the great disaster
of the past year. A very high proportion of the population
had died of plague – no one knew, any more than we do,
how many. This blood-letting was an attempt to staunch
God's anger by an act of sacrificial propitiation. Perhaps
after all it would work. The language and customs of the
flagellants were in many ways those of the most approved
piety: they said many *Paters* and *Aves* in the course of the
day; they sang hymns as they went along celebrating the
sufferings of Christ; they fasted and abstained from intercourse with women; in the course of their scourgings they
chanted a liturgy of penance. More dubiously, as a work
pleasing to God, they called for the killing of the Jews,
whom they believed to be the authors of their distress.
Whatever the learned might say, this attempt to identify the
culprits did nothing to lessen their popularity with the
people. On the whole the abbot who watched them going
through the town was inclined to suspend judgement.

Throughout the summer and autumn of 1349 the agita-
tion spread through the towns of Flanders and Germany.
Then, as the plague came to an end, it petered out as
quickly as it had begun. It left almost no mark on the institutions or thinking of the medieval church, but it leaves a
vivid impression of the way in which large numbers of
people behaved when subjected to great strain. They took
up the devotions of current piety and adapted them to
their own fierce resolve to make a sacrifice to God both of
their own bodies and of those whom they believed to be
God's enemies. They were immensely sure of themselves
and contemptuous of traditional disciplines and restraints.
In their zeal they swamped the ordinary organization of
the church, broke through the barrier between the illiterate
populace and the learned rulers of society, and spoke with
certainty about things to come. To a greater or less degree

these are the features of every popular movement of the Middle Ages. The plague only added an explosive energy to frustrations that were always present, and it showed more clearly than any other incident of the Middle Ages the permanent ingredients of mass religion. It is important to remember this strong undertow of popular feeling when we consider the new types of religious organization.

But before turning to this theme we must trace the development of another dominant influence in later medieval religion.

The influence of women in religious life

The provision of a suitably dignified religious retreat for unmarried women and widows had presented a difficult problem for the aristocracy of the early Middle Ages. An unmarried woman was an anomaly in secular society. Girls were commonly married at the age of thirteen or fourteen, and widows were expected to marry again without undue delay. It was only in this way that the obligation of family policy and the military responsibilities of property could be discharged. Yet, unattractive though the position of unmarried women in society in many ways was, it had its alleviations. Great families felt bound to make provision for girls who could not or would not marry, and widows with important connexions and an established place in society could not easily be coerced into disposing of themselves and their property otherwise than as they wished.

These considerations help to account for the very large number of monastic foundations for nuns in the early medieval centuries. The Merovingian and Anglo-Saxon kings of the seventh and eighth centuries were especially notable for the size and importance of the nunneries which they endowed. It was a main purpose of these endowments to provide a retreat for the widows and daughters of the great, and some of the most famous names in early Frankish and English monastic history are names of nuns of royal descent – Hilda at Whitby, Etheldreda at Ely, Radegunde at Poitiers, Bathilda at Chelles, and very many others. They were masterful and formidable ladies and they did not forget that they belonged to a ruling caste. Communities of monks were commonly attached to their nunneries in order to provide the necessary services of sacraments and temporal administration, and the great lady abbess ruled the whole organization in the spirit of one accustomed to command. These ladies of the Dark Ages have some remarkable religious and literary achievements to their credit, but their period of splendid independence did not last long. As society became better organized and ecclesiastically more right-minded, the necessity for male dominance began to assert itself.

DECLINE

In the great period of monastic foundation from the early tenth to the early twelfth century the position of women in the monastic life suffered a sharp decline. The institution of double monasteries, and more especially the dominant position of the women in them, came under attack. Moreover, the new and more exacting conception of the monastic duty of liturgical specialization and of the intercessory value of monastic masses necessarily emphasized the importance of monks who could most efficiently perform these duties. The double monasteries therefore disappeared.

Nunneries of course continued to be founded, but in contrast to their earlier importance they played only a small part in the monastic development of this period. The evidence of Cluny, where the ideals of the new monasticism were most fully displayed, is particularly striking in this regard. In the tenth and eleventh centuries scores of monasteries were founded in association with Cluny, but they included only one foundation for nuns before the beginning of the twelfth century. This was at Marcigny, and it was founded at the suggestion of Hugh, abbot of Cluny, for the special purpose of providing a retreat for women whose husbands had become monks of Cluny at his instigation.[6] The abbot had felt some compunction in advising men to become monks when there were so few

6. *Vita S. Hugonis Abbatis Cluniacensis*, in M. Marrier and A. Quercetanus, *Bibliotheca Cluniacensis*, 1815, p. 455.

opportunities for their wives to do likewise. He therefore
encouraged his brother to provide land for a nunnery. The
circumstances and terms of the foundation illustrate the
lowered esteem of women in religion. They no longer
directed their own affairs; still less did they rule monks.
On the contrary, those who entered 'this glorious prison'
were placed under the rule of a prior appointed by the
abbot of Cluny. The nuns were strictly enclosed lest 'in
appearing in the world they either made others desire
them, or saw things which they themselves desired'.[7] The
nunnery was to be

a place where mature women who were tired of matrimonial
licence might purge their past errors and be worthy of attaining
the embraces of Christ. Noble women who had been freed from
matrimony chose this place, resigning themselves the more patiently to the loss of matrimonial joys as they had discovered how short
and full of sorrow are its pleasures.[8]

These words of Abbot Hugh and his biographer do not
express any very high notion of the spiritual vocation or
capacity for self-discipline of the ladies who found a refuge
at Marcigny. Yet the emphasis on providing an escape
from matrimony which obtrudes itself in these documents
was probably not ill-judged. Disgust at the recollection or
prospect of marriage seems to have played a very large part
in recommending the monastic life to women, and this
disgust certainly did not diminish in the course of the
twelfth century. It is often thought that the lofty position
accorded to women in the romantic and devotional literature of this century is evidence of their increasing ease and
freedom in the world. But the inference is false. The growth
of a romantic and erotic literature only strengthened belief
in the moral and social dangers of feminine wantonness;
and the devotional literature of the twelfth century, with
its intense interest in virginity, helped to create in many
minds a strong and sometimes hysterical aversion to the

7. ibid., 455–6. For the imagery of the prison, see Peter the Venerable,
Epp., ii, 17; iv, 21; vi, 39 (*The Letters of Peter the Venerable*, ed.
G. Constable, 1967, i, pp. 161, 306, 428).
   8. Hildebert, *Vita S. Hugonis*, ii, 11 (*P.L.* 159, 868).

state of matrimony. As a result of these influences, and still more as a result of the insecure position of women in a rapidly growing population, the number of women who desired a religious life greatly outran the number of monastic foundations available for their reception.

NEW OPPORTUNITIES AND FRUSTRATIONS

The need for new opportunities for women in religion and the difficulty of meeting this need can be most clearly seen in the history of the new religious Orders. Around the year 1100, when the new Orders were beginning to make their appearance, there were several religious leaders whose teaching made a wide appeal to women. The earliest of these was Robert of Arbrissel, an itinerant preacher in the towns and villages of the Loire valley in the last years of the eleventh century. He gathered a large following of women 'rich and poor, widows and virgins, old and young, prostitutes and man-haters alike', as his biographer reports.[9] The control of this heterogeneous body must have presented alarming difficulties, but he finally settled many of these women in a new monastery at Fontevrault. Very soon the donations began to pour in.[10] They came from people of all ranks, sometimes accompanied by the gift of a daughter of the donor to add to the community. The need was evidently great, and the social composition of the nunnery was at first very varied. But within a generation Fontevrault had become a very aristocratic house indeed, the burial place of the counts of Anjou, and a refuge for women from the greatest families of northern France.

Another example of a strong initial impulse, followed by a speedy reaction, is to be found in the work of St Norbert, the founder of the Premonstratensian canons. In the rising towns of northern France and Flanders he struck an even more fertile soil than Robert of Arbrissel. Preaching in Valenciennes and the neighbouring towns from 1118 to 1125 he met the same kind of enthusiastic reception that

9. Baudry, *Life of Robert of Arbrissel*, *P.L.* 162, 1052–8.
10. *P.L.* 162, 1085–1118, and more fully in J. de la Mainferme, *Clypeus Fontebaldensis*, 3 vols., 1648–91, and Cosnier, *Exordium Fontis Ebraldensis*.

the friars were to find a century later – notably from the women of these towns.[11] A canon of Laon reported that by about 1150 there were more than a thousand women in various places belonging to the single church of Prémontré 'serving God in such severity and silence that you could scarcely find the like in the strictest monasteries of monks'.[12] A few sentences later the same writer says that more than ten thousand women had been drawn into the Premonstratensian Order. It revived the institution of double monasteries, which had been in disfavour since the tenth century. They were no longer governed by an abbess as they had been in the Merovingian foundations, but in numbers and esteem they restored women to a position of respect and importance. We need not take the chronicler's estimates of numbers too seriously, but it is evident that eyewitnesses were astonished by the number of women who chose this escape from the world.

Yet even while the chronicler of Laon was writing, the reaction had set in. Norbert's double monasteries aroused the same anti-feminine criticisms as those of an earlier period. By the middle of the century there were powerful influences at work to get rid of the intruders. Successive popes tried in vain to protect the rights of the women. In 1138 Innocent II insisted that the Order must give adequate maintenance to its women members, from whom, or on whose behalf, it had received a large part of its property. Celestine II, Eugenius III, and Adrian IV repeated this humane insistence in 1143, 1147, and 1154. But the exhortations of popes have little force when they run against the stream of common religious opinion. While the popes issued their bulls, the Order began suppressing its double monasteries and the sisters of Prémontré began their wanderings. Before the end of the century the General Chapter of Prémontré had decreed that no more women were to be admitted to the Order:

11. *Vita S. Norberti, P.L.* 170, 1273.
12. *Miracula S. Mariae Laudunensis,* iii, c. 7 (*P.L.* 156, 996–7). See also A. Erens, 'Les sœurs dans l'ordre de Prémontré', *Analecta Praemonstratensia,* 1929, v, 6–26.

Since the times are dangerous and the church is burdened beyond measure, we have decided by common consent that we will henceforward receive no more sisters.[13]

One of the abbots, Conrad of Marchtal, put the reason for rejecting women with brutal frankness:

We and our whole community of canons, recognizing that the wickedness of women is greater than all the other wickedness of the world, and that there is no anger like that of women, and that the poison of asps and dragons is more curable and less dangerous to men than the familiarity of women, have unanimously decreed for the safety of our souls, no less than for that of our bodies and goods, that we will on no account receive any more sisters to the increase of our perdition, but will avoid them like poisonous animals.[14]

Whatever might be said officially about the difficulties of discipline and the pressure on resources, this outburst gives us a glimpse of the popular religious conceptions which long continued to depress the status of women in the religious life.

Yet, however persistent these repressive views might be, they could not resist the strong social pressure to make more room for women in the religious life. The most striking illustration of the strength of this pressure is provided by the inability of even the Cistercian Order to keep women out. There was no religious body more thoroughly masculine in its temper and discipline than the Cistercians, none that shunned female contact with greater determination, or that raised more formidable barriers against the intrusion of women. To St Bernard every woman was a threat to his chastity, and he saw vast and nameless dangers in that easy association of men and women which marked the early evangelistic efforts of Robert of Arbrissel and St Norbert:

To be always with a woman and not to have intercourse with her is more difficult than to raise the dead. You cannot do the less

13. E. Martène, *De Antiquis Ecclesiae Ritibus*, 1737, iii, 925, quoted by Erens, op. cit.
14. Quoted by Erens from E. L. Hugo, *Annales Praemonstratenses*, ii, 147.

difficult: do you think I will believe that you can do what is more difficult?[15]

Unlike the Premonstratensians, the early Cistercians' legislation simply ignored the existence of women; and when they recognized their existence, it was in order to keep them at a distance. And yet, almost as soon as the Order began to expand, we find nunneries springing up following the customs of Cîteaux, and claiming the protection, if not of the Order, at least of influential members of the Order. They appeared everywhere in Europe by the middle years of the twelfth century, and especially in those least developed parts of Europe where there was still plenty of vacant land, and where the Cistercian monks were most strongly settled. In Spain especially, the great families, who were responsible for the settlement of Cistercian monks, also created some of the largest and most aristocratic houses of Cistercian nuns. These nunneries had no formal place in the structure of the Order, but were created with the good-will and under the supervision of individual Cistercian abbots. They were remarkably free to develop as they pleased. In a primitive aristocratic environment, the Cistercian abbesses of large foundations in Spain recall the feminine grandeur of the Merovingian age. Innocent III was scandalized to learn that they undertook the benediction of their own nuns, heard their confessions, and preached in the pulpits.[16] Although they had no place in the Cistercian organization, they behaved like Cistercians, and the greatest of them had their own dependent houses and held their own Chapters.

All this happened without the slightest notice being taken of it in the official acts of the Cistercian Order. It is a remarkable example of demand creating supply. The existence of Cistercian nunneries was an affront to the carefully integrated organization of the Order, but it appealed to another side of the Cistercian movement – to its expansive and missionary zeal, which gladly extended

15. *Sermones in Cantica*, lxv (*P.L.* 183, 1091).
16. Potthast, *Regesta*, no. 4143 (*P.L.* 216, 356).

the influence of the Order in every possible direction. Moved by this zeal, and acting independently of the organization in response to pressure from outside, Cistercian abbots had already carved out a large area for feminine initiative before the Order took any official cognizance of the new force that had arisen in its midst.

It was not until 1191 that the official records of the Order mentioned the nuns. A brief note in the decisions of the General Chapter of this year shows the difficulty of knowing how to deal with these unwelcome adherents. It appears that the independent abbesses of Spain had been refusing to attend the meetings of their local Chapter, and the king had appealed to the Cistercian General Chapter to compel their attendance. But it too was powerless: this most authoritarian of all governing bodies resolved merely to

write to the King of Castile and say that we cannot force his abbesses to go to the Chapter about which he writes; but if they wish to go – as we should advise them to do – it would please us greatly. [17]

From this time the General Chapter became increasingly aware of the contrast between the discipline of the Order and the freedom of the large and rapidly growing number of women who adhered to its customs without being subject to its organization or control. The result was a long struggle to discipline the women. From 1213 onwards the General Chapter tried to enforce a regime of strict enclosure; it insisted that the number of nuns should be limited by the abbot to whose supervision they were committed; that there should be no new settlements of nuns without the licence of the General Chapter; that the nuns should receive no visitors without permission; that they should make their confessions only to a confessor appointed by the supervising abbot; and finally that no more nunneries were to be attached to the Order.[18] Thus the Cistercians

17. *Statuta Cisterciensia*, A.D. 1191, c. 27.
18. ibid.: A.D. 1213, c. 3, 4; 1218, c. 4, 84; 1219, c. 12; 1220, c. 4; 1225, c. 1; 1228, c. 16; 1233, c. 12; 1239, c. 7. The first declaration that no more nunneries were to be admitted to the Order is 1228, c. 16.

tried to impose the authority of the abbot and the General Chapter, to restrict the freedom of abbesses and nuns, and to stifle the whole development. But it was too late. The attempt to prevent new foundations of Cistercian nunneries was a complete failure. In several parts of Europe, especially in the areas of most rapid settlement – in Germany, Belgium, Holland, Portugal, and also in Switzerland – the number of Cistercian nunneries came in the course of the thirteenth century greatly to exceed the number of foundations for Cistercian monks. Over the Order as a whole, the number of nunneries – though not their wealth – was not far behind that of the male monasteries.[19] The combined pressures of lay founders and their families, often supported by the popes, defeated the restrictions which the General Chapter attempted to impose.

Meanwhile, the attempt to bring the nunneries under a stricter supervision had only a limited success. The Cistercians found too late that they could not treat the nuns with the peremptory firmness that they were accustomed to display towards their monks. In the years 1242–4 when the policy of subordinating the nuns to the supervision of Cistercian abbots reached its peak, there were disturbances in the nunneries. The high-spirited abbess and nuns of Parc-aux-Dames in northern France shouted and stamped and walked out of the chapter-house when the official visitors told them of the recent legislation.[20] The General Chapter attempted – whether with success we cannot tell – to discipline the ringleaders of this demonstration, but it rescinded the most offensive passage in its legislation in the following year.[21] In practice the legislators had to bow before the force of feminine liberty.

19. According to the most recent estimate, the total number of Cistercian nunneries at the end of the Middle Ages was 654 (and the figure for Italy is very incomplete) against 742 foundations for monks. The nunneries were in the majority in Germany (255: 75), Belgium (45: 18), Switzerland (21: 8), and Holland (23: 14). See F. Vongrey and F. Hervay, 'Kritische Bemerkungen zum "Atlas de l'ordre cistercien" von Fred. van der Meer', *Analecta Cisterciensia*, 1967, xxiii, 137–8.

20. *Stat. Cist.*, A.D. 1242, c. 15–18; 1243, c. 6–8, 61–8.

21. ibid., A.D. 1244, c. 8.

The Cistercian struggle took place at a high social level. Fundamentally it was a struggle between a central legislative body and aristocratic ladies who resented any interference with their accustomed liberties, especially by a body in which they had no voice and to which they owed only the most shadowy obedience. In its outcome the struggle demonstrated that those who stand on the fringe of an organization and have no part in its deliberations are in a strong position for resisting control. The vigour of the feminine side of the Cistercian movement is very surprising. It is less surprising that in course of time it created an official reaction against it. But by the time that this reaction had reached its full development, a new feminine movement had begun in a quite different social environment. It is to this movement and the situation from which it arose that we must now turn.

II. A CONFUSION OF TONGUES

We may begin by looking at the new situation in one clearly defined local environment; and we may note that one of the chief characteristics of the novelties of the later Middle Ages lies in the strong influence of locality in their development. The organizations we have so far examined have all shown their vitality by their ability to subordinate local conditions to the requirements of a universal system. But the vitality of the new movements is shown in their resistance to overall control, and in the preservation of their local peculiarities in the face of all attempts to plane down eccentricities and impose the stamp of universal legislation upon them.

One result of this localism is that the historian must himself become more local, and this makes it necessary to be highly selective in the choice of examples. In the pages that follow we shall trace the fortunes of two groups of women and men: the beguines of Cologne in the late thirteenth and fourteenth, and the religious brethren of Deventer and its neighbourhood in the fourteenth and fifteenth centuries. These groups do not impose themselves on the historian in the same way as the Cistercians and the friars. The Cistercians and the friars belong to Europe as a whole; the beguines and brethren do indeed belong in the most general sense to a widespread movement, but the movement is not European-wide, still less does it create a universal corporate framework suitable and necessary for its development. It is not even in any strict sense a single movement at all: it is simply a series of reactions to the conditions of urban life and commercial wealth, combined with disillusionment about elaborate structures of government and systems of theoretical perfection. But since these conditions are to be permanent features of European life, the early reactions to them have an importance out of all proportion to the numbers and institutional strength of the groups we are to study. In the history of these reactions women play a leading part and it is with them that we begin.

The beguines of Cologne

THE ORIGINS

In 1243, the year in which the nuns of Parc-aux-Dames were stamping out of their chapter-house and hurling insults at their visitatorial board, Matthew Paris – surveying the European scene from his English monastery – made an entry in his Chronicle to which he attached great importance:

At this time and especially in Germany, certain people – men and women, but especially women – have adopted a religious profession, though it is a light one. They call themselves 'religious', and they take a private vow of continence and simplicity of life, though they do not follow the Rule of any saint, nor are they as yet confined within a cloister. They have so multiplied within a short time that two thousand have been reported in Cologne and the neighbouring cities.[22]

We know that the chronicler was greatly impressed by the news of this new movement because in 1250, when he

22. Matthew Paris, *Chronica Majora*, iv, 278.

summarized the main events of the previous half century,
he repeated his information in a slightly different form and
placed the new movement alongside the friars as a notable
development in the religious life:

In Germany [he wrote] there has arisen an innumerable multitude of celibate women who call themselves beguines: a thousand
or more of them live in Cologne alone.[23]

When he came to write a précis of his chronicle he still
found room for these women, and he added the additional
information that 'they live a frugal life on the labour of
their own hands'.[24] That was all he had to say about them,
and we may wonder why he thought them sufficiently
important to be mentioned in every version of his chronicle
and in the same company as the friars.

Part of the answer is to be found in an almost exactly
contemporary remark made by the great bishop of Lincoln,
Robert Grosseteste. The English Franciscan chronicler,
Thomas of Eccleston, reports that Grosseteste one day
preached a sermon to the Franciscans in which he extolled
the life of begging as the highest kind of poverty next to
heaven itself. But later in private he told the Franciscans
that there was a still higher kind of poverty: this was to
live by one's own labour 'like the beguines'. These people,
he declared, had the most perfect and holy form of religious
life because they lived by their own efforts and did not
burden the world with their demands.[25] If Grosseteste, the
greatest champion of the Franciscans in English public

23. ibid., v, 194.

24. *Historia Angliae*, ii, 476; iii, 93; *Abbreviatio Chronicorum*, iii, 288, 318.
For a general treatment of the subject, see H. Grundmann, *Religiöse
Bewegungen im Mittelalter*, 1961, c. 6, 'Die Beginen im xiii Jht.'; E. G.
Neumann, *Rheinisches Beginen– u. Begardenwesen*, 1960. The fullest details
on the beguines of Cologne are given in J. Asen, 'Die Beginen in Köln',
Annalen des Hist. Vereins f. den Niederrhein, 1927–8, cxi, 81–180; cxii, 71–
148; cxiii, 13–96. The statistics given below have been extracted from
these articles, which made use of the property registers in the city
archives.

25. Thomas of Eccleston, *De Adventu Fratrum Minorum in Angliam*, ed.
A. G. Little, p. 99.

life, could think that the beguines had discovered the highest form of religious life, they certainly deserved all the space they occupied in Matthew Paris's chronicle.

Between them, Grosseteste and Matthew Paris surveyed a very large slice of European life, and they were both impressed by the new and strange phenomenon. The beguine movement differed substantially from all earlier important movements within the western church. It was basically a women's movement, not simply a feminine appendix to a movement which owed its impetus, direction, and main support to men. It had no definite Rule of life; it claimed the authority of no saintly founder; it sought no authorization from the Holy See; it had no organization or constitution; it promised no benefits and sought no patrons; its vows were a statement of intention, not an irreversible commitment to a discipline enforced by authority; and its adherents could continue their ordinary work in the world.

Of course no new movement is ever wholly new in all its features. Several of the characteristics of the beguines had been anticipated in some degree in the religious Orders of the previous hundred years. The Franciscans had started without a definite Rule, and both they and the Dominicans had from the beginning operated in the world. Many of the early groups of hermits, preachers, and seekers who later adopted the Rule of St Augustine had started with intentions as ill-defined as those of the beguines. But in many of their features, and above all in their combination of them, the beguines presented a new front to the ecclesiastical hierarchy. They were part of that popular ferment that had been working sporadically within the church ever since western society had begun its great expansion in the mid-eleventh century. This ferment had taken many forms, but hitherto it had always spilled over into heresy. Indeed, it was from the hated name Albigensian that the name 'beguine' had been derived. It was a label of contempt given by their enemies to women who claimed to be holier than other women, who resisted the advances of lascivious priests (there is evidence that this often got them into trouble), and rejected the inducements of lawful matrimony.[26]

The name 'beguine' was intended as a smear, but it was difficult to make the charge of heresy stick. When the movement began in the first quarter of the thirteenth century many beguines suffered, and some died, as a result of the suspicion of heresy. But they were remarkably innocent. They had no quarrel with orthodoxy; they had no distinctive theological ideas at all; they were not perfectionists or Manicheans; they had no new revelation, only a desire to live 'religiously'. And so, although they met with much dislike, they also found protectors and made their way forward imperceptibly. Their Albigensian affiliations, if they had ever existed, were soon forgotten, and Matthew Paris could write, 'No one knows why they are called beguines, nor how they began.'

Modern research has been able to discover 'how they began' and it points to the area round Liège about the year 1210 as the time and place. From here they spread throughout the cities of Flanders, and in the course of time throughout the whole area from the Baltic to the Alps, and eastwards from Flanders to Bohemia. But it was Cologne that aroused the interest of Matthew Paris, and it happens that the remarkable archives of the city make it possible to reconstruct the history of the movement in this important centre in considerable detail. A brief investigation at this point will throw light on a widespread phenomenon.

GROWTH

We may look first at the urban setting of the movement. The growth of Cologne in the thirteenth and fourteenth centuries can be traced in only very rough outline, but it seems likely that the population grew from about 15,000 at the beginning of the thirteenth century to a medieval maximum of around 37,000 about 1320. After this date there are some wild fluctuations punctuated by the onset

26. For the early persecution of these women see H. Grundmann, op. cit., pp. 171–2, and James of Vitry's *Life* of Mary of Oignies (1177–1213) in *Acta Sanctorum*, 23 June, vol. iv.

of the plague. These cannot be traced in any detail, but the visitation of 1348–50 must for a time have reduced the population to a level not much above 20,000. If, as is generally thought, the number of women in the population was significantly higher than that of men, the rapid growth of the town in the thirteenth and early fourteenth centuries would clearly leave an increasing number of women in a very insecure position. For unmarried and widowed women a religious house would be the obvious refuge, but the number of nunneries was small, and the resources of the unmarried female members of even quite prosperous urban families must often have been exiguous. It is against a general background of this kind that we must examine the evidence for the growth of the number of women who wished to live a religious life, singly in their family homes or in small groups living in houses which one of their number had inherited, or which they bought by pooling inheritances.

The survival of systematic records of property transactions in the city from the year 1223 makes it possible to trace the development of the movement in some detail.[27] The first beguines appear in 1223. In this year two sisters, Elizabeth and Sophie, described as beguines, members of an important local family, sold small properties which they had inherited on the banks of the Rhine: Sophie's share was no more than the twelfth part of a house and courtyard, and there was a third beguine called Rigmunde, who sold the sixth part of a similar property. After this beginning there is a gap in the recorded transactions of beguines in the city until 1250. Then there comes a dramatic change and the number of such transactions rises steeply until 1310. The facts may most conveniently be summarized in a graph showing the number of beguines mentioned in

27. Some 200 registers have preserved the records of more than 150,000 property transactions in the city between about 1220 and 1400. There is an account of these books and the literature on them, together with the text of about 2,500 documents, in H. Planitz and T. Buyken, *Die Kölner Schreinsbücher des xiii u. xiv Jahrhunderts* (Publikationen der Gesellschaft für Rheinische Geschichtskunde, xlvi), 1937.

property transfers in the city in each decade between 1250 and 1400:[28]

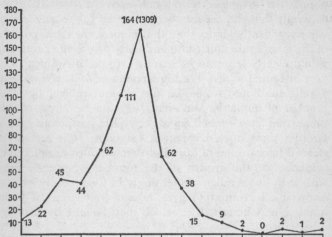

BEGUINES MENTIONED IN PROPERTY
TRANSACTIONS IN COLOGNE, 1250–1400

It will be seen from this graph, that the number of beguines recorded in these transactions declines even more steeply after 1310 than it had risen in the previous sixty years. There is of course no exact correlation between the number of beguines buying or selling property and their total number in the city, but the steep rise in their property transactions between 1250 and 1310 must correspond to a rapid growth in the number of beguines. The decline in transactions after 1310 is not quite so simply explained. The earliest beguines had lived singly or in small informal groups. They were therefore much involved in buying and selling small tenements in order to set up their establishments. Gradually however small permanent convents came to be set up, and these increased very rapidly in number around the end of the thirteenth century. The facts

28. See Asen, op. cit., cxi, 93.

relating to their foundation may be summarized in another graph showing the number of permanent beguine convents known to have been founded in each decade between 1260 and 1400:[29]

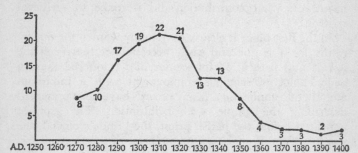

FOUNDATIONS OF BEGUINE CONVENTS
IN COLOGNE, 1260–1400*

*Of 169 convents the exact date of foundation of only 108 is known: with regard to the others there is an element of conjecture in assigning them to the appropriate decade, and 23 are left unaccounted for in the graph.

By the end of the fourteenth century there were a hundred and sixty-nine beguine convents in the city. The convents provided a home for about fifteen hundred beguines, and they gradually – partly as a result of ecclesiastical pressure and partly for simple convenience – drew in the whole beguine population. By 1400 all beguines lived in convents. The initial impetus which had astonished observers in the mid thirteenth century had long ago died away, and there was no need for any new foundations. The common fate of medieval religious movements suggests that, when the first energy had departed, the number of beguines would shrink; but there were beguines in Cologne till the end of the eighteenth century, and in the early sixteenth century they were still sufficiently numerous for a contemporary satirist to compare them to the drops in the ocean or the hairs of an ass.

29. ibid., pp. 93–4.

THE APPEAL OF THE BEGUINES

What are we to say about this history of an Order that was not an Order? What function did it serve; what people did it attract; what contribution did it make to medieval religion?

In the first place it clearly gave many women the opportunity for a simple and easily accessible retreat from the storms and frustrations of secular life. It offered them a wide choice of religious employment with a minimum amount of complication. Many records have been preserved describing the simple acts of initiation. The aspirant appeared before the parish priest, the bishop's official, the warden of the Franciscans, or the prior of the Dominicans, and took an oath in one of many different forms. Some just 'offered themselves to Christ'; others 'desired to live religiously all their lives'; others declared that they wished 'to serve the Lord Jesus Christ in the habit of a beguine'. Most frequently, they renounced marriage and took an oath of chastity, though sometimes they expressly left open the possibility of a later change of mind. The ceremony of profession took place after Mass, when the confessor of the new beguine offered her a beguine's dress at the altar, and she vowed to wear it as 'a girl dedicated and offered to God'.[30]

The main theme of the beguine's life was dedication to God. Her employments were of various kinds and were combined in varying proportions: working in a hospital, weaving and embroidery, simple prayer and meditation. The way of life precluded any great development of learning or literature, but two or three beguines of the thirteenth century have left considerable records of their prayers and visions. It is not surprising that their records are full of ecstatic and visionary experiences with a strong element of naive sexuality in their imagery. Without pretending to reach out to any new truths, and wholly unsystematic though they are, they have a fresh individuality and pathos in their vernacular outpourings:

30. Many of the formulas of dedication have been preserved in the city archives: see Asen, op. cit., cxi, pp. 89–90.

I send this book out as a messenger to all the clergy good or bad. It describes myself alone, and reveals my secrets with thanksgiving. Hi, Lord God, who has made this book? I have made it in my weakness, for I would not withhold my gift. Hi, Lord, what shall it be called to serve thy honour? It shall be called 'a streaming light of my Godhead' into all the hearts that live here without falsehood.[31]

Or again:

> My body is in great distress.
> My soul is in highest bliss,
> for she has seen
> and thrown her arms around
> her Loved One all at once.
> Poor thing,
> she is distressed by him:
> he so draws and delights her,
> she cannot withhold herself,
> and he brings her into himself.
>
> Then the body speaks to the soul:
> 'Where have you been? I cannot bear it any more.'
> And the soul says, 'Shut up, you fool,
> I want to be with my beloved;
> You will never enjoy me any more –
> I am his joy; he is my distress –
> Your distress is, that you can no longer enjoy me:
> You must put up with this distress
> for it will never leave you.'[32]

These and similar outpourings provide a remarkable testimony to the release which these women found in their religious profession and the freedom with which they expressed their visionary flights. No doubt they owed a great deal to the encouragement and guidance of the friars in whom they found their chief support. Independent though they were in their origin and plan of life, they clustered round the friaries: of the hundred and sixty-seven individual beguines whose exact address in Cologne is

31. Mechthild of Magdeburg, *Das fliessende Licht der Gottheit*, ed. P. Gall Morel, 1869 (reprinted 1963), p. 3.

32. ibid., pp. 7–8.

known between 1263 and 1389 a hundred and thirty-six lived in the neighbourhood of the Dominicans and Franciscans.[33]

In many ways it is an idyllic picture – women escaping from the sordid frustrations of the world into the liberty of an unpretentious spiritual life: enjoying vivid experiences of a loving God, and occupied in useful services ranging from the care of the sick to the embroidery of ecclesiastical vestments. Yet these women and their way of life raised up enemies, all in some degree afraid and not all unreasonably. We may leave aside the vulgar scoffers and ecclesiastical witch-hunters who pursued them in their early days and turn to some of the more mature critics, who tried and in the end partly succeeded in turning the movement back into the familiar channels of the religious Orders.

THE CRITICS OF THE MOVEMENT AND ITS DECLINE

Until the middle years of the thirteenth century the beguine movement was treated with great sympathy by those in authority. In their attitudes to the new religion Robert Grosseteste and Matthew Paris reflected the range of opinion that seems to have prevailed around 1250, varying from cautious interest and approval to wholehearted enthusiasm. The papal legates in Germany were especially helpful. In 1250 the legate Peter, bishop of Alba, placed the beguines of Cologne under the protection of the provost of the cathedral to save them from the oppression of clergy and laity in the city; and in the following year the legate, Cardinal Hugh, reinforced the protection of religious women in the city 'who were not sheltered by cloister-walls or established Rule, but lived in the midst of a sea of secular dangers'.[34]

Yet the fact that this protection was needed shows that there were many people in the city who disapproved of the new liberty which these women enjoyed. Parish priests who lost parishioners to the friars, fathers who lost daughters,

---

33. Asen, op. cit., cxi, pp. 90–91.   34. ibid., p. 104.

men who resented the women who got away, were all the
enemies of the beguines. In the end these enemies gained a
partial victory, partly because the impetus of the movement
began to slacken, partly because the movement itself was
not immune from corruption and absurdities, partly
because the views of the common man always in the end
prevail. These views were first forcibly expressed by a
bishop of East Germany, Bruno, bishop of Olmütz, writing
to the pope in 1273. He complained that the 'religion' of
the beguines had not been approved by the Holy See, that
the women used their liberty as a veil of wickedness in
order to escape the yoke of obedience to their priests and
'the coercion of marital bonds'. Above all, he was indignant
that young women should assume the status of widowhood
against the authority of the Apostle who approved no
widows under the age of sixty. For these evils Bruno had a
single remedy: 'I would have them married or thrust into
an approved Order.'[35]

No doubt this was how many men felt. The General
Council of Lyons in 1274 took up the theme and began the
official repression of fringe-communities like those of the
beguines:

> The frenzied eagerness of applicants has forcibly obtained a
> multiplication of religious Orders, and the reckless foolhardiness
> of some of these various Orders, especially those mendicants whose
> own foundation has not yet been approved, has set loose an
> unbridled multitude of such Orders. We therefore repeat with
> greater stringency the earlier prohibition: no one from now on-
> wards shall found any new Order or assume the habit of any new
> religious life; and we declare that all the aforesaid mendicant
> orders and religious organizations founded since the aforesaid council
> [of 1215], which have not obtained papal confirmation, are forever
> prohibited and quashed, no matter how far they have progressed.[36]

It can scarcely be doubted that the beguines were among
the unauthorized religious organizations referred to in this

35. C. Höfler, *Analecten zur Geschichte Deutschlands und Italiens* (Abh. der
Königl. Akademie zu München, Hist. Kl.), 1846, iv, 27. For the background of this report, see H. Grundmann, op. cit., p. 334.

36. c.23 (*Conciliorum Oecumenicorum Decreta*, ed. J. Alberigo, p. 302).

prohibition, and the General Council of Vienne in 1312 made the reference explicit and more sharply hostile:

We have been told that certain women commonly called Beguines, afflicted by a kind of madness, discuss the Holy Trinity and the divine essence, and express opinions on matters of faith and sacraments contrary to the catholic faith, deceiving many simple people. Since these women promise no obedience to anyone and do not renounce their property or profess an approved Rule, they are certainly not 'religious', although they wear a habit and are associated with such religious orders as they find congenial. . . . We have therefore decided and decreed with the approval of the Council that their way of life is to be permanently forbidden and altogether excluded from the Church of God.[37]

This decree illustrates very well the perplexity of the ecclesiastical authorities in the face of the beguines. They did not fit into the well-regulated category of the religious orders; it was difficult to get information about them; much of the information was biased. Yet it was hard to see why people should not live a common life in a harmless Christian way following the practices of religious Orders even though they followed no Rule and took no vows. The Council evidently felt the difficulty; having started its decree with the bold and hostile words I have quoted, it finished in a milder fashion:

In saying this we by no means intend to forbid any faithful women from living as the Lord shall inspire them, provided they wish to live a life of penance and to serve God in humility, even if they have taken no vow of chastity, but live chastely together in their lodgings.

Here we see in a single paragraph, at the end of the great legislative period of the medieval church, the tension between the forces of authority and liberty and the growing difficulty in giving clear-cut authoritative directives.

The issue, however, which was left undecided at the highest level, had somehow to be resolved in practice. In 1318 the archbishop of Cologne required the dissolution of all beguine associations and their integration into Orders

37. c.16 (ibid., p. 350).

approved by the pope. This local decision was followed by a series of decrees of successive archbishops and popes which finally brought about the concentration of beguines into established convents. The process had gone so far by 1421 that Pope Martin V ordered the archbishop of Cologne to search out and destroy any small convents of persons living under the cloak of religion without a definite Rule. It is not known whether the archbishop took any action as a result of this mandate, but in any case the free flowering of the beguine movement had by now long since come to an end, leaving as its memorial a large number of hospitals and old people's homes which persisted into modern times.

Despite this slow process of attrition, the freedom of religious association which the beguines had helped to pioneer was never lost, but it is not to be traced any further in the history of the beguines themselves. By the middle of the fourteenth century they had exhausted the initial impulse that had so greatly impressed contemporary observers. For a further phase in its development we must turn to another area of Europe.

The Religious brethren of Deventer and its Neighbourhood

THE ENVIRONMENT

We may take as our point of departure some developments in a group of small but active towns in the valley of the River Ijssel in eastern Holland during the late fourteenth century. The whole area is shown in the map on the following page. We are here far away from the main centres of earlier medieval religious life and it is possible to observe new developments with comparative ease. In the last thirty miles before it enters the Zuider Zee the Ijssel flows past the towns of Zutphen, Deventer, Zwolle (on a neighbouring stream), and Kampen. In the late fourteenth century they were towns with populations ranging from about six to twelve thousand, so they were small in comparison with the greatest cities of Europe. But they were all – and especially Deventer and Kampen – growing centres of trade with a high concentration of commercial

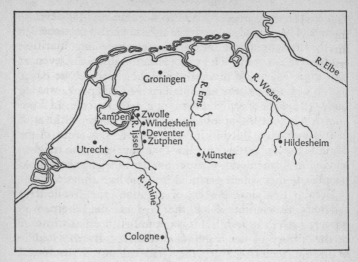

DEVENTER AND ITS NEIGHBOURHOOD

wealth and municipal independence.[38] They were all
members or associates of the Hanseatic confederation of
towns, but they had neither the size nor the geographical
position to give them a commanding position in this alliance of commercial interests. They were on the western
fringe of the main Hanseatic area, and their interests –
being closely tied up with local wool-growers and farmers –
were in many ways different from those of their greater
commercial allies. Their situation called for great coolness
and vigilance on the part of their ruling oligarchies: the
cautious independence and quiet opportunism which are
so important and necessary a part of Dutch history are
already apparent in the politics of these small towns. They
had no one to depend on but themselves. Their political
connexions were slight. Kampen, Deventer, and Zwolle
belonged to the bishop of Utrecht, and Zutphen to the county
of Gueldre. They paid dues to their nominal rulers, but

38. For a general account of the area, see P. Dollinger, *La Hanse,
xii-xvii siècles*, 1964; Z. W. Sneller, *Deventer, die Stadt der Jahrmärkte*, 1936.

they had to shape their policies to meet the rapidly developing trade of the Baltic and North Sea. Kampen stood out
among its neighbours in the importance of its maritime
trade with England, Norway, and the Baltic. Deventer,
which had been a port connecting the towns of the Rhine
valley with the North Sea since the ninth century, was the
scene of a very large fair for cloth, metalware, and food-
stuffs. These were the two most important towns of the area.

From a religious point of view the development of the
Ijssel towns was distinctly retarded. Before 1370 the religious
Orders had made only a slight penetration into the region.
In the country near Deventer there were Premonstratensian
canons and Cistercian nuns; in Kampen and Zwolle there
were small houses of Augustinian canons; there were
Franciscans at Kampen and Deventer, and Dominicans at
Zwolle and Zutphen. But none of these foundations made a
strong appeal to the commercial population. They belonged
rather to the rural aristocracy, and even the Franciscan
house at Deventer owed its foundation and development
to the Count of Gueldre and his English wife, Eleanor, the
daughter of Edward II. By the time the friars reached
these outposts of northern Europe they had lost their
inflammatory power; and even if they had retained their
primitive force it is doubtful whether begging could ever
have appealed to zealous spirits in small, damp, northern,
maritime cities, as it had appealed in Assisi, Siena, and
Naples.

Nevertheless the symptoms of urban religious development were beginning to appear. In 1349 we hear of a large
party of flagellants being entertained by the town council
of Deventer at public expense. At Deventer too and at
Zwolle there had been houses of beguines, though they
seem to have disappeared before 1380; and in this year at
Kampen a popular preacher gained a large following for
his doctrines of a natural union between God and man and
the uselessness of institutional religion.[39] These things were

39. There is an account of a sermon delivered in 1382 by this preacher,
Bartholomew of the Order of hermits of St Augustine in Dordrecht, in
Gerardi (Groote) Magni Epistolae, ed. W. Mulder, 1933, Ep. 31.

faint ripples of the great wave of emotionalism and anti-ecclesiasticism which were always the first signs of the entry of the urban laity into the religious field.

GERHARD GROOTE

About 1380 a new and indigenous religious energy began to appear, which was suited to the somewhat sombre life of these towns. This energy did not express itself in the colourful and extravagant gestures of the early Franciscans, but it found release in more prosaic ways. The man responsible for giving it a local expression was Gerhard Groote, the son of a cloth merchant and the inheritor of a considerable property in and around the town of Deventer.[40] In 1374 he was thirty-four years old, and at this date he seemed in every way acclimatized to the cosmopolitan intellectual and ecclesiastical life of the time. He had studied law and theology at Paris, and he had a consuming interest in the sciences of medicine and astrology – the two sciences which in the late fourteenth century promised the most immediate practical results. Academically he was armed at all points, though he was perhaps not moving as fast as would have been prudent towards his higher degree. Probably he was afflicted by the common academic difficulty of choosing a subject for specialization. Like all successful students he was engaged in a double race for academic distinction and worldly success, and they pulled him in different directions. He had followed the common university routine in applying to the pope for ecclesiastical preferment, but it was late in coming. From 1365 to 1367 he had represented his home town in a dispute with the bishop of Utrecht at the papal court at Avignon, and in 1368 (perhaps as a result of his

40. For the career of Gerhard Groote see T. P. van Zijl, *G. Groote, Ascetic and Reformer (1340–84)* (Catholic University of America Studies in Medieval History, New Series, 18), 1963; and for his works, *Werken van Geert Groote*, ed. J. G. J. Tiecke, 1941. There are some valuable recollections of his life in Thomas à Kempis, *Vita Gerardi Magni, Opera Omnia*, ed. M. J. Pohl, vii, 31–115. There is a very large modern literature on the movement which he inspired: see especially the works of R. R. Post, *De Moderne Devotie* (2nd ed., 1950) and 'Studien over de Broeders van het Gemeine Leven', *Nederl. Historiebledin*, i–ii, 1938–9.

opportunities for pressing his claims at Avignon) he became a canon of Aachen. Three years later he had a papal
provision entitling him to a canonry at Utrecht, but it is
doubtful whether he ever received it. In a modest way he
was becoming a local magnate, edging his way forward
inch by inch. Then in 1372 he fell ill in Deventer, and in
his weeks of illness his life began to take a different direction. By the standards of a St Francis he moved painfully
slowly. In 1374 he had only got so far as to give his parental
home to the town of Deventer for charitable purposes, and
he retired for a time to live with the Carthusians near
Arnhem to think out his position.

The record of his reflections and resolutions taken at
this time has survived and it gives us a vivid picture of the
state of mind of a fourteenth-century academic drop-out at
the moment of crisis. He was quite unclear about his
future. He showed no inclination to become a Carthusian
or a member of any other religious Order. He was clear
only about his determination to keep clear of everything
that he had hitherto sought. His jottings are repetitive and
unformed, sometimes in the first person and sometimes in
the second, sometimes resolving, sometimes admonishing
himself:

I will seek no further benefice. . . . You will serve no temporal
lord for gain; you will not seek to be any lord's astrologer; you
will not exercise any forbidden art for anyone; you will not choose
times [i.e. by astrology or the like] for journeys or blood-letting
except in a general way in consideration of the weather. . . .

You will not waste time in geometry, arithmetic, rhetoric,
judicial astrology, etc., which are arts reproved by Seneca, and
are much more to be rejected by a spiritual man or a Christian. . . .

You will never take a degree in medicine, because I intend to
seek neither gain nor benefices through having a degree. . . .

I will pursue no studies to increase my fame; avoid all public
disputations such as those in theology or arts at Paris – don't
even go to them to learn – they are useless and full of discord. . . .
You will not study for a degree in theology because I desire
neither gain nor benefices nor fame, and I can learn equally well
without a degree. . . . You will not be a counsel in any law-suit
unless there is some evident injustice or beating down of the poor

. . . not even for a friend or relative . . . not even in Deventer . . . even if a relative is beaten, killed, or molested you will not molest his attacker or give counsel against him to injure him.[41]

These were his resolves. What was to follow was much less clear. He determined to concentrate mainly on books of devotion, on regular religious observances, on frugal living. Beyond that he could not see. But he resolved – and this was a characteristic touch that became part of the way of life which he slowly evolved – to put aside some time every day to read his collection of reflections and resolutions 'because this outlines your position'.[42]

These words strike the note of experiment which was an essential part of Groote's contribution to the religious life of the late Middle Ages. He had no plans, no theories, no visions, no pet aversions; he just wanted to be free. He was no revolutionary, no Wycliffe; but he was in some ways much more modern than Wycliffe – more modern in the academic subjects that interested him, and even more modern in his rejection of these interests. He had no use for ancient controversies. Like every successful religious innovator of the Middle Ages he combined extreme, even violent, conservatism on social and dogmatic questions with considerable freedom and novelty in organization and sentiment.

The ten years of life which were left to him after he abandoned the race for success were a time of experiment and unfinished achievement. The chronology of these years is very difficult to establish. We hear of him preaching in Deventer, Zwolle, and Kampen, and gradually extending his activities to the surrounding towns and villages, wearing an old grey cloak and patched garments which became a legend among his followers. Despite his resolution to give up academic work, his interest in books never faltered: we hear of him making an expedition to Paris to buy books, and of his going on preaching expeditions on which he carried a barrel-load of volumes so that he could engage

41. The personal memoranda from which these extracts are taken are printed in Thomas à Kempis, *Opera omnia*, vii, 87–107.

42. ibid., p. 105.

in discussions after his sermons and confound his critics. He had a scribe who kept a record of what he said, and the atmosphere of learned, yet unacademic, controversy which he created wherever he went takes us back to a much earlier period in the history of the church – to the time of St Augustine, when doubts existed about the possibility of any religious truth; doubts such as we know today, but scarcely find in the Middle Ages. He was only a deacon, and he needed a special episcopal licence to preach; then, as the outcry of the religious Orders against him grew in intensity, he was silenced by the bishop on a technicality. After this we hear of him getting students to copy theological books, and he preached to them in private when they came to his house to be paid. So he died, a silenced and suspected man.

GROOTE'S RELIGIOUS FOUNDATIONS

Towards the end of his life Groote had turned his parental home in Deventer, which he had given up in 1374, into a house for religious women, and he made statutes for them which are remarkable for their lack of ecclesiastical paraphernalia. The women were to take no binding vows and wear no distinctive habit; they were to be lay people subject to the secular courts; they were to belong to no religious Order, but simply to serve God and work for their living. It is not surprising that his enemies said these were simply beguines under another name. But Groote was no friend of feminine freedom. His conversion had left him with an extreme aversion to sexuality, and he kept the women under his direction to a strict regime of prayer and toil. Meanwhile in a neighbouring street a group of clerks and laymen began to live together in St Paul's vicarage under Groote's general direction; and in the last months of his life he was engaged in founding a community of Augustinian canons at Windesheim a few miles north of Deventer in the Ijssel valley.

This last step was probably taken with reluctance, but it was a wise one. The opposition against him, led by the Dominicans who attacked his communities as unlawful assemblies of begards and beguines, had risen to such a height that he felt it necessary to demonstrate his lack of hostility to the religious Orders. Besides, he rightly saw that the community of regular canons would provide a secure defence for his more informal communities in time of need.[43] After all, as he told the brethren, the Augustinian Rule was 'not much different from our religious way of life except that those who profess it are bound by a vow'. This was a large exception, but without this base at Windesheim the communities which were not bound by a vow could scarcely have survived.

When Groote died in 1384 he seemed to have achieved very little, and the movement which he initiated never competed in popularity with the great Orders of the earlier centuries. It scarcely spread beyond the towns of Holland and Westphalia, and even within this area its numerical success was modest. According to one calculation the number of communities of Groote's brethren rose to thirty-four in Holland and eleven in the Rhineland and Westphalia; of similar communities for women there were perhaps three times that number.[44] The significance of the movement lay not in its numbers, but in its power of survival outside the ranks of the formal religious Orders without scandal, without suppression, and without radical change. The survival of these irregular communities ran counter to some of the deepest convictions of the medieval church, and the reasons for their survival will require careful consideration.

As a first step to understanding what it was that Groote's foundations stood for, and why, and how far, they managed to preserve their original character, we may begin by looking at them through the eyes of contemporaries. The two accounts which follow were written a few years after

43. *Scriptum Rudolphi Dier de Muden de Magistro Gherardo Grote*, ed. G. Dumbar, *Analecta*, 3 vols., 1719–22, i, 13.

44. The number of communities of women is always more uncertain than those of men. Most of the sisters were probably in the towns of Holland. In the Münster–Cologne area the records of meetings between 1431 and 1476 show that eleven communities of men and fifteen of women took part (K. Löffler, *Hist. Jahrbuch der Görres Gesellschaft*, 1909, xxx, 762–98).

Groote's death, but the first was written by a friend, the second by an enemy. The friend wrote thus:

> In various places many people have started living together like clergy in a single house in which they copy books for sale; and those who cannot write exercise whatever mechanical skills they have, or do other manual work for profit in a neighbouring house. These people work with their hands, and they live on what they can earn by their labours or on their private income. They share everything and seek increase of harmony by having all things in common. They eat together, and they do not beg. They place one of their number in charge of the house, and they follow his advice and obey him, as pupils obey their master. They follow this mode of life for convenience in providing the necessities of life; but principally they hope that by living thus, they will better please God and serve Him.[45]

To the hostile observer the emphasis was rather different:

> There are persons of both sexes who have assumed the habits of a new religious Order and hold conventicles. They profess no approved Rule, and they set up superiors for themselves at their own pleasure. Under the pretence of devotion they draw people to them, doing many things contrary to the truth of Holy Scripture and the sacred canons. From the offerings of the faithful they build sumptuous houses like regular monasteries, and within them they practise rites which have not been approved by the church.[46]

Leaving aside for the moment the hint of heresy in the second passage, there are three things to be noticed in these accounts which could shock, surprise, or exasperate contemporary opinion. These were: the absence of a Rule and binding vow; the choice of ordinary work as a source of livelihood; and the freedom with which laymen mixed with clerks in these communities and lived 'like clergy'.

45. This comes from a consultation on the legitimacy of living as a community without a Rule by Arnold, Abbot of Dickeninge, O.S.B., professor of Canon Law, in 1397 (L. Korth, 'Die ältesten Gutachten über die Brüderschaft des gemeinsamen Lebens', *Mittheilungen aus den Stadtarchiv von Köln*, ed. K. Höhlbaum, 5 Band, xiii Heft, 1887, p. 8).

46. This comes from the address of Matthew Grabow O.P. to Martin V in 1419 (H. Keussen, 'Der Dominikaner Matthaus Grabow u. die Brüder vom gemeinsamen Leben', ibid., pp. 28–47).

To a large extent we have already found these features in the beguine movement, and many of the criticisms of Groote's brethren followed the same lines as the criticisms of the beguines. But the struggle was now more intense: Groote's brethren were learned men who knew what they were doing and could defend themselves. The beguines' best defence had been inoffensive silence, and in the end this was not enough. Groote's brethren answered their critics in their own terms, and exchanged blow for blow. Since the whole institutional importance of Groote's brethren arises from their ability to retain their freedom intact, the time has come to consider the basis of their way of life and the pressures to which they were subjected in clinging to it.

The absence of Rule or binding vow. We have already seen that the absence of an authorized Rule was a major cause of hostility to the beguines. Groote and his followers aroused similar hostility: not unnaturally, for they presented a more articulate challenge to the traditional organization of religious life than the beguines. They had considered the question and had made a distinct choice. Despite Groote's recognition that the Rule of St Augustine was not very different from the rule of life he voluntarily observed, he did not choose to adopt it or any other Rule. His brethren, or many of them, persisted in this refusal. Here then on a small stage we meet a situation similar to the one which we have already observed on a grand scale in the relations of the Greek and Latin churches: the very smallness of the issue dividing the brethren from the regular religious Orders was an aggravation of their offence. Persistent nonconformity in a small matter is more vexatious than downright opposition in great matters, expecially when it comes from learned and intelligent men. It suggests that they have some deeper criticism which they fear to utter. It creates a breach between men of similar aims by raising issues which are either too small or too great for discussion.

The need for a binding vow was one of the common assumptions that had bound together all religious Orders in the Middle Ages. They were all based on one fundamental idea – that a life fully pleasing to God could not be lived in the secular world. Strictly speaking, perhaps it could not be lived anywhere in man's fallen state. But the gap could be closed until it was very small if men dedicated themselves entirely to a life of penitential discipline, self-abnegation, and prayer, making the following of Christ a regular, full-time, authorized activity. The forms that this life could take varied considerably – that was the reason for the diversity of religious Orders – but whichever form was adopted it had to be a life-long commitment. Anything less than this was a practical denial of the announced intention of a total dedication to God. It was only this total dedication that gave religious Orders a claim to the privileges they enjoyed; and no great religious leader in the West since the eighth century had questioned the necessity for irrevocability in any acceptable form of dedicated religious life.

This did not of course mean that laymen living in the world could not adopt some of the forms of piety developed by the religious Orders; they both could, and were encouraged to, do this. But it aroused hostility when men or women came together in a semi-permanent, semi-organized way to carve out for themselves some unknown form of religious life. The hostility to this existed at every level of seriousness, and it came from all sides. It came from members of religious Orders who saw their place in society and even their means of livelihood threatened by the rivalry of unauthorized groups. It came from the formally religious laity who always hate the unco' guid. And in a more serious way it came from thoughtful men who saw that these half-organized communities threatened some of the basic principles of traditional order. They substituted a changeable will for a definite and authoritative law. They made it impossible to be certain of a person's status under ecclesiastical or secular law. And finally, under the appearance of giving up everything for God's service, they encouraged men to think that they could find a full acceptance with God through a merely conditional obedience. These were very serious matters both in their social and religious implications.

It is easy to see that many of the opponents of Groote's brethren were short-sighted and selfish men who saw their influence and status threatened by the new movement. But, whatever ulterior motives they may have had, they were defending an ancient and respectable tradition. In the circumstances of the late fourteenth century they saw that the new freedom claimed by Groote and his followers was one more threat to the already battered ideal of a papally controlled and systematically organized Christian society. If people could form associations without authorization, choose a superior in some unknown manner, adopt a monastic type of life without the sanction of a monastic Rule, read the Scriptures together in the common tongue, confess their sins to one another and receive counsel and correction from no one knew whom, there would be an end to all order in the church.

The controversies surrounding the communities of Groote's brethren came to a head at the time of the Council of Constance. A friar called Martin Grabow, who was a lecturer to the Dominicans at Groningen, wrote a treatise in which he drew together all the legal and philosophical arguments that could be urged against the brethren.[47] He carried the dispute beyond the confines of law and authority and appealed to the fundamental sanctity of the natural order to prove the need for a Rule and permanent vow in practising a life of total religion. He argued that it was contrary to nature and an offence against society for men to renounce this world's goods without joining an authorized religious Order. To act thus was to deprive a man's dependants of their just expectations, even of life itself. It was therefore equivalent to homicide, and it was a mortal sin for men to believe that by measures contrary to nature they could merit eternal life. No authority, not even the pope, could condone that which affronted both reason and nature.

47. The contents of the treatise are summarized in Grabow's speech at the Council of Constance. See H. Keussen, op. cit.

This was an extreme position but it simply gave a new
generality and philosophical dignity to an ancient argument.
The decrees of the Councils of 1215, 1274, and 1312 against
new and unauthorized forms of religious communities had
all presupposed a background of thought not very different
from that of Martin Grabow. In a sense any completely
religious life flies in the face of nature, the universal rule of
life. The full religious life could therefore only be lawful
if it were stamped with the authority of a system higher
than that of nature – otherwise chaos would ensue.

When we consider the strength and antiquity of this
point of view, it is surprising to observe the confidence with
which the brethren attacked their enemy. As soon as they
got wind of Grabow's treatise, they leaped into the fray as
if they scented victory from afar. At Deventer they worked
through the night to copy the hostile tract.[48] They des-
patched it to the canons of Northorn, who went at once to
Groningen with a notary to secure legal testimony to
Grabow's authorship. They brought their enemy before
the bishop of Utrecht, and he only escaped condemnation
by appealing to the Council of Constance. But he did not
escape for long. After several months of inquiry and discussion the treatise was condemned and ordered to be
burned as 'erroneous, scandalous, injurious, rash, pre-
sumptuous, offensive to pious ears, heretical, and an
incitement to heresy'; its author was imprisoned on bread
and water till he 'recanted, revoked, and abhorred his
heretical depravity'; he was forbidden ever again to set
foot in the province of Cologne, and more especially the
diocese of Utrecht, on pain of perpetual imprisonment;
and, if he refused to recant, he was to be degraded as a
heretic and handed over to the secular authority to be
burnt.[49]

The menacing tone of this judgement stands in sharp
contrast to the liberality of its substance. Possibly the two

48. The extraordinary efficiency and dispatch with which the brethren
prepared their defence are described by J. Busch, *Chronicon Windesheimense*,
ed. K. Grube (*Geschichtsquellen der Provinz Sachsen*, 1886, xix); pp. 172–4.
49. H. Keussen, op. cit., pp. 44–7.

features are not unconnected. As the belief in system and authority waned, and a greater area was cleared for individual liberty, there appeared an ever stronger need to reaffirm the supreme penalties of disobedience. Violence and liberty grew together. Yet in a small way this judgement was a victory for liberty, and the success of the brethren bears witness to a major shift in ecclesiastical opinion since the thirteenth century.

But when we ask why they won, and still more why they were so sure of winning, it is not easy to give an answer. We can only indicate why they attached so much importance to their freedom from binding vows; and then we can understand why lawyers who shared their feelings interpreted the law in their favour.

At the root of everything there was a persistent desire for experiment, a desire to discover for oneself a way of life suited to one's own experience. There was a fear and distrust of the great religious Orders which had claimed so much and aroused such great hopes, only to produce (as it seemed) so little except disillusion. The brethren insisted that they were not hostile to the religious Orders. Indeed many of them in the end became Augustinian canons; but many held out, although the attractions of a binding commitment were strongly felt, especially when a brother left the community. At such a time those who remained felt themselves betrayed, and they looked with envy at communities which could call for legal sanctions against a deserter. The remarkable thing is not that men should have felt the charms of legal sanctions, but that they continued to resist them. In 1490 the rector of the brethren at Hildesheim was asked for his views on this thorny problem, and he replied in a letter which shows the lasting power of the freedom which Groote had secured for his followers:

We are not [he wrote] members of an Order, but religious men trying to live in the world. If we get a papal order compelling those who leave us either to return to us or to enter another Order, we shall be selling our liberty – that liberty which is the singular glory of the Christian religion – to buy chains and prison walls, in order to fall into line and conform to the religious Orders. We too will then be subject to servitude, like slaves who can be corrected only by punishment. I myself indeed once thought that we should accept a Rule and make a profession; but Master Gabriel Biel corrected me, saying that there were already enough members of religious Orders. Our way of life springs and has always sprung from an inner kernel of devotion. Let us therefore not bring upon ourselves at once the destruction of our good name, our peace, our quiet, our concord, and our charity. Our voluntary life as brethren is very different from the irrevocable necessity of those who live under the Rule and statutes of a religious Order. *Their* monasteries fall into decay through the presence of unstable and undisciplined members: think then how much more *our* life would be destroyed by the enforced presence of such people.[50]

It would have been difficult to make these words intelligible to St Anselm or St Bernard. They show a desire for the danger in being constantly exposed to freedom, which it was a main aim of earlier religious leaders to shield men from. The certainty and safety of an irrevocable decision, which earlier religious leaders had desired so eagerly for their followers, the brethren sought to avoid.

Above all they sought to avoid any distinctive label, such as the most successful of the great Orders had been proud to bear. Modern scholars habitually call the followers of Groote 'the Brethren of the Common Life', but even this is too precise a label. The 'Common Life' was simply the irreducible residue that was left when they had cut away all other distinguishing features. They commonly called themselves merely 'the brethren living together at Zwolle' – or wherever it might be. If they wanted a word to describe their inner purpose the word they added was *devoti*, 'devout'. No more than that. About this unendearing adjective I shall have something to say later. Meanwhile we must only notice that silence may convey a criticism quite as effectively as any invective; and existing religious Orders felt rebuked by the silent aversion of Groote and his followers. The brethren avoided Rules and vows principally because they

50. *Annalen u. Akten der Brüder des Gemeinsamen Lebens im Lüchtenhofe zu Hildesheim*, ed. R. Doebner (*Quellen u. Darstellungen zur Gesch. Niedersachsens*, 1903, ix), p. 113.

desired immediacy in their religion; but also because they saw that these things had led to formalism and indifference. Their attitude survived all attacks and inducements to change, not because it was logically very sound but because many people thought with Master Gabriel Biel that there were already enough, not to say too many, members of religious Orders.[51]

The doctrine of work. The place of manual labour in the religious life had always been a matter of great difficulty. It was clearly enjoined in the Rule of St Benedict; but the purpose it served was not so clear. 'Idleness' wrote Benedict 'is the enemy of the soul; therefore at definite times of the day the brethren should be engaged on manual work and at other times on the reading of sacred texts.'[52] But if the purpose was simply to avoid idleness there were other, perhaps better, remedies than manual labour. Again, St Benedict admonished his monks to be content to labour in the harvest if poverty or necessity forced them to do so, for in living by the labour of their hands they were following the ancient Fathers and Apostles. But neither St Benedict nor his followers seem to have thought that there was any special virtue in earning a living by manual work: it was simply to be borne with resignation in time of need. In fact it was seldom needed. Monks and canons soon found better ways of spending their time than working for their living.

The flight from manual work reached its logical conclusion with the friars and their dedication to a life of begging, which is the antithesis of work. By 1240, as we have already seen, Bishop Grosseteste could draw a contrast between the friars who lived by begging and the beguines who lived by work. Yet no more than fifteen years earlier the contrast would have seemed outrageous to St Francis:

I have worked [he wrote in his Testament in 1226] with my hands and I wish to continue to do so; and I want all my other

51. For a similar view from a quite different quarter see Thomas Gascoigne, *Loci e Libro Veritatum,* ed. J. E. Thorold Rogers, 1881, 107–13,
52. *Reg. Ben.,* c. 48

brethren to work at an honest craft. Let those who have no craft learn one, not out of greed for the reward of their labour, but as an example, and for the avoidance of idleness. If we are not given the reward of our labour, then let us seek alms from door to door, for this is the Lord's table.[53]

It would seem from this that for St Francis begging was not so much a principle of life as a reply to the world's injustice, a way of turning the other cheek instead of demanding a just price. But mendicancy became so quickly established as the highest form of renunciation – higher than penitential labour or necessitous toil – that within a few years Grosseteste could equate Franciscan poverty with begging; and the beguine practice of working for a livelihood appeared to him a new idea.

More than a century passed before this idea had any important new development. During this time the friars ceased to beg, without starting to work. When this happened, the time had come for a new attempt to explore the possibility of bringing manual labour back into the religious life. Groote and his followers were the chief agents in this attempt.

As soon as Groote's views began to take shape after his conversion he discovered that he had a strong aversion to begging as a means of supporting a religious life. He also discovered that he had a strong belief in the virtue of manual work – not simply as an escape from idleness or as an occasional necessity – but as an essential tool of a religious life:

I have often told you [he wrote to the head of the brethren at Zwolle with regard to the women under his direction] that labour is wonderfully necessary to mankind in restoring the mind to purity. I have experience of those who (as Paul writes to Timothy) 'learn to be idlers, gadding about from house to house; and not only idlers but gossips and busybodies, saying what they should not'. When women have free meals and alms, they are freed from the need for earning a living by work, and so they reject the useful medicine which God first gave man. . . . Don't think however that I wish men or women to be occupied in secular business or human entanglements – let them simply work on those things which bring a daily subsistence from hand to mouth without superfluity. . . . Labour is holy, but business is dangerous.[54]

Groote therefore envisaged his communities of men and of women working for their living. But the conditions of town-life in the later Middle Ages put many difficulties in the way of achieving this ideal – difficulties quite different from those experienced by the earlier Orders, but no less frustrating. Nearly all urban crafts and industries were the monopoly of gilds. These were authorized by the towns, and in many cases they controlled the municipal government. A main purpose of these gilds was to frustrate the attempts of non-members to interfere with their monopoly, and any religious body which attempted to do this found itself at once an object of hostility and unable to live peacefully with its neighbours in the town. However hard it struggled to maintain its right to support itself by manual work, it was bound in the end to fail.

We can see the stages of defeat very clearly exemplified at Hildesheim.[55] Here the brethren managed to keep one of their body employed as a shoemaker almost to the end of the fifteenth century. But in 1476 the shoemakers' gild took up the fight in earnest. They began by sending a delegation to complain to the brethren about the violation of their privileges, and at first they received a very haughty reply: 'if you have your privileges from the town, we have ours from the pope: go away; we have nothing to do with you'. For the moment they were subdued, but they came back four years later in a more truculent mood and received a more civil answer: 'we have no desire to harm anyone. Only one of us works on shoes, and he is more of a cobbler than a shoemaker; besides he is so old that he cannot stand upright. Delay your prohibition till he dies, which can't be long, and we shall be obliged.' The poorer members of the

---

54. *Gerardi Magni Epistolae*, ed. W. Mulder, Ep. 32.
55. For what follows see R. Doebner, op. cit., pp. 71, 85–6, 112.

delegation wanted to insist on an immediate capitulation by the brethren, but their leaders finally agreed to allow the old shoemaker to continue to work till he died, provided that he made shoes only for the brethren and not for sale. So peace was patched up; but the rector of the brethren was sufficiently alarmed by the bellicose disposition of the gildsmen to tell the old shoemaker to avoid trouble in future by putting a little old leather into every shoe he made. Privately, he added, 'Don't think that just because we spoke civilly to these shoemakers we have submitted – or even will submit – to their senseless, envious, and base machinations.'

The old shoemaker who had been at the point of death in 1480, was still working in 1489 when the gildsmen appeared once more to protest. This time there was no escape: the old man was called forward and told to stop work. The brethren at Hildesheim had carried on a long battle with the gild for their freedom to work. In this fight, they showed all the toughness that we associate with the communities of Groote's followers. But in the end it was a hopeless struggle against the forces of municipal trading interests. Groote's teaching about the sanctity of labour and its power to cleanse the mind did not succumb to the ordinary forces of internal relaxation that had brought manual labour to an end in the earlier religious Orders: but it succumbed none the less – to the power of late medieval gild organizations.

There was, however, one field of production which municipal gilds barely touched. The whole business of book production was in the hands of stationers, parchment makers, illuminators, and book-binders who had little or no organization in the towns of Holland and North Germany. Here the brethren found a whole range of crafts which they could make their own. Groote with his life-long passion for books had pointed the way, and his disciples followed it with zest. They organized themselves into associations for copying books. They developed their own styles of writing and their own distinctive bindings. They perfected the processes for the rapid multiplication of handwritten books, and they were ready when the time came to be among the first in the business of printing.[56]

Of course the copying of books was a very ancient activity in religious communities. The splendid manuscripts of Jarrow and Monkwearmouth in the seventh and eighth centuries, of Canterbury in the eleventh and twelfth, and of St Albans in the thirteenth are examples of work either written or supervised by monks. But no religious community had ever concentrated its energies on book production as Groote's brethren did. Besides, most monastic libraries were already full by the fourteenth century, and they relied on gifts and the services of professional scribes for any further accessions. Like every other kind of manual labour, the copying of books had come to be unnecessary in the religious Orders. It was here that the brethren saw their chance. They saw that the world needed books in ever-increasing quantity. Besides writing books for themselves, they supplied parochial, collegiate, and cathedral churches with rapidly produced and accurate texts of devotional and liturgical works. So here at least they succeeded, where others had failed, in combining a religious way of life with the task and virtue of earning a living with their hands.

Besides contributing to their livelihood and their religious stability, the copying of books made an important contribution to the defence of their way of life. It kept them alert to learned opinion and made it possible for them to react quickly to any attack. We have already seen how effectively the brethren at Deventer mobilized their scribal resources when Matthew Grabow attacked them. But their books did more than serve the purpose of self-defence. They carried far and wide the forms of devotion practised and

56. For an account of the various styles of writing practised by the brethren, see the articles of B. Kruitwagen in *Het Boek*, 1933–4, xxii, 209–30; 1935–6, xxiii, 1–54; also K. Löffler 'Das Schrift u. Buchwesen der Brüder vom gemeinsamen Leben', *Zeitschrift f. Bücherfreunde*, 1907–8, xi, 286–93. For an example of the transition from this professional scribal activity to printing, see Jacobus Traiecti alias de Voecht, *Narratio de Inchoatione Domus Clericorum in Zwollis*, ed. M. Schoengen, 1908, pp. 163–5.

developed by the brethren, and made these forms part of
the general piety of Christendom.

The mixing of clergy and laity. A deep division between clergy
and laity was one of the most persistent features of medieval
life. It was a division perpetuated by the legal and educational systems, and exacerbated by the rights and privileges
which were attached to clerical status. In practical life
there were many mitigations of the crude division in society,
but when Boniface VIII declared that 'the experience of
modern times clearly demonstrates the hostility of the laity
to the clergy' he expressed a truth that could be widely
documented.

The religious Orders made their own contribution to this
division in society by giving a conspicuous physical existence to wealthy and privileged corporations of clergy standing apart from every other social group. Yet in their origins
several religious Orders had broken down the barrier and
had included both laymen and clergy in a single community.
The most striking example of this coexistence had been
given by the Franciscans. The earliest communities had
included a large, and even a predominant, lay element; but
laymen disappeared from Franciscan convents very quickly
for the same reasons that they had disappeared from the
communities of earlier religious Orders: it was in every way
easier to organize and support a religious community if all
its members were in holy orders. Besides, the higher aims of
preaching, evangelization, and spiritual direction could
only be served by the clergy.[57] So among the Franciscan
friars, as in the other Orders, the lay element was quickly
banished to the kitchen or disappeared altogether.

Groote was the last religious reformer of the Middle
Ages to attempt once more to combine clergy and laity in
a single community. It might seem that he had a better

57. For the clearest justification of this development see St Bonaventura,
Determinationes Questionum circa Regulam Fratrum Minorum, ii, 16: *Cur
Fratres non Promovent Ordinem Poenitentium* (*Opera Omnia*, viii, 368–9),
defending the Franciscans against the charge that, if they were genuinely
concerned about the salvation of souls, they would have tried to extend
the Order of lay penitents founded by St Francis.

chance of success than his predecessors. The absence of the vows and privileges of a religious Order removed a main ground of the division between the clergy and laity; and so long as manual work provided a source of livelihood laymen had a natural place in the community. Yet, despite these advantages, the association of clergy and laity in the communities of brethren was scarcely more successful than it had been in the past. As we have seen, the only kind of manual labour that could be successfully maintained was book-production, and this was labour especially suitable for clerks. So the old story of the exclusion of laymen from the communities was repeated. In the early days clerks and laymen worked together building houses and fitting them for occupation. But when the communities settled down to their steady routine of study, prayer, and copying books, there was little left for the layman to do but cook.

By far the greater number of lay members of the communities mentioned in the abundant biographies of the brethren were cooks. They were sometimes remembered with affection and respect, but the case of the cook at Hildesheim illustrates the limitations of their rôle: he tried to escape to the schools 'lest he should spend all his days toiling as a layman'. His effort failed and he was induced to return. The brethren sympathized with him, but there was nothing they could do about it except be glad for his sake when he died quickly.[58]

Slowly therefore the laity were squeezed out or relegated to an inferior status because there was no important rôle for them. The struggle to retain them as effective members of the community was more prolonged than it had been among the Franciscans; but in the long-run the old established inferiority remained and the laity faded out.

THE NEW RELIGIOUS TEMPER

We have now examined the main contrasts between Groote's brethren and the members of earlier religious Orders. This inquiry has illustrated the extent to which it was possible

58. R. Doebner, op. cit., p. 24. There are further details of the gradual squeezing out of the laity on pp. 64, 260, 270.

in the fifteenth century to break away from the traditional organization of a religious Order without incurring judicial condemnation or suffering a total collapse of religious ideals. The survival of the brethren is a singular testimony to the religious freedom of the later Middle Ages growing alongside the violence of ecclesiastical tribunals and the persistence of deep-seated divisions between clergy and laity. The brethren survived largely because of their mediocrity. The great and successful religious Orders of the earlier centuries had tended quickly to be moulded by the conditions which ensured their success. In protest against this social conformity several of the Orders produced groups of dissidents, who either founded a new organization or cherished private revelations and apocalyptic expectations which brought them into trouble and condemnation. For various reasons the followers of Groote avoided both these fates. They were not rich or powerful enough to become thoroughly worldly, nor poor or resentful enough to cherish truths which the world ignored.

Their spirit of calm withdrawal from the world is one of their most paradoxical features. On the one hand they were extremely businesslike. We have seen several examples of this in their organization of book-production and in the steps they took in their own defence. Their organization, unpretentious though it was, showed great power of survival in a not too friendly world. Their schools were among the most popular and effective in northern Europe. Yet, although the brethren lived in towns which were humming with commercial activity, and although their occupations brought them into constant contact with this tough and abundant life, ultimately their only claim to a place in the history of the medieval church arises from their intense preoccupation with the interior life of religion and the solitude of individual experience. A canon of Windesheim of the second generation, who looked back with veneration to Groote as the master he had never seen, expressed this interior message in imperishable form in the *Imitation of Christ*. This is one of the few books which breaks down without an effort the barrier between the medieval and modern worlds, and it was written by a man who could scarcely hold down even the least responsible administrative post in his community.

Thomas à Kempis is the greatest name in the whole movement inspired by Groote, but it seems almost an accident that it was he who wrote the words that give the movement its place in history. In his writings apart from the *Imitation* he is scarcely distinguishable from many other followers of Groote. All the writers in the movement aimed at an intensity of individual perception arising from a regular routine of labour and liturgy. The brethren meditated over their daily tasks and found a source of devotion in the humblest activities. They neither withdrew from the world nor threw themselves upon it. They were sheltered from its fiercest struggles. Consequently, though they are admirable examples of ordinary life, they produced only one book which displays to the world the intensity which they sought in their mild retirement from the storms of city life.

In contrast to those for whom the faith was simply a matter of formal adherence or intellectual assent, Groote's followers sought an effective, personal, experimental faith. Their detestation of merely formal religion was unbounded. What they wished to put in its place was something that they could never define, but it is abundantly illustrated in their spiritual diaries and collections of *memorabilia*.

Groote and his followers were great writers of these intimate and rambling documents. It had been one of Groote's first acts on his conversion to make a record of his resolutions, and to resolve frequently to read it. So with his followers: they were forever recording notable sayings and reflections for future use[59]. They attached great importance to their personal records as an aid to meditation. They rediscovered the uses of spiritual autobiography in religious development, and they carried further than ever before the process, which first began to be perceptible in the eleventh

59. See J. Busch, *Chron. Windesheimense,* pp. 206–7, for the place of commonplace books *(rapiaria)* in the school at Zwolle in the time of the great master John Cele.

century, of emphasizing individual devotions at the expense
of the corporate Offices of the church. Here is a sample of
the daily life of one of the brethren in the mid fifteenth
century, which illustrates the adaptation of the old corporate
Offices to serve the purposes of private devotion:

From midday till one o'clock I work, sometimes singing a
hymn to drive away boredom or excite devotion. Then at three
o'clock I read vespers and go over the subject-matter of the day's
Office. After this I study or prepare parchment till four o'clock
when I take up my allotted task [of copying] till supper-time. At
supper I behave as I did at dinner [taking no notice of others,
etc.] and immediately after supper I read compline. After this I
examine myself for my failings and sins for some time, and when I
have done this I rule or scrape parchment till eight o'clock.[60]

These and other similar records show how the monastic
ideal of a strictly regulated day had been taken over by the
brethren and turned into a personal act of prolonged
devotion. The steady liturgical routine was made a servant
of their personal life, and this egocentricity gives a very
private, self-conscious, and puritanical appearance to
everything they did.

The communities were all small, so the members all
knew each other very well. They looked at one another
with an appreciative eye, and in their abundant domestic
chronicles they wrote of their companions, who were
certainly not saints or heroes of a traditional kind, with
unenvious admiration. These chronicles are remarkable
among the great mass of monastic histories for the abundance
and vivacity of their biographical and domestic detail, and
for their utter indifference to the great events of the world at
large. They abound in such sketches as this:

James Enckhuysen came of well-to-do parents. He came to
school at Zwolle and entered our house. He was a very accurate
scribe, and he copied many books, Missals, Graduals, Psalters,
Canons, and a Bible worth 500 florins. This was made at the

60. W. Jappe Alberts, *Consuetudines Fratrum Vitae Communis* (Fontes
minores medii aevi, viii), 1959, p. 3.

expense of Herman Droem, dean of Utrecht, where the book now is. For a time he was in charge of the sisters at the *Maat*, but they needed a stricter and more rigorous control than it was in his nature to provide, so he asked to be relieved of this task. He then devoted himself to writing, and he was for a long time librarian and keeper of the clock. He did both these jobs to perfection. His books were always accurate and he produced them on time; and we were never wakened at the wrong time when he was in charge of the clock. He had a good voice, with a slight stammer which made him ashamed to preach in public; but he overcame this defect when he read to the clergy and laity, as he often did, in a clear and sonorous voice. For four or five days before his death he lost his appetite, and his strength waned so that he could scarcely walk without a stick. We said to him, 'James, do you want to die?' He replied, 'Yes; it's high time; I've lived long enough.' His strength continued to ebb, though no one knew the cause of his illness. The day before he died the brethren asked him about receiving the sacraments of the Church, and he said 'Whenever you like'; and so he received them devoutly and died the same night.[61]

The similarity in temper of all these biographies is very striking. They all record the same mild usefulness and satisfaction in efficient service, alongside a total absorption in domestic affairs. Perhaps for this reason they leave, as the records of few religious movements, an impression of persistent harmony and sweetness with very little blemish. They neither reached the heights nor touched the depths of the religious Orders.

It may then reasonably be asked why we should end this survey of medieval ecclesiastical society with the spiritual and material adventures of this not very extensive or heroic organization. The best reason is that they illustrate the virtues that were possible in a religious group at a time when the systematic intellectual and organizational enterprises of the earlier centuries were breaking down. In the late fourteenth century religious men had some shattering paradoxes and failures before their eyes. The Benedictines had retreated from the world, and had become great

61. M. Schoengen, op. cit., pp. 190–93.

centres of government and instruments of social cohesion. The Cistercians had gone into the wilderness, and had become the greatest organizers of economic forces before the Fuggers and Medicis. The Franciscans had dedicated their lives to poverty, and were comfortably installed in every large town in Europe. In all this, effective religion (so it seemed) was lost in superficiality.

With these examples before their eyes Groote and his followers proposed to follow an ideal substantially different from any earlier one: moderation, absence of organization, and a persistent unfrenzied search for interior illumination. They made their living as scribes and schoolmasters, they owned houses, and they seem never to have been short of ready money. They retreated indeed from the world's excesses and were indifferent to its large affairs; but their real retreat was into the inner sanctuary of the soul where, as Eckhart had said, 'the birth of Christ takes place as it does in eternity and with no difference'. Eckhart had also said that he who entered into this true spiritual experience in the soul's sanctuary was freed from all external vows.

These two things – the retreat into the soul and the retreat from formal vows – lie at the centre of the brethren's way of life. Moderation was an essential part of their outlook – without it they would not have survived. They were not in any respect disciples of Eckhart, but they came from a similar, though more provincial, environment, and they shared the same sense of alienation from the systems of the past. They trod more carefully than Eckhart, and they never incurred his condemnation. Though they spoke with reverence of an ecstatic religion as the goal of a lifetime's devotion, they were generally content with that degree of internal warmth of feeling which stops far short of ecstasy. At this level they were very communicative. Their business of copying books and teaching helped to make them articulate, and even voluble. Their retreat from the world was of a kind that was compatible with great practical activity; it required no desert places, no entire seclusion, no withdrawal even from the main streets of the town for its achievement. Their type of devotion was therefore well fitted to become the model for busy and articulate people whose numbers were increasing rapidly towards the end of the Middle Ages. This helps to explain why the *Imitation of Christ* was the medieval work which had the widest success in later centuries and why the retreat into the soul provided an acceptable religion for busy modern men.

Epilogue

WE have now surveyed the main types of ecclesiastical organization that made up the medieval church, beginning with western Christendom as a whole and descending to the communities of beguines and devout brethren, the smallest of the corporate religious bodies which could claim a more than local significance. Even at this lowly level we are still among the élite, still among the macro-organisms of Christendom. Below the limits of our survey lie the parishes and parochial gilds; and outside lie the fraternities and assemblies of heretical sects. But we stop at this point for two reasons. The first is that our study has chiefly been concerned to trace the shaping of ecclesiastical institutions by their environment, and to note the effect of the wind and weather of social and economic change on the greatest corporate expressions of medieval religious energy. Below the level to which we have come, the generality of the picture is lost in a cloud of detail: the omens have been sufficiently clear already in the last pages of our survey, and to go further would require a different scale of treatment.

The second reason for stopping at this point is that our survey of outward forms is only a preliminary step towards understanding the inner energy of the organizations of which the outer forms alone have so far been sketched. This is a task of the greatest complexity, and the area already extends beyond the hope of any adequate survey. Yet it is not an entirely impossible task. The men and women we have been dealing with were the most articulate members of their society. If we descend to the lower levels of parish and gild, we come up against the large mass of inarticulate Christians, who have left no record of their thoughts and experience; and if we go further afield to the heretical sects, we find that whatever was most articulate has been destroyed. No doubt much still remains to be done in examining and classifying the records of medieval religious protest, and in understanding the religious life of medieval Europe at its least privileged level, but at best it is likely to remain a collection of fragments.

It is far otherwise with the experience of those who were responsible for developing the institutions that we have surveyed. Here the materials are immensely abundant, and the bulk of material available for study continues to grow. It is probably not an exaggeration to say that the amount of evidence available for studying the thoughts which shaped the Christian experience of the Middle Ages has doubled in the course of this century – the amount of evidence, that is to say, which has been printed, edited, and prepared for scholarly use. A very high proportion of the evidence of religious thought and sentiment which has lain unused and almost unusable for centuries is now at last available for close inspection. The present survey is no more than an introduction to the study of this huge deposit of Christian thought and experience. But it is a necessary introduction. The habit of separating ecclesiastical history from secular history has tended to make everything ecclesiastical appear more rarefied than it really is. It is only when we study church history as an aspect of secular history that we can begin to understand the limitations and opportunities of the medieval church and the vast distance that separates it from every modern church.

List of Popes, 590–1513

The names of popes who are mentioned in the text are printed in CAPITALS; anti-popes and their dates in *italics*. The first date is that of election, the second is the date of death unless marked res. (resigned), dep. (deposed) or exp. (expelled). For further details see *List of Popes* in C. R. Cheney, *Handbook of Dates for Students of English History* (Royal Historical Society, Guides and Handbooks no. 4, 1st ed. 1948, 2nd ed. 1970), on which this list is based.

From 590 to 999 the list contains only the popes who are mentioned in the text; thereafter it is complete.

GREGORY I	590–604	Gregory VI	1045–6 (dep.)
GREGORY II	715–31	Clement II	1046–7
		Damasus II	1047–8
ZACHARIAS	741–52	LEO IX	1048–54
STEPHEN II	752–7	Victor II	1054–7
		Stephen IX	1057–8
ADRIAN I	772–95	Benedict X	1058–9 (dep.)
LEO III	795–816		
NICHOLAS I	858–67	NICHOLAS II	1058–61
		Alexander II	1061–73
JOHN X	914–28 (dep.)	*Honorius II*	*1061–72*
		GREGORY VII	1073–85
		Clement III	*1080–1100*
SILVESTER II	999–1003	Victor III	1086–7
John XVII	June–Dec. 1003	URBAN II	1088–99
John XVIII	1004–9	PASCHAL II	1099–1118
Sergius IV	1009–12	*Theodoric*	*1100 (exp.)*
Gregory	*1012 (exp.)*	*Albert*	*1102 (dep.)*
BENEDICT VIII	1012–24	*Silvester IV*	*1105–11 (dep.)*
JOHN XIX	1024–32	Gelasius II	1118–19
BENEDICT IX	1032–45 (res.)	*Gregory VIII*	*1118–21 (dep.)*
	1046 (dep.)	CALIXTUS II	1119–24
Silvester III	*1045 (dep.)*	Honorius II	1124–30

INNOCENT II	1130–43	John XXI	1276–7
Anacletus II	*1130–38*	NICHOLAS III	1277–80
Victor IV	*1138* (res.)	MARTIN IV	1281–5
CELESTINE II	1143–4	HONORIUS IV	1285–7
LUCIUS II	1144–5	Nicholas IV	1288–92
EUGENIUS III	1145–53	CELESTINE V	July–Dec.
Anastasius IV	1153–4		1294 (res.)
ADRIAN IV	1154–9	BONIFACE VIII	1294–1303
ALEXANDER III	1159–81	Benedict XI	1303–4
Victor IV	*1159–64*	CLEMENT V	1305–14
Paschal III	*1164–8*	JOHN XXII	1316–34
Calixtus III	*1168–78* (res.)	*Nicholas V*	*1328–30* (*res.*)
Innocent III	*1179–80* (*dep.*)	BENEDICT XII	1334–42
		CLEMENT VI	1342–52
Lucius III	1181–5	Innocent VI	1352–62
Urban III	1185–7	Urban V	1362–70
Gregory VIII	Oct.–Dec. 1187	Gregory XI	1370–78
		URBAN VI	1378–89
Clement III	1187–91	*Clement VII*	*1378–94*
CELESTINE III	1191–8	Boniface IX	1389–1404
INNOCENT III	1198–1216	*Benedict XIII*	*1394–1409* (*dep.*)[1]
HONORIUS III	1216–27		
GREGORY IX	1227–41	Innocent VII	1404–6
Celestine IV	Oct.–Nov. 1241	Gregory XII	1406–9 (dep.)[2]
INNOCENT IV	1243–54	ALEXANDER V	1409–10
ALEXANDER IV	1254–61	*John XXIII*	*1410–15* (*dep.*)[3]
URBAN IV	1261–4		
CLEMENT IV	1265–8	MARTIN V	1417–31
GREGORY X	1271–6	*Clement VIII*	*1423–9* (res.)
Innocent V	Jan.–June 1276	Eugenius IV	1431–9 (dep.)[4]
Adrian V	July–Aug. 1276	*Felix V*	*1439–49* (*res.*)

1. *Benedict XIII* was deposed by the Council of Pisa in 1409 and by the Council of Constance in 1417.

2. Gregory XII was deposed by the Council of Pisa in 1409 and resigned in 1415.

3. *John XXIII* was deposed by the Council of Constance in 1415 and died in 1419.

4. Eugenius IV was deposed by the Council of Basel in 1439 and died in 1447.

Nicholas V	1447–55	Innocent VIII	1484–92
Calixtus III	1455–8	Alexander VI	1492–1503
PIUS II	1458–64	Pius III	Sept.–Oct.
PAUL II	1464–71		1503
SIXTUS IV	1471–84	JULIUS II	1503–13

Index

MORE ABOUT PENGUINS
AND PELICANS

Penguinews, which appears every month, contains details of all the new books issued by Penguins as they are published. From time to time it is supplemented by *Penguins in Print*, which is our complete list of almost 5,000 titles.

A specimen copy of *Penguinews* will be sent to you free on request. Please write to Dept EP, Penguin Books Ltd, Harmondsworth, Middlesex, for your copy.

In the U.S.A.: For a complete list of books available from Penguins in the United States write to Dept CS, Penguin Books, 625 Madison Avenue, New York, New York 10022.

In Canada: For a complete list of books available from Penguins in Canada write to Penguin Books Canada Ltd, 2801 John Street, Markham, Ontario L3R 1B4.

THE PELICAN HISTORY OF
MEDIEVAL EUROPE

Maurice Keen

A tradition of insularity has tended to deprive the English-speaking world of some of the most fascinating history of all – that of Europe in the Middle Ages. As a subject it is seldom taught outside universities.

The unity of Christendom, which bound together religion and politics and found its fullest expression in the crusades, provides the theme of this book, in which an Oxford medievalist traces the history of Europe from barbarous beginnings in the ruins of the Roman Empire. Maurice Keen shows how the feudal order of a world driven back upon its natural resources was gradually transformed into the self-confident, expansionist society of the twelfth century.

Discussing the struggles of Empire and Papacy for mastery of the Christian community, Dr Keen explains how Papal victories served to blur the distinction between temporal and spiritual matters and eventually undermined the spiritual authority of the Church. And he demonstrates how the Hundred Years War developed from a feudal dispute into dynastic rivalry and finally into national conflict, until by the fifteenth century new economic and social conditions had made the unity of Christendom merely a pious phrase.

This outline history assumes no knowledge in the reader and yet engages him in a stimulating discussion of most of the important issues of the Middle Ages.

THE PELICAN HISTORY OF ENGLAND

While each volume is complete in itself, the whole series has been planned to provide an intelligent and consecutive guide to the development of English society in all its aspects. The nine volumes are:

'As a portent in the broadening of popular culture the influence of this wonderful series has yet to receive full recognition and precise assessment. No venture could be more enterprising or show more confidence in the public's willingness to purchase thoughtful books . . .' – *Listener*

The Pelican History of the Church

THE OTHER VOLUMES

THE EARLY CHURCH
Henry Chadwick

The story of the early Christian church from the death of Christ to the Papacy of Gregory the Great. Professor Henry Chadwick makes use of the latest research to explain the astonishing expansion of Christianity throughout the Roman Empire.

THE REFORMATION
Owen Chadwick

In this volume Professor Owen Chadwick deals with the formative work of Erasmus, Luther, Zwingli, Calvin, with the special circumstances of the English Reformation, and with the Counter-Reformation.

THE CHURCH AND THE AGE OF REASON
1648–1789
G. R. Cragg

This span in the history of the Christian church stretches from the age of religious and civil strife before the middle of the seventeenth century to the age of industrialism and republicanism which followed the French Revolution.

THE CHURCH IN AN AGE OF REVOLUTION
Alec R. Vidler

'A most readable and provocative volume and a notable addition to this promising and distinguished series' – *Guardian*

A HISTORY OF CHRISTIAN MISSIONS
Stephen Neill

This volume of *The Pelican History of the Church* represents the first attempt in English to provide a readable history of the worldwide expansion of all the Christian denominations – Roman Catholic, Orthodox, Anglican, and Protestant.